Practical Cooking

Soups

Practical Cooking

Soups

p

This is a Parragon Publishing Book
This edition published in 2002

Parragon Publishing
Queen Street House
4 Queen Street
Bath BA1 1HE, UK

ISBN: 0-75258-326-3

Printed in China

NOTE

Cup measurements in this book are for American cups.
Tablespoons are assumed tobe 15ml. Unless otherwise stated,
milk is assumed to be full fat, eggs are medium
and pepper is freshly ground black pepper.

Recipes using uncooked eggs should be
avoided by infants, the elderly, pregnant women and anyone
suffering from an illness.

Contents

Oriental Soups (continued)

European Soups

International Soups

Traditional British Soups

Low Fat

Special Occasion Soups

Introduction

Soup is one of the fundamental forms of food. Its traditions go back to the earliest days of civilized man with the advent of fire. It remains a favorite source of nourishment and pleasure today and homemade soup has become a special treat.

The benefits of soups are numerous. It is nutritious, satisfying to eat, and generally lean. It is economical to make, especially using abundant seasonal produce, but even expensive ingredients go further when made into soups.

Making soup can be a very creative endeavor, as well as satisfying for the cook as for the recipients. Practice hones skills and promotes confidence. This book offers an array of different styles of soup, using a variety of ingredients and techniques. Consider the recipes as a framework of proportions, and experiment with alternative ingredients if you wish.

Equipment

Soup-making requires little in the way of basic equipment. A good knife or two and a large saucepan with a lid are essential. A stockpot or soup kettle, or a large-capacity cast-iron casserole is also useful. Other things required to expedite your efforts are probably already in your kitchen – a cutting board,

colander, strainers, vegetable peeler, scissors, ladle, and spoons. A fat-separator or de-greasing pitcher is helpful, as is a large-capacity measuring container.

A wide range of specialised equipment is available but not necessarily essential to making soups. For puréeing soups, the various options produce differing results. A food mill, the most economical choice, will do the basic job of producing relatively smooth soups and it also strains at the same time. For the smoothest and best texture, nothing beats a blender. A food processor may be used for chopping and slicing ingredients as well as puréeing cooked soups, so it performs a variety of functions. A hand-held blender can purée right in the saucepan, as long as the depth of liquid is appropriate.

These pieces of equipment may each have a role to play in soup-making, but it is best to experiment first and see what you really need for the soups you like to make before investing. For most people there is no need for a battery of equipment. Always follow the manufacturer's directions and recommendations for safe operation of electrical appliances.

Ingredients

Soups are only as good as the ingredients in them. While leftovers are traditionally used as a springboard for creativity in soup-making, and may certainly provide useful components, fresh ingredients at their peak provide optimum nutritional benefits and taste.

Water is the most basic ingredient for soup. Even stock is essentially flavored water. Many soups taste best made with water, as the pure flavors are highlighted; this is especially true of vegetable soups.

Introduction

Be careful with your use of stock ingredients; it is easy to overdo strong-tasting vegetables or meats, which will drown the taste of the main flavor in your soup. Carrots and chicken form the basis of excellent stock.

Some soups make their own stock during the cooking process. Others call for stock as an ingredient. This can be homemade, bought ready-made, made up from bouillon cubes, powder, or liquid stock base, or canned consommé or clear broth. It is useful to know how to make stock, as homemade is more economical and normally has a superior flavor.

Stock-making

Making stock is easy. After getting it under way, it requires little attention, just time. You can save stock ingredients in the freezer until you need them; chicken carcasses, giblets, necks, backs, and trimmings; scraps and bones from meat roasts; vegetable trimmings such as leek greens, celery leaves and stems, mushroom stalks, pieces of carrot, and unused onion halves.

Fresh ingredients are determined by the kind of stock you want. Chicken or turkey wings are inexpensive and provide excellent flavors for poultry stock. Veal bones give more flavor than beef and pork lends sweetness. Lamb or ham bones are not suitable for a general purpose meat stock, as flavors are too pronounced, but can make delicious stocks when their flavors are appropriate, such as ham stock for split pea or bean soup.

Aromatic vegetables –carrots, onions, leeks, and garlic, for instance, are almost always included in stock. Strongly flavored vegetables such as cabbage should be used sparingly as the stock produced would be unsuitable for delicate soups. Avoid dark greens as they make pale stock murky.

Brown the main ingredients first, either by roasting or frying, as this adds color and flavor to the stock. Adding a roast chicken carcass is an easy way to do this.

Use cold water to make the stock; it helps extract the impurities. For a flavorful stock, keep the amount of water in proportion to the ingredients, which should be covered with about 2 inches of water. Skim off the scum or foam that rises to the surface as stock is heated, as it contains impurities

Introduction

that can make stock cloudy. Cook stock uncovered and do not allow it to boil at any time or fat may be incorporated into the liquid, which will not be removable.

Stock needs slow cooking over a low heat. Beef or meat stock takes 4–6 hours to extract maximum flavor, chicken or other poultry stock 2–3 hours. Fish stock requires about half an hour.

Remove the fat from stock before using. The easiest way to do this is to refrigerate it, allowing the fat to congeal, and then lift it off. If time is short, use a fat separator (a pitcher with the spout at the bottom) to remove the fat from warm stock, or spoon off the fat, although that is not always as effective as other methods. For greater flavor, stock can be reduced – cooked slowly,

uncovered, to reduce it and concentrate it. This procedure may also be useful to reduce the volume for storage. Stock keeps refrigerated for about three days, or frozen for up to three months.

Serving Soup

Soup is more flexible in terms of portions than many other foods. In this book, a range of servings may be indicated as a soup will provide more servings as a starter than as the main focus of a meal. Starter portions vary from 1 cup for very rich recipes to 1.5 cups; main courses from 1.75 cups to about 2 cups.

Soup is a perfect food for almost any occasion, from the most casual to the most formal. It can set the tone for the rest of the meal or be the meal itself. It

brings satisfaction to those who make it as well as those who eat it and nourishes both the body and the soul.

Basic Recipes

Chinese Stock

This basic stock is used in Chinese cooking not only as the basis for soup-making, but also whenever liquid is required instead of plain water.

MAKES 2½ QUARTS

10 oz chicken pieces

10 oz pork spare ribs

3½ quarts cold water

3-4 pieces gingerroot, minced

3-4 scallions, each tied into
  a knot

3-4 tbsp Chinese-rice wine or dry sherry

1 Trim off any excess fat from the chicken and spare-ribs; chop them into large pieces.

2 Place the chicken and pork in a large pan with the water; add the ginger and scallion knots.

3 Bring to a boil, and skim off the scum. Reduce the heat and simmer uncovered for at least 2-3 hours.

4 Strain the stock, discarding the chicken, pork, ginger, and scallions; add the wine and return to boil, simmer for 2-3 minutes.

5 Refrigerate the stock when cool; it will keep for up to 4-5 days. Alternatively, it can be frozen in small containers and be defrosted as required.

Fresh Chicken Stock

MAKES 1½ QUARTS

2 lb chicken, skinned

2 celery stalks

1 onion

2 carrots

1 garlic clove

few sprigs of fresh parsley

2 Quarts

salt and pepper

1 Put all the ingredients into a large saucepan.

2 Bring to a boil. Skim away surface scum using a large flat spoon. Reduce the heat to a gentle simmer, partially cover, and cook for 2 hours. Allow to cool.

3 Line a strainer with clean cheesecloth and place over a large pitcher or bowl. Pour the stock through the strainer. The cooked chicken can be used in another recipe. Discard the other solids. Cover the stock and chill.

4 Skim away any fat that forms before using. Store in the refrigerator for 3-4 days, until required, or freeze in small batches.

Fresh Vegetable Stock

This can be kept chilled for up to three days or frozen for up to three months. Salt is not added when cooking the stock: it is better to season it according to the dish in which it its to be used.

MAKES 1½ QUARTS

9 oz shallots

1 large carrot, diced

1 celery stalk, chopped

½ fennel bulb

1 garlic clove

1 bay leaf

a few fresh parsley and tarragon sprigs

2 quarts water

pepper

1 Put all the ingredients in a large saucepan and bring to a boil.

2 Skim off the surface scum with a flat spoon and reduce to a gentle simmer. Partially cover and cook for 45 minutes. Leave to cool.

3 Line a strainer with clean cheesecloth and put over a large pitcher or bowl. Pour the stock through the strainer. Discard the herbs and vegetables.

4 Cover and store in small quantities in the refrigerator for up to three days.

Fresh Lamb Stock

MAKES 1½ QUARTS

about 2 lb bones from a cooked
joint or raw chopped lamb bones

2 onions, studded with 6 cloves, or sliced or
chopped coarsely

2 carrots, sliced

1 leek, sliced

1-2 celery stalks, sliced

1 Bouquet Garni

about 2 quarts water

1 Chop or break up the bones and place in a large saucepan with the other ingredients.

2 Bring to a boil and remove any scum from the surface with a draining spoon. Cover and simmer gently for 3-4 hours. Strain the stock and leave to cool.

3 Remove any fat from the surface and chill. If stored for more than 24 hours the stock must be boiled every day, cooled quickly and chilled again. The stock may be frozen for up to 2 months; place in a large plastic bag and seal, leaving at least 1 inch of headspace to allow for expansion.

Fresh Fish Stock

MAKES 1½ QUARTS

1 head of a cod or salmon, etc, plus the
trimmings, skin, and bones or just the
trimmings, skin, and bones

1-2 onions, sliced

1 carrot, sliced

1-2 celery stalks, sliced

good squeeze of lemon juice

1 Bouquet Garni or 2 fresh or dried bay
leaves

1 Wash the fish head and trimmings and place in a saucepan. Cover with water and bring to a boil.

2 Remove any scum with a draining spoon, then add the remaining ingredients. Cover and simmer for about 30 minutes.

3 Strain and cool. Store in the refrigerator and use within 2 days.

Cornstarch Paste

Cornstarch paste is made by mixing 1 part cornstarch with about 1½ parts of cold water. Stir until smooth. The paste is used to thicken sauces.

How to Use This Book

Each recipe contains a wealth of useful information, including a breakdown of nutritional quantities, preparation, and cooking times, and level of difficulty. All of this information is explained in detail below.

The nutritional information provided for each recipe is per serving or per portion. Optional ingredients, variations or serving suggestions have not been included in the calculations.

The number of chef's hats represents the difficulty of each recipe, ranging from easy (1 chef's hat) to difficult (5 chef's hats).

This amount of time represents the preparation of ingredients, including cooling, chilling, and soaking times.

This represents the cooking time.

The ingredients for each recipe are listed in the order that they are used.

The method is clearly explained with step-by-step directions that are easy to follow.

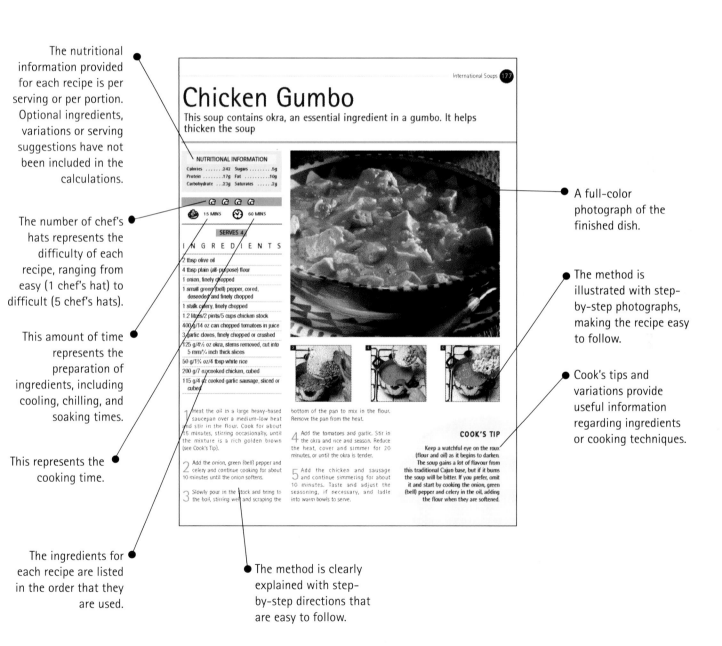

A full-color photograph of the finished dish.

The method is illustrated with step-by-step photographs, making the recipe easy to follow.

Cook's tips and variations provide useful information regarding ingredients or cooking techniques.

Vegetable Soups

Vegetables are endlessly variable and eminently enjoyable. Each vegetable can be used in many ways – in creamy soups, broths, and thick, hearty ones. They provide a light

start to a meal or a satisfying main course, can be cooked quickly and last longer than other soups. Choose plump, fresh vegetables, as they have more flavor than tired ones, and use plenty to give a pleasing density. Use the recipes that follow freely and don't be afraid to experiment with them.

Beet Soup

Here are two variations using the same vegetable: a creamy soup made with puréed cooked beetroot and a traditional clear soup, Bortsch.

NUTRITIONAL INFORMATION

Calories 106	Sugars 11g
Protein 3g	Fat 5g
Carbohydrate . . .13g	Saturates 3g

🍲 25 MINS   🕐 35–55 MINS

SERVES 6

I N G R E D I E N T S

B O R T S C H

2 oz raw beet, peeled
  and grated

2 carrots, finely chopped

1 large onion, finely chopped

1 garlic clove, minced

1 bouquet garni

5 cups vegetable stock

2–3 tsp lemon juice

salt and pepper

⅔ cup soured cream, to serve

C R E A M E D   B E E T   S O U P

¼ cup butter or margarine

2 large onions, finely chopped

1–2 carrots, chopped

2 celery stalks, chopped

1 lb cooked beet, diced

1–2 tbsp lemon juice

3½ cups vegetable stock

1¼ cups milk

salt and pepper

T O   S E R V E

grated cooked beet or 6 tbsp
  heavy cream, lightly whipped

1 To make bortsch, place the beet, carrots, onion, garlic, bouquet garni, stock, and lemon juice in a saucepan and season to taste with salt and pepper. Bring to a boil, cover, and simmer for 45 minutes.

2 Press the soup through a fine strainer or a strainer lined with cheesecloth, then pour into a clean pan. Taste and adjust the seasoning and add extra lemon juice, if necessary.

3 Bring to a boil and simmer for 1–2 minutes. Serve with a spoonful of soured cream swirled through.

4 To make creamed beet soup, melt the butter or margarine in a saucepan. Add the onions, carrots and celery and fry until just beginning to color.

5 Add the beet, 1 tablespoon of the lemon juice, the stock, and seasoning and bring to a boil. Cover and simmer for 30 minutes, until tender.

6 Cool slightly, then press through a strainer or process in a food processor or blender. Pour into a clean pan. Add the milk and bring to a boil. Adjust the seasoning and add extra lemon juice, if necessary. Top with grated beet or heavy cream.

Fresh Tomato Soup

Made with fresh tomatoes, the taste of this soup is subtle and complex. Basil is a proven partner for tomatoes, but you could also try tarragon.

NUTRITIONAL INFORMATION

Calories	222	Sugars	........13g
Protein	.........3g	Fat	..........17g
Carbohydrate	...15g	Saturates	......9g

10 MINS   60 MINS

SERVES 4

I N G R E D I E N T S

2 lb ripe plum tomatoes, skinned

2 tsp olive oil

1 large sweet onion, finely chopped

1 carrot, finely chopped

1 stalk celery, finely chopped

2 garlic cloves, finely chopped or minced

1 tsp fresh marjoram leaves, or ¼ tsp dried marjoram

2 cups water

4–5 tbsp heavy cream, plus extra to garnish

2 tbsp chopped fresh basil leaves

salt and pepper

1 Cut the tomatoes in half and scrape the seeds into a strainer set over a bowl to catch the juice. Reserve the juice and discard the seeds. Chop the tomato flesh into large chunks.

COOK'S TIP

For the best flavor, this soup needs to be made with ripe tomatoes. If supermarket tomatoes are pale and hard, leave them to ripen at room temperature for several days. This is especially important in winter when most tomatoes are picked and shipped before they are ripe.

2 Heat the olive oil in a large saucepan. Add the onion, carrot, and celery and cook over a medium-low heat for 3–4 minutes, stirring occasionally.

3 Add the tomatoes and their juice, with the garlic and marjoram. Cook for 2 minutes. Stir in the water, reduce the heat and simmer, covered, for about 45 minutes until the vegetables are very soft, stirring occasionally.

4 Allow the soup to cool slightly, then transfer to a blender or food processor and purée until smooth, working in batches, if necessary. (If using a food processor, strain off the cooking liquid and reserve. Purée the soup solids with enough cooking liquid to moisten them, then combine with the remaining liquid.)

5 Return the soup to the saucepan and place over a medium-low heat. Add the cream and stir in the basil. Season with salt and pepper and heat through; do not allow to boil.

6 Ladle the soup into warm bowls and swirl a little extra cream into each serving. Serve at once.

Speedy Beet Soup

Quick and easy to prepare in a microwave oven, this deep red soup of puréed beet and potatoes makes a stunning first course.

NUTRITIONAL INFORMATION

Calories . . . . . . .120 Sugars 11g
Protein . . . . .4g Fat 2g
Carbohydrate . . .22g Saturates 1g

 20 MINS   30 MINS

SERVES 6

I N G R E D I E N T S

1 onion, chopped

12 oz potatoes, diced

1 small cooking apple, peeled,
   cored and grated

3 tbsp water

1 tsp cumin seeds

1 lb cooked beet,
   peeled and diced

1 bay leaf

pinch of dried thyme

1 tsp lemon juice

2½ cups hot vegetable stock

4 tbsp soured cream

salt and pepper

few dill sprigs, to garnish

1 Place the onion, potatoes, apple, and water in a large bowl. Cover and cook on HIGH power for 10 minutes.

2 Stir in the cumin seeds and cook on HIGH power for 1 minute.

3 Stir in the beet, bay leaf, thyme, lemon juice, and hot vegetable stock. Cover and cook on HIGH power for 12 minutes, stirring halfway through the cooking time.

4 Leave to stand, uncovered, for 5 minutes. Remove and discard the bay leaf. Strain the vegetables and reserve the liquid. Process the vegetables with a little of the reserved liquid in a food processor or blender until they are smooth and creamy. Alternatively, either mash the vegetables with a potato masher or press them through a strainer with the back of a wooden spoon.

5 Pour the vegetable purée into a clean bowl with the reserved liquid and mix well. Season to taste. Cover and cook on HIGH power for 4–5 minutes, until the soup is very hot.

6 Serve the soup in warmed bowls. Swirl 1 tablespoon of soured cream into each serving and garnish with a few sprigs of fresh dill.

Eggplant Soup

The parsnip and carrot bring a balancing sweetness to the eggplants in this delicious soup.

NUTRITIONAL INFORMATION

Calories	131	Sugar	.........9g
Protein	.........3g	Fats	...........8g
Carbohydrates	...12g	Saturates	......3g

20 MINS   1¼ HOURS

SERVES 4

INGREDIENTS

1 tbsp olive oil, plus extra for brushing

1 lb 10 oz eggplants, halved lengthways

1 carrot, halved

1 small parsnip, halved

2 onions, finely chopped

3 garlic cloves, finely chopped

4 cups chicken or vegetable stock

¼ tsp fresh thyme leaves, or a pinch of dried thyme

1 bay leaf

⅛ tsp ground coriander

1 tbsp tomato paste

⅔ cup light cream

freshly squeezed lemon juice

salt and pepper

LEMON-GARLIC SEASONING:

grated rind of ½ lemon

1 garlic clove, finely chopped

3 tbsp chopped fresh parsley

1 Oil a shallow roasting pan and add the eggplant, cut sides down, and the carrot and parsnip. Brush the vegetables with oil. Roast in a preheated oven at 400oF for 30 minutes, turning once.

2 When cool enough to handle, scrape the eggplant flesh away from the skin, or scoop it out, then roughly chop. Cut the parsnip and carrot into chunks.

3 Heat the oil in a large saucepan over a medium-low heat. Add the onions and garlic and cook for about 5 minutes, stirring frequently, until softened. Add the eggplant, parsnip, carrot, stock, thyme, bay leaf, coriander, and tomato paste, with a little salt. Stir to combine. Cover and simmer for 30 minutes, or until very tender.

4 Allow the soup to cool slightly, then transfer to a blender or food processor and purée until smooth, working in batches if necessary. (If using a food processor, strain off the cooking liquid and reserve. Purée the soup solids with enough cooking liquid to moisten them, then combine with the remaining liquid.)

5 Return the puréed soup to the saucepan and stir in the cream. Reheat the soup over a low heat for about 10 minutes until hot. Adjust the seasoning, adding lemon juice to taste.

6 To make the lemon-garlic seasoning, chop together the lemon rind, garlic and parsley until very fine and well mixed. Ladle the soup into warm bowls, then garnish with some freshly chopped parsley.

Smoky Green Bean Soup

For the most robust flavor, use bacon that has been fairly heavily smoked and has a pronounced taste.

NUTRITIONAL INFORMATION

Calories 192   Sugars 7g
Protein . . . . .9g   Fat 8g
Carbohydrate . . .22g   Saturates 2g

15 MINS   60 MINS

SERVES 4

INGREDIENTS

1 tbsp oil

3½ oz lean smoked back bacon, finely
   chopped

1 onion, finely chopped

1–2 garlic cloves, finely chopped or minced

2 tbsp all-purpose flour

5 cups water

1 leek, thinly sliced

1 carrot, finely chopped

1 small potato, finely chopped

1 lb green beans

1 bay leaf

freshly grated nutmeg

salt and pepper

garlic croûtons, to garnish

VARIATION

**Use frozen green beans
instead of fresh if you wish.
There is no need to defrost them.**

1 Heat the oil in a large wide saucepan over a medium heat. Add the bacon and cook for 8–10 minutes until golden. Remove the bacon from the pan with a draining spoon and drain on paper towels. Pour off all the fat from the pan.

2 Add the onion and garlic to the pan and cook for about 3 minutes, stirring frequently, until the onion begins to soften.

3 Stir in the flour and continue cooking for 2 minutes. Add half of the water and stir well, scraping the bottom of the pan to mix in the flour.

4 Add the leek, carrot, potato, beans, and bay leaf. Stir in the remaining water and season with salt and pepper. Bring just to a boil, stirring occasionally, reduce the heat and simmer, partially covered, for 35–40 minutes, or until the beans are very tender.

5 Allow the soup to cool slightly, then transfer to a blender or food processor, and purée until smooth, working in batches if necessary. (If using a food processor, strain off the cooking liquid and reserve. Purée the soup solids with enough cooking liquid to moisten them, then combine with the remaining liquid.)

6 Return the soup to the saucepan, add the bacon and simmer over a low heat for a few minutes until heated through, stirring occasionally. Taste and adjust the seasoning, adding nutmeg, pepper, and, if needed, more salt. Sprinkle with croûtons to serve.

Fava Bean Soup

Fresh fava beans are best for this scrumptious soup, but if they are unavailable, use frozen beans instead.

NUTRITIONAL INFORMATION

Calories	224	Sugars	.........4g
Protein	........12g	Fat	...........6g
Carbohydrate	...31g	Saturates	.......1g

15 MINS   40 MINS

SERVES 4

I N G R E D I E N T S

2 tbsp olive oil

1 red onion, chopped

2 garlic cloves, minced

2 potatoes, diced

3 cups fava beans,
    thawed if frozen

3¾ cups vegetable stock

2 tbsp freshly chopped mint

mint sprigs and unsweetened yogurt,
    to garnish

1 Heat the olive oil in a large saucepan. Add the onion and garlic and sauté for 2–3 minutes, until softened.

2 Add the potatoes and cook, stirring constantly, for 5 minutes.

3 Stir in the beans and the stock, cover and simmer for 30 minutes, or until the beans and potatoes are tender.

4 Remove a few vegetables with a draining spoon and set aside until required. Place the remainder of the soup in a food processor or blender and process until smooth.

5 Return the soup to a clean saucepan and add the reserved vegetables and chopped mint. Stir thoroughly and heat through gently.

6 Transfer the soup to a warm tureen or individual serving bowls. Garnish with swirls of yogurt and sprigs of fresh mint and serve immediately.

VARIATION

Use fresh cilantro and ½ tsp ground cumin as flavorings in the soup, if you prefer.

Dwarf Soup

This fresh-tasting soup with dwarf beans, cucumber, and watercress can be served warm, or chilled on a hot summer day.

NUTRITIONAL INFORMATION

Calories 121   Sugars 2g
Protein . . . . .2g   Fat 8g
Carbohydrate . . .10g   Saturates 1g

 5 MINS   25–30 MINS

SERVES 4

INGREDIENTS

1 tbsp olive oil

1 onion, chopped

1 garlic clove, chopped

7 oz potato, peeled and cut into
    1 inch cubes

scant 3 cups vegetable or chicken stock

1 small cucumber or ½ large cucumber,
    cut into chunks

3 oz bunch watercress

4 ½ oz dwarf beans, trimmed
and halved lengthwise

salt and pepper

1 Heat the oil in a large pan and fry the onion and garlic for 3–4 minutes or until softened.

2 Add the cubed potato and fry for a further 2–3 minutes.

3 Stir in the stock, bring to a boil and leave to simmer for 5 minutes.

4 Add the cucumber to the pan and cook for a further 3 minutes or until the potatoes are tender. Test by inserting the tip of a knife into the potato cubes–it should pass through easily.

5 Add the watercress and allow to wilt. Then place the soup in a food processor and blend until smooth. Alternatively, before adding the watercress, mash the soup with a potato masher and push through a strainer, then chop the watercress finely and stir into the soup.

6 Bring a small pan of water to a boil and steam the beans for 3–4 minutes or until tender.

7 Add the beans to the soup, season, and warm through.

VARIATION

Try using 4½ oz snow peas instead of the beans, if you prefer.

Tarragon Pea Soup

This soup is simple and quick to make using frozen peas and stock made from a cube, ingredients you are likely to have on hand.

NUTRITIONAL INFORMATION

Calories . . . . . . .147 Sugars 6g
Protein . . . . .9g Fat 4g
Carbohydrate . . .20g Saturates 2g

15 MINS   60 MINS

SERVES 4

INGREDIENTS

2 tsp butter

1 onion, finely chopped

2 leeks, finely chopped

1 ½ tbsp white rice

1 lb frozen English peas

4 cups water

1 chicken or vegetable bouillon cube

½ tsp dried tarragon

salt and pepper

chopped hard-cooked egg or croûtons, to
   garnish

1 Melt the butter in a large saucepan over a medium-low heat. Add the onion, leeks and rice. Cover and cook for about 10 minutes, stirring occasionally, until the vegetables are soft.

2 Add the peas, water, bouillon cube, and tarragon and bring just to a boil. Season with a little pepper. Cover and simmer for about 35 minutes, stirring occasionally, until the vegetables are very tender.

3 Allow the soup to cool slightly, then transfer to a blender or food processor and purée until smooth, working in batches if necessary. (If using a food processor, strain off the cooking liquid and reserve. Purée the soup solids with enough cooking liquid to moisten them, then combine with the remaining liquid.)

4 Return the puréed soup to the saucepan. Taste and adjust the seasoning, adding plenty of pepper and, if needed, salt. Gently reheat the soup over a low heat for about 10 minutes until hot.

5 Ladle into warm bowls and garnish with egg or croûtons.

COOK'S TIP

The rice gives the soup a little extra body, but a small amount of raw or cooked potato would do the same job.

VARIATION

Substitute frozen green beans for the peas and omit the tarragon, replacing it with a little dried thyme and/or marjoram.

Broccoli Soup

This soup highlights the rich flavor of broccoli. It is a popular vegetable with almost everyone and particularly healthy.

NUTRITIONAL INFORMATION

Calories	208	Sugar	.........5g
Protein	.........6g	Fats	..........16g
Carbohydrates	...10g	Saturates	......9g

15 MINS   40 MINS

SERVES 4

I N G R E D I E N T S

14 oz broccoli (from 1 large head)

2 tsp butter

1 tsp oil

1 onion, finely chopped

1 leek, thinly sliced

1 small carrot, finely chopped

3 tbsp white rice

3¾ cups water

1 bay leaf

4 tbsp heavy cream

3½ oz cream cheese

freshly grated nutmeg

salt and pepper

croûtons, to serve (see Cook's Tip)

1 Divide the broccoli into small florets and cut off the stems. Peel the large stems and chop all the stems into small pieces.

2 Heat the butter and oil in a large saucepan over a medium heat and add the onion, leek, and carrot. Cook for 3–4 minutes, stirring frequently, until the onion is soft.

3 Add the broccoli stems, rice, water, bay leaf, and a pinch of salt. Bring just to a boil and reduce the heat to low. Cover and simmer for 15 minutes. Add the broccoli florets and continue cooking, covered, for 15–20 minutes until the rice and vegetables are tender. Remove the bay leaf.

4 Season the soup with nutmeg, pepper and, if needed, more salt. Stir in the cream and cream cheese. Simmer over a low heat for a few minutes until heated through, stirring occasionally. Taste and adjust the seasoning, if needed. Ladle into warm bowls and serve sprinkled with croûtons.

COOK'S TIP

To make croûtons, remove the crusts from thick slices of bread, then cut the bread into dice. Fry in vegetable oil, stirring constantly, until evenly browned, then drain on paper towels.

Silky Spinach Soup

This soup has a rich brilliant color and an intense pure flavor. You can taste the goodness!

NUTRITIONAL INFORMATION

Calories	69	Sugars	........4g
Protein	........4g	Fat	..........4g
Carbohydrate	....5g	Saturates	......1g

10 MINS   40 MINS

SERVES 4

I N G R E D I E N T S

1 tbsp olive oil

1 onion, halved and thinly sliced

1 leek, split lengthways and thinly sliced

1 potato, finely diced

4 cups water

2 sprigs fresh marjoram or ¼ tsp dried

2 sprigs fresh thyme or ¼ tsp dried

1 bay leaf

14 oz young spinach, washed

freshly grated nutmeg

salt and pepper

4 tbsp light cream, to serve

 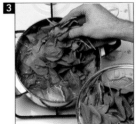 

1 Heat the oil in a heavy-bottomed saucepan over a medium heat. Add the onion and leek and cook for about 3 minutes, stirring occasionally, until they begin to soften.

2 Add the potato, water, marjoram, thyme, and bay leaf, along with a large pinch of salt. Bring to a boil, reduce the heat, cover, and cook gently for about 25 minutes until the vegetables are tender. Remove the bay leaf and the herb stems.

3 Add the spinach and continue cooking for 3–4 minutes, stirring frequently,

just until it is completely wilted.

4 Allow the soup to cool slightly, then transfer to a blender or food processor and purée until smooth, working in batches if necessary. (If using a food processor, strain off the cooking liquid and reserve. Purée the soup solids with enough cooking liquid to moisten them, then combine with the remaining liquid.)

5 Return the soup to the saucepan and thin with a little more water, if wished. Season with salt, a good grinding of pepper and a generous grating of nutmeg. Place over a low heat and simmer until reheated.

6 Ladle the soup into warm bowls and swirl a table-spoonful of cream into each serving.

Cream Cheese & Herb Soup

Make the most of home-grown herbs to create this wonderfully creamy soup with its marvellous garden-fresh fragrance.

NUTRITIONAL INFORMATION

Calories	275	Sugars	.........5g
Protein	.........7g	Fat	..........22g
Carbohydrate	...14g	Saturates	......11g

🕐 15 MINS   🕐 35 MINS

SERVES 4

INGREDIENTS

2 tbsp butter or margarine

2 onions, chopped

3½ cups vegetable stock

25 g/1 oz coarsely chopped mixed
    herbs, such as parsley, chives, thyme,
    basil and oregano

1 cup full-fat soft cheese

1 tbsp cornstarch

1 tbsp milk

chopped chives, to garnish

1 Melt the butter or margarine in a large, heavy-bottomed saucepan. Add the onions and fry over a medium heat for 2 minutes, then cover and turn the heat to low. Continue to cook the onions for 5 minutes, then remove the lid.

2 Add the vegetable stock and herbs to the saucepan. Bring to a boil over a moderate heat. Lower the heat, cover, and simmer gently for 20 minutes.

3 Remove the saucepan from the heat. Transfer the soup to a food processor or blender and process for about 15 seconds, until smooth. Alternatively, press it through a strainer with the back of a wooden spoon. Return the soup to the saucepan.

4 Reserve a little of the cheese for garnish. Spoon the remaining cheese into the soup and whisk until it has melted and is incorporated.

5 Mix the cornstarch with the milk to a paste, then stir the mixture into the soup. Heat, stirring constantly, until thickened and smooth.

6 Pour the soup into warmed individual bowls. Spoon some of the reserved cheese into each bowl and garnish with chives. Serve at once.

Onion & Fava Bean Soup

This soup has well-balanced vegetable flavors and a satisfying crunch from the crispy bacon. It makes a good lunch, served with crusty bread.

NUTRITIONAL INFORMATION

Calories	213	Sugar	. . . . .8g
Protein	. . . . .10g	Fats	. . . . .9g
Carbohydrates	. . .24g	Saturates	. . . . . .4g

15 MINS   1 HOUR 10 MINS

SERVES 4

INGREDIENTS

1 tbsp butter

2 tsp oil

2 large onions, finely chopped

1 leek, thinly sliced

1 garlic clove, minced

5 cups water

6 tbsp white rice

1 bay leaf

½ tsp chopped fresh rosemary leaves

½ tsp chopped fresh thyme leaves

12 oz fresh or defrosted frozen fava beans

3½ oz rindless sliced bacon, finely chopped

1½ cups milk, plus extra if needed

freshly grated nutmeg

salt and pepper

1 Heat the butter and half the oil in a large saucepan over a medium heat. Add the onions, leek, and garlic. Season with salt and pepper and cook for 10–15 minutes, stirring frequently, until the onion is soft.

2 Add the water, rice, and herbs with a large pinch of salt. Bring just to a boil and reduce the heat to low. Cover and simmer for 15 minutes.

3 Add the fava beans, cover again and continue simmering for a further 15 minutes, or until the vegetables are tender.

4 Allow the soup to cool a bit, transfer to a blender or food processor and purée until smooth, working in batches if necessary. (If using a food processor, strain off the cooking liquid and reserve. Purée the soup solids with enough cooking liquid to moisten them, then combine with the remaining liquid.)

5 Heat the remaining oil in a small skillet over a medium-low heat. Add the bacon and cook until crispy, stirring occasionally. Drain on paper towels.

6 Return the soup to the sauce-pan and stir in the milk, adding a little extra for a thinner soup. Taste and adjust the seasoning, adding salt and pepper to taste and a good grating of nutmeg. Simmer over a low heat for about 10 minutes until heated through, stirring occasionally. Ladle the soup into warm bowls and sprinkle with bacon. Serve immediately.

Parsnip & Orange Soup

The exotic flavors give this simple soup a lift. If you wish, use bought gin purée instead of grating it.

NUTRITIONAL INFORMATION

Calories	142	Sugars	........16g
Protein	.........4g	Fat	...........3g
Carbohydrate	...27g	Saturates	......0g

15 MINS   60 MINS

SERVES 4

INGREDIENTS

2 tsp olive oil

1 large onion, chopped

1 large leek, sliced

2 carrots, thinly sliced

1 lb 12 oz parsnips, sliced

4 tbsp grated peeled fresh ginger
    root (about 2 oz)

2–3 garlic cloves, finely chopped

grated rind of ½ orange

1½ quarts water

1 cup orange juice

salt and pepper

snipped chives or slivers of scallion,
    to garnish

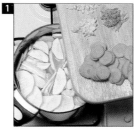

1 Heat the olive oil in a large saucepan over a medium heat. Add the onion and leek and cook for about 5 minutes, stirring occasionally, until softened,

VARIATION

You could make the soup using equal amounts (1 lb each) of carrots and parsnips.

2 Add the parsnips, carrots, ginger, garlic, grated orange rind, water, and a large pinch of salt. Reduce the heat, cover and simmer for about 40 minutes, stirring occasionally, until the vegetables are very soft.

3 Allow the soup to cool slightly, then transfer to a blender or food processor and purée until smooth, working in batches if necessary. (If using a food processor, strain off the cooking liquid and reserve. Purée the soup solids with enough

cooking liquid to moisten them, then combine with the remaining liquid.)

4 Return the soup to the saucepan and stir in the orange juice. Add a little water or more orange juice, if you prefer a thinner consistency. Taste and adjust the seasoning with salt and pepper

5 Then simmer for about 10 minutes to heat through. Ladle into warm bowls, garnish with chives or slivers of scallion and serve.

Wild Mushroom Soup

This soup has an intense, earthy flavor that brings to mind woodland aromas. It makes a memorable, rich tasting starter.

NUTRITIONAL INFORMATION

Calories 118   Sugars 5g
Protein . . . . .4g   Fat 7g
Carbohydrate . . . .7g   Saturates 4g

15 MINS   1 HOUR 20 MINS

SERVES 4

I N G R E D I E N T S

1 oz dried porcini mushrooms

1 ½ cups boiling water

4 ½ oz fresh porcini mushrooms

2 tsp olive oil

1 stalk celery, chopped

1 carrot, chopped

1 onion, chopped

3 garlic cloves, minced

5 cups vegetable stock or water

leaves from 2 thyme sprigs

1 tbsp butter

3 tbsp dry or medium sherry

2–3 tbsp soured cream

salt and pepper

chopped fresh parsley, to garnish

1 Put the dried mushrooms in a bowl and pour the boiling water over them. Allow to stand for 10–15 minutes.

2 Brush or wash the fresh mushrooms. Trim and reserve the stalks; slice large mushroom caps.

3 Heat the oil in a large sauce-pan over a medium heat. Add the celery, carrot, onion, and mushroom stems. Cook for about 8 minutes, stirring frequently, until the onion begins to color. Stir in the garlic and continue cooling for 1 minute.

4 Add the stock and thyme leaves with a large pinch of salt. Using a draining spoon, transfer the soaked dried mushrooms to the saucepan. Strain the soaking liquid through a cheesecloth-lined strainer into the pan. Bring to a boil, reduce the heat and simmer, partially covered, for 30–40 minutes, or until the carrots are tender.

5 Allow the soup to cool slightly, then transfer the soup solids with enough of the cooking liquid to moisten to a blender or food processor and purée until smooth. Return it to the saucepan, combine with the remaining cooking liquid and simmer gently, covered.

6 Melt the butter in a skillet over a medium heat. Add the fresh mushroom caps and season with salt and pepper. Cook for about 8 minutes until they start to color, stirring occasionally at first, then stirring more often as the liquid evaporates. When the pan becomes dry, add the sherry and bubble briefly.

7 Add the mushrooms and sherry to the soup. Taste and adjust the seasoning, if necessary. Ladle into warm bowls, put a dollop of cream in each and garnish with parsley.

Beans & Greens Soup

Include some pungent greens in this soup, if you can. They add a wonderful flavor, and of course are very good for you!

NUTRITIONAL INFORMATION

Calories	257	Sugar	.........9g
Protein	........16g	Fats	...........4g
Carbohydrates	...41g	Saturates	......1g

🍲 15 MINS   🕐 2 HOURS

SERVES 4

INGREDIENTS

9 oz dried green or cannellini beans

1 tbsp olive oil

2 onions, finely chopped

4 garlic cloves, finely chopped

1 stalk celery, thinly sliced

2 carrots, halved and thinly sliced

5 cups water

¼ tsp dried thyme

¼ tsp dried marjoram

1 bay leaf

4½ oz leafy greens, such as chard, mustard, spinach, and kale, washed

salt and pepper

1 Pick over the beans, cover generously with cold water and leave to soak for 6 hours or overnight. Drain the beans, put in a saucepan and add enough cold water to cover by 2 inches. Bring to a boil and boil for 10 minutes. Drain and rinse well.

2 Heat the oil in a large sauce-pan over a medium heat. Add the onion and cook, covered, for 3–4 minutes, stirring occasionally, until the onion is just softened. Add the garlic, celery and carrots, and continue cooking for 2 minutes.

3 Add the water, drained beans, thyme, marjoram, and bay leaf. When the mixture begins to bubble, reduce the heat to low. Cover and simmer gently, stirring occasionally, for about 1¼ hours until the beans are tender; the cooking time will vary depending on the type of bean. Season with salt and pepper.

4 Allow the soup to cool slightly, then transfer 2 cups to a blender or food processor. Purée until smooth and recombine with the soup.

5 A handful at a time, cut the greens crossways into thin ribbons, keeping tender leaves like spinach separate. Add the thicker leaves and cook gently uncovered, for 10 minutes. Stir in any remaining greens and continue cooking for 5–10 minutes, until all the greens are tender.

6 Taste and adjust the seasoning, if necessary. Ladle the soup into warm bowls and serve.

Split Pea & Ham Soup

A hearty and heartwarming soup, this is perfect for weekend lunches—
or make it ahead for a nourishing mid-week supper, all ready to reheat.

NUTRITIONAL INFORMATION

Calories ....275 Sugar 5g
Protein ....21g Fats 7g
Carbohydrates ...36g Saturates 1g

10 MINS   1¾ HOURS

SERVES 6

I N G R E D I E N T S

1 lb split green peas

1 tbsp olive oil

1 large onion, finely chopped

1 large carrot, finely chopped

1 stalk celery, finely chopped

4 cups chicken or vegetable stock

4 cups water

8 oz lean smoked ham, finely diced

¼ tsp dried thyme

¼ tsp dried marjoram

1 bay leaf

salt and pepper

1 Rinse the peas under cold running water. Put in a saucepan and cover generously with water. Bring to a boil and boil for 3 minutes, skimming off the foam from the surface. Drain the peas.

2 Heat the oil in a large saucepan over a medium heat. Add the onion and cook for 3–4 minutes, stirring occasionally, until just softened.

3 Add the carrot and celery and continue cooking for 2 minutes. Add the peas, pour over the stock and water and stir to combine.

4 Bring just to a boil and stir the ham into the soup. Add the thyme, marjoram, and bay leaf. Reduce the heat, cover and cook gently for 1–1½ hours until the ingredients are very soft. Remove the bay leaf.

5 Taste and adjust the seasoning. Ladle into warm soup bowls and serve.

VARIATION

You could add sliced, cooked sausages instead of or in addition to the ham. If you have a ham bone, use in place of the diced ham. Trim off the fat and cook the bone in the soup. Before serving, remove the bone, cut off the meat and return the meat to the soup.

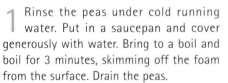

Split Pea & Parsnip Soup

This soup is surprisingly delicate. The yellow peas give it an appealing light color, while the parsnips add an aromatic flavor.

NUTRITIONAL INFORMATION

Calories 293   Sugars 9g
Protein . . . . .16g   Fat 7g
Carbohydrate . . .44g   Saturates 1g

 15 MINS   1 HOUR

SERVES 4

I N G R E D I E N T S

9 oz split yellow peas

1 tbsp olive oil

1 onion, finely chopped

1 small leek, finely chopped

3 garlic cloves, finely chopped

2 parsnips, sliced (about 225 g/8 oz)

2 quart water

10 sage leaves, or ¼ tsp dried sage

⅛ tsp dried thyme

¼ tsp minced coriander

1 bay leaf

salt and pepper

freshly grated nutmeg

chopped fresh cilantro leaves or parsley, to garnish

2 Heat the oil in a large saucepan over a medium heat. Add the onion and leek and cook for about 3 minutes, stirring frequently, until just softened. Add the garlic and parsnips and continue cooking for 2 minutes, stirring occasionally.

3 Add the peas, water, sage, thyme, coriander, and bay leaf. Bring almost to a boil, reduce the heat, cover and cook gently for about 40 minutes until the vegetables are very soft. Remove the bay leaf.

4 Allow the soup to cool slightly, then transfer to a blender or food processor and purée until smooth, working in batches if necessary. (If using a food processor, strain off the cooking liquid and reserve. Purée the soup solids with enough cooking liquid to moisten them, then combine with the remaining liquid.)

5 Return the soup to the saucepan and thin with a little more water, if wished. Season generously with salt, pepper, and nutmeg. Place over a low heat and simmer until reheated. Ladle into warm soup plates and garnish with fresh cilantro leaves or parsley.

1 Rinse the peas well under cold running water. Put in a saucepan and cover generously with water. Bring to a boil and boil for 3 minutes, skimming off the foam from the surface. Drain the peas.

Garbanzo Bean & Chorizo

This soup is satisfying and colorful, with an appealing piquancy from the chorizo.

NUTRITIONAL INFORMATION

Calories . . . . . . .382 Sugar 11g
Protein . . . . .23g Fats 12g
Carbohydrates . . .50g Saturates 3g

🥪 15 MINS   🕐 1¾ HOURS

SERVES 4

INGREDIENTS

9 oz dried garbanzo beans, soaked overnight in cold water to cover generously

4½ oz lean chorizo, peeled and finely diced

1 onion, finely chopped

1 shallot, finely chopped

1 carrot, thinly sliced

2 garlic cloves, finely chopped

14 oz can chopped tomatoes in juice

5 cups water

1 bay leaf

¼ tsp dried thyme

¼ tsp dried oregano

8 oz pumpkin, diced

8 oz potato, diced

4½ oz curly kale leaves, finely chopped

salt and pepper

COOK'S TIP

You can easily chop the kale in a food processor; it should be like chopped parsley. Alternatively, slice crosswise into very thin ribbons.

1 Drain the garbanzo beans and put in a saucepan with enough cold water to cover generously. Bring to a boil over a high heat and cook for 10 minutes. Drain.

2 Put the chorizo in a large saucepan over a medium-low heat. Cook for 5–10 minutes, stirring, frequently to render as much fat as possible. Remove with a draining spoon and drain on paper towels.

3 Pour off the fat and add the onion, shallot, carrot, and garlic. Cook for 3–4 minutes.

4 Add the garbanzo beans, tomatoes, water, herbs, and chorizo. Bring almost to a boil, reduce the heat, cover and cook gently for 30 minutes.

5 Stir in the pumpkin and potato, cover and continue cooking for about 30 minutes until the garbanzo beans are tender. Season with salt and pepper.

6 Stir in the kale and continue to cook, uncovered, for 15–20 minutes, or until it is tender. Taste and adjust the seasoning. Ladle into warm bowls and serve.

Potato & Split Pea Soup

Split green peas are sweeter than other varieties of split pea and reduce down to a paste when cooked, which acts as a thickener in soups.

NUTRITIONAL INFORMATION

Calories 260	Sugars 5g	
Protein 11g	Fat 10g	
Carbohydrate ...32g	Saturates 3g	

  5–10 MINS   45 MINS

SERVES 4

I N G R E D I E N T S

2 tbsp vegetable oil

2 unpeeled mealy potatoes, diced

2 onions, diced

2¾ oz split green peas

4½ cups vegetable stock

5 tbsp grated Gruyère cheese

salt and pepper

C R O U T O N S

3 tbsp butter

1 garlic clove, minced

1 tbsp chopped parsley

1 thick slice white bread, cubed

1 Heat the vegetable oil in a large saucepan. Add the potatoes and onions and sauté over a low heat, stirring constantly, for about 5 minutes.

VARIATION

For a richly colored soup, red lentils could be used instead of split green peas. Add a large pinch of brown sugar to the recipe for extra sweetness if red lentils are used.

2 Add the split green peas to the pan and stir to mix together well.

3 Pour the vegetable stock into the pan and bring to a boil. Reduce the heat to low and simmer for 35 minutes, until the potatoes are tender and the split peas cooked.

4 Meanwhile, make the croûtons. Melt the butter in a skillet. Add the garlic, parsley, and bread cubes and cook, turning frequently, for about 2 minutes, until the bread cubes are golden brown on all sides.

5 Stir the grated cheese into the soup and season to taste with salt and pepper. Heat gently until the cheese is starting to melt.

6 Pour the soup into warmed individual bowls and sprinkle the croûtons on top. Serve at once.

Vegetable Chili Soup

This is a hearty and flavorful soup that is good on its own or spooned over cooked rice or baked potatoes for a more substantial meal.

NUTRITIONAL INFORMATION

Calories 209   Sugar 10g
Protein . . . . .12g   Fats 10g
Carbohydrates . . .19g   Saturates 5g

10 MINS   1 HOUR 15 MINS

SERVES 4

I N G R E D I E N T S

1 medium eggplant, peeled if wished, cut into 1 inch slices

1 tbsp olive oil, plus extra for brushing

1 large red or yellow onion, finely chopped

2 bell peppers, finely chopped

3–4 garlic cloves, finely chopped or minced

14 oz cans chopped tomatoes in juice

1 tbsp mild chili powder, or to taste

½ tsp ground cumin

½ tsp dried oregano

2 small zucchini, quartered lengthways and sliced

14 oz can kidney beans, drained and rinsed

2 cups water

1 tbsp tomato paste

6 scallions, finely chopped

4 oz grated Cheddar cheese

salt and pepper

1 Brush the eggplant slices on one side with olive oil. Heat half the oil in a large skillet over a medium-high heat. Add the eggplant, oiled side up, and cook for 5–6 minutes until browned on one side. Turn, brown the other side and transfer to a plate. Cut into bite-sized pieces.

2 Heat the remaining oil in a large saucepan over a medium heat. Add the onion and bell peppers, cover and cook for 3–4 minutes, stirring occasionally, until the onion is just softened. Add the garlic and continue cooking for 2–3 minutes, or until the onion begins to color.

3 Add the tomatoes, chili powder, cumin, and oregano. Season with salt and pepper. Bring just to a boil, reduce the heat, cover, and simmer for 15 minutes.

4 Add the zucchini, eggplant pieces, and beans. Stir in the water and tomato paste. Cover again and continue simmering for about 45 minutes, or until the vegetables are tender. Taste and adjust the seasoning. If you prefer it hotter, stir in a little more chili powder.

5 Season to taste. Ladle into bowls, and top with scallions and cheese.

Tomato & Lentil Soup

This soup is simple and satisfying, with subtle, slightly exotic flavors.

NUTRITIONAL INFORMATION

Calories . . . . . . .195 Sugar 9g
Protein . . . . .12g Fats 3g
Carbohydrates . . .33g Saturates 0g

 10 MINS   55 MINS

SERVES 6

INGREDIENTS

1 tbsp olive oil

1 leek, thinly sliced

1 large carrot, quartered and thinly sliced

1 large onion, finely chopped

2 garlic cloves, finely chopped

9 oz split red lentils

5 cups water

1½ cups tomato juice

14 oz can chopped tomatoes in juice

¼ tsp ground cumin

¼ tsp ground coriander

1 bay leaf

salt and pepper

chopped fresh dill or parsley, to garnish

1 Heat the oil in a large saucepan over a medium heat. Add the leek, carrot, onion, and garlic. Cover and cook for 4–5 minutes, stirring frequently, until the leek and onion are slightly softened.

2 Rinse and drain the lentils (check for any small stones). Add the lentils to the pan and stir in the water, tomato juice, and tomatoes. Add the cumin, coriander, and bay leaf with a large pinch of salt. Bring to a boil, reduce the heat, and simmer for about 45 minutes, or until the vegetables are tender.

3 If you prefer a smooth soup, allow it to cool slightly, then transfer to a blender or food processor and purée until smooth, working in batches if necessary. (If using a food processor, strain off the cooking liquid and reserve. Purée the soup solids with enough cooking liquid to moisten them, then combine with the remaining liquid.) Only purée about half of the soup, if you prefer a more chunky soup.

4 Return the puréed soup to the saucepan and stir to blend. Season with salt and pepper to taste. Simmer over a medium-low heat until reheated.

5 Ladle the soup into warm bowls, garnish with dill or parsley and serve.

Curried Lentil & Onion Soup

This soup is a typical Indian treatment of lentils, called dal.

NUTRITIONAL INFORMATION

Calories . . . . . . .232 Sugars 6g
Protein . . . . .11g Fat 8g
Carbohydrate . . .31g Saturates 1g

🍲 10 MINS   🕐 55 MINS

SERVES 4

INGREDIENTS

2 tsp olive oil

1 large onion, finely chopped

1 large leek, thinly sliced

1 large carrot, grated

1–2 garlic cloves, finely chopped

½ tsp chili paste

½ tsp grated peeled fresh gingerroot or ginger paste

½ tsp garam masala or curry powder

¼ tsp ground cumin

⅛ tsp ground turmeric

5 cups water

9 oz split red lentils or yellow split peas

salt and pepper

TO GARNISH

1 red onion, halved and thinly sliced into half-rings

oil, for frying

1 Heat the olive oil in a large saucepan over a medium heat. Add the onion and cook for 4–5 minutes, stirring frequently, until it just begins to brown. Add the leek, carrot and garlic and continue cooking for 2 minutes, stirring occasionally.

2 Stir in the chili paste, ginger, garam masala or curry powder, cumin, and turmeric. Add the water and stir to mix well.

3 Rinse and drain the lentils (check for any small stones). Add to the saucepan. Bring to a boil, reduce the heat, cover, and simmer gently for 35 minutes, or until the lentils and vegetables are very soft, stirring occasionally.

4 Allow the soup to cool slightly, then transfer to a blender or food processor and purée until smooth, working in batches if necessary. (If using a food processor, strain off the cooking liquid and reserve. Purée the soup solids with enough cooking liquid to moisten them, then combine with the remaining liquid.)

5 Return the soup to the saucepan and simmer over a low heat. Season with salt and pepper to taste.

6 For the fried onion garnish, heat oil to a depth of about ½ inch in a small skillet over a medium-high heat until it begins to smoke. Drop in about one-third of the onion slices and fry until deep golden brown. Using a draining spoon, transfer to paper towels and drain. Cook the remainder of the onion slices in batches and drain.

7 Ladle the soup into warm bowls and scatter the fried onions over the top. Serve the soup immediately.

Lentil, Potato, & Ham Soup

A comforting and satisfying cold-weather soup, this is good served with bread as a light main course,

NUTRITIONAL INFORMATION

Calories	254	Sugar	.........6g
Protein	........19g	Fats	...........4g
Carbohydrates	...38g	Saturates	......1g

   10 MINS   45 MINS

SERVES 5

INGREDIENTS

10½ oz Puy lentils

2 tsp butter

1 large onion, finely chopped

2 carrots, finely chopped

1 garlic clove, finely chopped

2 cups water

1 bay leaf

¼ tsp dried sage or rosemary

8 oz potatoes, diced
  (see Cook's Tip)

4 cups chicken stock

1 tbsp tomato paste

4 oz smoked ham, finely diced

salt and pepper

chopped fresh parsley, to garnish

1 Rinse and drain the lentils and check for any small stones.

2 Melt the butter in a large saucepan or flameproof casserole over a medium heat. Add the onion, carrots, and garlic, cover and cook for 4–5 minutes until the onion is slightly softened, stirring frequently.

3 Add the lentils to the vegetables with the water, bay leaf, and sage or rosemary. Bring to a boil, reduce the heat, cover, and simmer for 10 minutes.

4 Add the stock, potatoes, tomato paste, and ham. Bring back to a simmer. Cover and continue simmering for 25–30 minutes, or until the vegetables are tender.

5 Season to taste with salt and pepper and remove the bay leaf. Ladle into warm bowls, garnish with parsley and serve.

COOK'S TIP

Cut the potatoes into small dice, about ¼ inch, so they will be in proportion with the lentils.

Vegetable & Lentil Soup

In this simple-to-make soup, the flavors meld after blending to create a delicious taste. It is also very healthy and looks appealing.

NUTRITIONAL INFORMATION

Calories	165	Sugars	.........8g
Protein	........11g	Fat	..........3g
Carbohydrate	...25g	Saturates	......0g

15 MINS   50 MINS

SERVES 6

INGREDIENTS

1 tbsp olive oil

1 onion, finely chopped

1 garlic clove, finely chopped

1 carrot, halved and thinly sliced

1 lb young green cabbage, cored, quartered and thinly sliced

14 oz can chopped tomatoes in juice

½ tsp dried thyme

2 bay leaves

6¼ cups chicken or vegetable stock

7 oz Puy lentils

2 cups water

salt and pepper

fresh cilantro leaves or parsley, to garnish

1 Heat the oil in a large saucepan over a medium heat, add the onion, garlic, and carrot and cook for 3–4 minutes, stirring frequently, until the onion starts to soften. Add the cabbage and cook for a further 2 minutes.

2 Add the tomatoes, thyme and 1 bay leaf, then pour in the stock. Bring to a boil, reduce the heat to low and cook gently, partially covered, for about 45 minutes until the vegetables are tender.

3 Meanwhile, put the lentils in another saucepan with the remaining bay leaf and the water. Bring just to a boil, reduce the heat and simmer for about 25 minutes until tender. Drain off any remaining water, and set aside.

4 When the vegetable soup is cooked, allow it to cool slightly, then transfer to a blender or food processor and purée until smooth, working in batches, if necessary. (If using a food processor, strain off the cooking liquid and reserve. Purée the soup solids with enough cooking liquid to moisten them, then combine with the remaining liquid.)

5 Return the soup to the saucepan and add the cooked lentils. Taste and adjust the seasoning, and cook for about 10 minutes to heat through. Ladle into warm bowls and garnish with cilantro leaves or parsley.

Barley & Fennel Soup

This rustic vegetable soup is appealing in its simplicity. Serve it with ciabatta, focaccia, or garlic bread.

NUTRITIONAL INFORMATION

Calories . . . . .109 Sugar 3g
Protein . . . . .5g Fats 3g
Carbohydrates . . .16g Saturates 0g

 15 MINS   1¹/₄ HOURS

SERVES 4

INGREDIENTS

2 oz pearl barley

6¼ cups chicken or vegetable stock

1 bay leaf

½ tsp chopped fresh thyme leaves, or ⅛ tsp dried thyme

9 oz broccoli head

2 tsp olive oil

1 large leek, halved lengthways and finely chopped

2 garlic cloves, finely chopped

1 stalk celery, thinly sliced

1 large fennel bulb, thinly sliced
  1 tbsp chopped fresh basil

freshly grated Parmesan cheese, to serve

2 Cut the florets off the broccoli head and peel the stem. Cut the stem into very thin matchsticks, about 1 inch long, along with any large stems from the florets. Cut the florets into small slivers and reserve them seperately.

3 Heat the oil in a large pan over a medium-low heat and add the leek and garlic. Cover and cook for about 5 minutes, stirring frequently, until softened. Add the celery, fennel, and broccoli stems and cook for 2 minutes.

4 Stir in the remaining stock and bring to a boil. Add the barley with its cooking liquid. Season with salt and pepper. Reduce the heat, cover, and simmer gently for 10 minutes, stirring occasionally.

5 Uncover the pan and adjust the heat so the soup bubbles gently. Stir in the broccoli florets and continue cooking for 10–12 minutes, or until the broccoli is tender. Stir in the basil. Taste and adjust the seasoning, if necessary. Ladle into warm bowls and serve with plenty of Parmesan cheese to sprinkle over.

1 Rinse the barley and drain. Bring 2 cups of the stock to a boil in a small saucepan. Add the bay leaf and thyme. If the stock is unsalted, add a large pinch of salt. Stir in the barley, reduce the heat, partially cover, and simmer for 30–40 minutes until tender.

Wild Rice & Spinach Soup

Although it is generally classed as a grain, wild rice is actually a native North American grass that grows in water.

NUTRITIONAL INFORMATION

Calories	602	Sugar	........12g
Protein	........14g	Fats	..........39g
Carbohydrates	...51g	Saturates	.....20g

🍲 15 MINS   ⏲ 1¼ HOURS

SERVES 4

INGREDIENTS

2 tsp olive oil

3 oz smoked Canadian bacon, finely chopped

1 large onion, finely chopped

⅔ cup wild rice, rinsed in cold water and drained

5 cups water

1–2 garlic cloves, finely chopped or minced

1 bay leaf

½ cup all-purpose flour

2 cups milk

8 oz spinach leaves, finely chopped

1 cup heavy cream

freshly grated nutmeg

salt and pepper

1 Heat the oil in a large saucepan over a medium heat. Add the bacon and cook for 6–7 minutes until lightly browned. Add the onion and wild rice and continue cooking for 3–4 minutes, stirring frequently, until the onion softens.

2 Add the water, garlic, and bay leaf and season with a little salt and pepper. Bring to a boil, reduce the heat, cover and boil very gently for about 1 hour, or until

some of the grains of wild rice have split open.

3 Put the flour in a mixing bowl and very slowly whisk in enough of the milk to make a thick paste. Add the remainder of the milk, whisking to make a smooth liquid. Put the flour and milk mixture in a saucepan and ladle in as much of the rice cooking liquid as possible. Bring to a boil, stirring almost constantly. Reduce the heat so that the liquid just bubbles gently and cook for 10 minutes, stirring occasionally. Add the spinach and cook for 1–2 minutes until wilted.

4 Allow the soup to cool slightly, then transfer to a blender or food processor and purée, working in batches if necessary. (If using a food processor, strain off the cooking liquid and reserve. Purée the soup solids with enough cooking liquid to moisten them, then combine with the remaining liquid.)

5 Combine the puréed soup with the rice mixture in a saucepan and place over a medium-low heat. Stir in the cream and a grating of nutmeg. Simmer the soup until reheated. Taste and adjust the seasoning, if needed, and ladle into warm bowls.

Tomato & Rice Soup

This is a good soup for impromptu entertaining, especially if you have leftover rice to hand.

NUTRITIONAL INFORMATION

Calories ....299 Sugars 14g
Protein ....5g Fat 19g
Carbohydrate ...30g Saturates 10g

  15 MINS 1¼ HOURS

SERVES 4

I N G R E D I E N T S

1 tbsp olive oil

1 large onion, finely chopped

2 garlic cloves, finely chopped or minced

2 carrots, grated

1 stalk celery, thinly sliced

14 oz cans plum tomatoes in juice

1 tsp dark brown sugar, or to taste

3¾ cups vegetable stock or water

1 bay leaf

1 cup cooked white rice

2 tbsp chopped fresh dill

6 tbsp heavy cream

salt and pepper

fresh dill sprigs, to garnish

1 Heat the olive oil in a large saucepan over a medium heat. Add the onion, cover, and cook for 3–4 minutes, stirring occasionally, until the onion is just softened.

2 Add the garlic, carrots, celery, tomatoes, brown sugar, and stock or water with the bay leaf to the saucepan. Reduce the heat, cover, and simmer for 1 hour, stirring occasionally.

3 Allow the soup to cool slightly, then transfer to a blender or food processor and purée until smooth, working in batches if necessary. (If using a food processor, strain off the cooking liquid and reserve. Purée the soup solids with enough cooking liquid to moisten them, then combine with the remaining liquid.)

4 Return the soup to the saucepan and stir in the rice and dill. Season with salt, if needed, and pepper. Cook gently over a medium-low heat for about 5 minutes, or until hot.

5 Stir in the cream. Taste the soup and adjust the seasoning, if necessary. Ladle into warm soup bowls and garnish each serving with a swirl of cream and dill sprigs. Serve at once.

Vegetable with Bulghur

This healthy and colorful soup makes good use of your herb garden. The fresh herbs give it a vibrant flavor.

NUTRITIONAL INFORMATION

Calories 110	Sugars 7g
Protein 5g	Fat 3g
Carbohydrate . . .17g	Saturates 0g

15 MINS   50 MINS

SERVES 5

I N G R E D I E N T S

1 tbsp olive oil

2 onions, chopped

3 garlic cloves, finely chopped or minced

⅓ cup bulghur wheat

5 tomatoes, skinned and sliced, or
    14 oz can plum tomatoes in juice

8 oz peeled pumpkin or acorn squash,
    diced

1 large zucchini, quartered lengthways and
    sliced

4 cups boiling water

2 tbsp tomato paste

¼ tsp chili paste

1½ oz chopped mixed fresh oregano, basil,
    and flat-leaf parsley

1 oz arugula leaves, coarsely chopped

1⅓ cups shelled fresh or
    frozen Englis peas

salt and pepper

freshly grated Parmesan cheese, to serve

1 Heat the oil in a large saucepan over a medium-low heat and add the onions and garlic. Cover and cook for 5–8 minutes until the onions soften.

2 Stir in the bulghur wheat and continue cooking for 1 minute.

3 Layer the tomatoes, pumpkin or squash and zucchini in the saucepan.

4 Combine half the water with the tomato paste, chili paste and a large pinch of salt. Pour over the vegetables. Cover and simmer for 15 minutes.

5 Uncover the saucepan and stir. Put all the herbs and the arugula on top of the soup and layer the peas over them.

Pour over the remaining water and gently bring to a boil. Reduce the heat and simmer for about 20–25 minutes, or until all the vegetables are tender.

6 Stir the soup. Taste and adjust the seasoning, adding salt and pepper if necessary, and a little more chili paste if you wish. Ladle into warm bowls and serve with Parmesan cheese.

Hot &
Spicy Soups

Soups are a part of nearly every meal in the Far East, and are usually served between courses to clear the palate. This chapter

provides a range of soups from all over the Far East, from thick Indian dal soups to hot, sour Chinese vegetarian soups and combinations of seafood and noodles. All the ingredients are readily available from good stores, and although several recipes demand a little time, all are worth any extra effort in the making.

Curried Parsnip Soup

Parsnips make a delicious soup as they have a slightly sweet flavor. In this recipe, spices are added to complement this sweetness.

NUTRITIONAL INFORMATION

Calories	152	Sugars	.........7g
Protein	.........3g	Fat	...........8g
Carbohydrate	...18g	Saturates	.......3g

 10 MINS   35 MINS

SERVES 4

INGREDIENTS

1 tbsp vegetable oil

1 tbsp butter

1 red onion, chopped

3 parsnips, chopped

2 garlic cloves, minced

2 tsp garam masala

½ tsp chili powder

1 tbsp all-purpose flour

3¾ cups vegetable stock

grated rind and juice of 1 lemon

salt and pepper

lemon rind, to garnish

1 Heat the oil and butter in a large saucepan until the butter has melted. Add the onion, parsnips, and garlic and sauté, stirring frequently, for about 5–7 minutes, until the vegetables have softened, but not colored.

2 Add the garam masala and chili powder and cook, stirring constantly, for 30 seconds. Sprinkle in the flour, mixing well and cook, stirring constantly, for a further 30 seconds.

3 Stir in the stock, lemon rind and juice and bring to a boil. Reduce the heat and simmer for 20 minutes.

4 Remove some of the vegetable pieces with a draining spoon and reserve until required. Process the remaining soup and vegetables in a food processor or blender for about 1 minute, or until a smooth purée. Alternatively, press the vegetables through a strainer with the back of a wooden spoon.

5 Return the soup to a clean saucepan and stir in the reserved vegetables. Heat the soup through for 2 minutes until very hot.

6 Season to taste with salt and pepper, then transfer to soup bowls, garnish with grated lemon rind and serve.

Curried Zucchini Soup

This soup is lightly curried to allow the delicate flavor of the zucchini to come through.

NUTRITIONAL INFORMATION

Calories	147	Sugars	........8g
Protein	.........6g	Fat	..........9g
Carbohydrate	...10g	Saturates	......5g

 10 MINS   35 MINS

SERVES 4

I N G R E D I E N T S

2 tsp butter

1 large onion, finely chopped

2 lb zucchini, sliced

2 cups chicken or vegetable stock

1 tsp curry powder

½ cup sour cream

salt and pepper

1 Melt the butter in a large saucepan over a medium heat. Add the onion and cook for about 3 minutes until it begins to soften.

2 Add the stock, zucchini, and curry powder, along with a large pinch of salt if using unsalted stock. Bring the soup to a boil, reduce the heat, cover and cook gently for about 25 minutes until the vegetables are tender.

3 Allow the soup to cool slightly, then transfer to a blender or food processor, working in batches if necessary. Purée the soup until just smooth, but still with green flecks. (If using a food processor, strain off the cooking liquid and reserve. Purée the soup solids with enough cooking liquid to moisten them, then combine with the remaining liquid.)

4 Return the soup to the saucepan and stir in the sour cream. Reheat gently over a low heat just until hot. (Do not boil.)

5 Taste and adjust the seasoning, if needed. Ladle into warm bowls and serve.

COOK'S TIP

Stock made from a cube or liquid stock base is fine for this soup. In this case, you may wish to add a little more sour cream. The soup freezes well, but freeze it without the cream and add before serving.

Indian Potato & Pea Soup

A slightly hot and spicy Indian flavor is given to this soup with the use of garam masala, chili, cumin, and coriander.

NUTRITIONAL INFORMATION

Calories	153	Sugars	.........6g
Protein	.........6g	Fat	...........6g
Carbohydrate	...18g	Saturates	.......1g

 10 MINS 35 MINS

SERVES 4

I N G R E D I E N T S

2 tbsp vegetable oil

8 oz mealy potatoes, diced

1 large onion, chopped

2 garlic cloves, minced

1 tsp garam masala

1 tsp ground coriander

1 tsp ground cumin

3¾ cups vegetable stock

1 red chili, chopped

scant 1 cup frozen English peas

4 tbsp unsweetened yogurt

salt and pepper

chopped cilantro,
  to garnish

warm bread, to serve

VARIATION

For slightly less heat, seed the chili before adding it to the soup. Always wash your hands after handling chilies as they contain volatile oils that can irritate the skin and make your eyes burn if you touch your face.

1 Heat the vegetable oil in a large saucepan. Add the potatoes, onion, and garlic and sauté over a low heat, stirring constantly, for about 5 minutes.

2 Add the garam masala, ground coriander, and cumin and cook, stirring constantly, for 1 minute.

3 Stir in the vegetable stock and chopped red chili and bring the mixture to a boil. Reduce the heat, cover the pan and simmer for 20 minutes, until the potatoes begin to break down.

4 Add the peas and cook for a further 5 minutes. Stir in the yogurt and season to taste with salt and pepper.

5 Pour into warmed soup bowls, garnish with chopped fresh cilantro and serve hot with warm bread.

Indian Bean Soup

A thick and hearty soup, nourishing and substantial enough to serve as a main meal with whole-wheat bread.

NUTRITIONAL INFORMATION

Calories 237	Sugars 9g
Protein 9g	Fat 9g
Carbohydrate . . .33g	Saturates 1g

 20 MINS   50 MINS

SERVES 6

I N G R E D I E N T S

4 tbsp vegetable ghee or vegetable oil

2 onions, peeled and chopped

1½ cups potato, cut
   into chunks

1½ cups parsnip, cut
   into chunks

1½ cups turnip or rutabaga, cut into chunks

2 celery stalks, sliced

2 zucchini, sliced

1 green bell pepper, seeded and cut into
   ½ inch pieces

2 garlic cloves, minced

2 tsp ground coriander

1 tbsp paprika

1 tbsp mild curry paste

5 cups vegetable stock

salt

14 oz can black-eye peas,
   drained and rinsed

chopped cilantro,
   to garnish (optional)

1 Heat the ghee or oil in a saucepan, add all the prepared vegetables, except the zucchini and green bell pepper, and cook over a moderate heat, stirring frequently, for 5 minutes. Add the garlic, ground coriander, paprika, and curry paste and cook, stirring constantly, for 1 minute.

2 Stir in the stock and season with salt to taste. Bring to a boil, cover, and simmer over a low heat, stirring occasionally, for 25 minutes.

3 Stir in the black-eye peas, sliced zucchini, and green bell pepper, cover, and continue cooking for a further 15 minutes, or until all the vegetables are tender.

4 Process 1¼ cups of the soup mixture (about 2 ladlefuls) in a food processor or blender. Return the puréed mixture to the soup in the saucepan and reheat until very hot. Sprinkle with chopped cilantro, if using and serve hot.

Dal Soup

Dal is the name given to a delicious Indian lentil dish. This soup is a variation of the theme–it is made with red lentils and curry powder.

NUTRITIONAL INFORMATION

Calories 284   Sugars 13g
Protein ....16g   Fat 9g
Carbohydrate ...38g   Saturates 5g

 5 MINS   40 MINS

SERVES 4

INGREDIENTS

2 tbsp butter

2 garlic cloves, minced

1 onion, chopped

½ tsp turmeric

1 tsp garam masala

¼ tsp chili powder

1 tsp ground cumin

2 lb canned, chopped
    tomatoes, drained

1 cup red lentils

2 tsp lemon juice

2½ cups vegetable stock

1¼ cups coconut milk

salt and pepper

chopped cilantro and lemon
    slices, to garnish

naan bread, to serve

1 Melt the butter in a large saucepan. Add the garlic and onion and sauté, stirring, for 2–3 minutes. Add the turmeric, garam masala, chili powder, and cumin and cook for a further 30 seconds.

2 Stir in the tomatoes, red lentils, lemon juice, vegetable stock, and coconut milk and bring to a boil.

3 Reduce the heat to low and simmer the soup, uncovered, for about 25–30 minutes, until the lentils are tender and cooked.

4 Season to taste with salt and pepper and ladle the soup into a warm tureen. Garnish with chopped cilantro and lemon slices and serve immediately with warm naan bread.

COOK'S TIP

You can buy cans of coconut milk from supermarkets and delicatessens. It can also be made by grating creamed coconut, which comes in the form of a solid bar, and then mixing it with water.

Spicy Dal & Carrot Soup

This delicious, warming and nutritious soup includes a selection of spices to give it a 'kick'. It is simple to make and extremely good to eat.

NUTRITIONAL INFORMATION

Calories 173   Sugars 11g
Protein ....9g   Fat 5g
Carbohydrate ...24g   Saturates 1g

10 MINS   50 MINS

SERVES 6

I N G R E D I E N T S

4½ oz split red lentils

5 cups vegetable
   stock

12 oz carrots, peeled and sliced

2 onions, peeled and chopped

1 x 9 oz can chopped tomatoes

2 garlic cloves, peeled and chopped

2 tbsp vegetable ghee or oil

1 tsp ground cumin

1 tsp ground coriander

1 fresh green chili, seeded and chopped,
   or use 1 tsp minced chili (from a jar)

½ tsp ground turmeric

1 tbsp lemon juice

salt

1¼ cups skimmed milk

2 tbsp chopped fresh cilantro

yogurt, to serve

1 Place the lentils in a strainer and wash well under cold running water. Drain and place in a large saucepan with 3½ cups of the vegetable stock, the carrots, onions, tomatoes and garlic. Bring the mixture to a boil, reduce the heat, cover, and simmer for 30 minutes.

2 Meanwhile, heat the ghee or oil in a small pan, add the cumin, coriander, chili and turmeric and fry gently for 1 minute.

3 Remove from the heat and stir in the lemon juice and salt to taste.

4 Purée the soup in batches in a blender or food processor. Return the soup to the saucepan, add the spice mixture, and the remaining 1¼ cups stock or water and simmer for 10 minutes.

5 Add the milk to the soup and adjust the seasoning according to taste.

6 Stir in the chopped cilantro and reheat gently. Serve hot, with a swirl of yogurt.

Indian Potato & Pea Soup

A slightly hot and spicy Indian flavor is given to this soup with the use of garam masala, chili, cumin, and coriander.

NUTRITIONAL INFORMATION

Calories	153	Sugars	.........6g
Protein	.........6g	Fat	...........6g
Carbohydrate	...18g	Saturates	......1g

 5 MINS   35 MINS

SERVES 4

INGREDIENTS

2 tbsp vegetable oil

8 oz mealy potatoes, diced

1 large onion, chopped

2 garlic cloves, minced

1 tsp garam masala

1 tsp ground coriander

1 tsp ground cumin

3¾ cups vegetable stock

1 red chili, chopped

3½ oz frozen English peas

4 tbsp low-fat unsweetened yogurt

salt and pepper

chopped fresh cilantro, to garnish

1 Heat the vegetable oil in a large saucepan and add the diced potatoes, onion, and garlic. Sauté gently for about 5 minutes, stirring constantly. Add the ground spices and cook for 1 minute, stirring all the time.

2 Stir in the vegetable stock and chopped red chili and bring the mixture to a boil. Reduce the heat, cover the pan, and simmer for 20 minutes.

3 Add the peas and cook for a further 5 minutes. Stir in the yogurt and season to taste.

4 Pour the soup into warmed bowls, garnish with the chopped fresh cilantro and serve hot with warm bread.

COOK'S TIP

For slightly less heat, seed the chili before adding it to the soup. Always wash your hands after handling chilies as they contain volatile oils that can irritate the skin and make your eyes burn if you touch your face.

Corn & Lentil Soup

This pale-colored soup is made with corn and green lentils, and is similar in style to the traditional crab and corn soup.

NUTRITIONAL INFORMATION

Calories 171   Sugars 9g
Protein . . . . .5g   Fat 2g
Carbohydrate . . .30g   Saturates 0.3g

5 MINS   30 MINS

SERVES 4

INGREDIENTS

2 tbsp green lentils

4 cups vegetable stock

½ inch piece gingerroot, chopped finely

2 tsp soy sauce

1 tsp sugar

1 tbsp cornstarch

3 tbsp dry sherry

11½ oz can corn

1 egg white

1 tsp sesame oil

salt and pepper

TO GARNISH

scallion, cut into strips

red chili, cut into strips

1 Wash the lentils in a strainer. Place in a saucepan with the stock, gingerroot, soy sauce, and sugar. Bring to a boil and boil rapidly, uncovered, for 10 minutes. Skim off any froth on the surface. Reduce the heat, cover and simmer for 15 minutes.

2 Mix the cornstarch with the sherry in a small bowl. Add the corn with the liquid from the can and cornstarch mixture to the saucepan. Simmer for 2 minutes.

3 Whisk the egg white lightly with the sesame oil. Pour the egg mixture into the soup in a thin stream, remove from the heat and stir. The egg white will form white strands. Season with salt and pepper to taste.

4 Pour into 4 warmed soup bowls and garnish with strips of scallion and red chili. Serve the soup immediately.

COOK'S TIP

To save time use a 15 oz can of green lentils instead of dried ones. Place the lentils and corn in a large saucepan with the stock and flavorings, bring to a boil and simmer for 2 minutes, then continue the recipe from step 2 as above.

Spinach & Bean Curd Soup

This is a very colorful and delicious soup. If spinach is not in season, watercress or lettuce can be used instead.

NUTRITIONAL INFORMATION

Calories	33	Sugar	.........1g
Protein	.........4g	Fat	...........2g
Carbohydrate	....1g	Saturates	.....0.2g

🍲 3½ HOURS   🕐 10 MINS

SERVES 4

INGREDIENTS

1 cake bean curd

4½ oz spinach leaves without stems

3 cups Chinese Stock
   (see page 14) or water

1 tbsp light soy sauce

salt and pepper

1 Using a sharp knife, cut the bean curd into small pieces about ¼ inch thick.

2 Wash the spinach leaves thoroughly under cold, running water and drain thoroughly.

3 Cut the spinach leaves into small pieces or shreds, discarding any discolored leaves and tough stalks. (If possible, use fresh young spinach leaves, which have not yet developed tough ribs. Otherwise, it is important to cut out all the ribs and stems for this soup.) Set the spinach aside until required.

4 In a preheated wok or large skillet, bring the Chinese stock or water to a rolling boil.

5 Add the bean curd cubes and light soy sauce, bring back to a boil and simmer for about 2 minutes over a medium heat.

6 Add the shredded spinach leaves and simmer for 1 more minute, stirring gently. Skim the surface of the soup to make it clear, adjust the seasoning to taste.

7 Transfer the spinach and bean curd soup to a warm soup tureen or individual serving bowls and serve with chopsticks, to pick up the pieces of food and a broad, shallow spoon for drinking the soup.

COOK'S TIP

Soup is an integral part of a Chinese meal; it is usually presented in a large bowl placed in the center of the table, and consumed as the meal progresses. It serves as a refresher between different dishes and as a beverage throughout the meal

Vegetarian Hot & Sour Soup

This popular soup is easy to make and very filling. It can be eaten as a meal on its own or served as an appetizer before a light menu.

NUTRITIONAL INFORMATION

Calories	.61	Sugars	.1g
Protein	.5g	Fat	.2g
Carbohydrate	.8g	Saturates	.0.2g

30 MINS 10 MINS

SERVES 4

INGREDIENTS

4 dried shiitake mushrooms
  (if unavailable, use open-cup
  mushrooms)

4½ oz firm bean curd

1 cup canned bamboo shoots

2½ cups vegetable stock or water

⅓ cup English peas

1 tbsp dark soy sauce

2 tbsp white wine vinegar

2 tbsp cornstarch

salt and pepper

sesame oil, to serve

1 Place the Chinese dried mushrooms in a small bowl and cover with warm water. Leave to soak for about 20–25 minutes.

2 Drain the mushrooms and squeeze out the excess water, reserving this. Remove the tough centers and cut the mushrooms into thin shreds. Shred the bean curd and bamboo shoots.

3 Bring the stock or water to a boil in a large saucepan. Add the mushrooms, bean curd, bamboo shoots, and peas. Simmer for 2 minutes.

4 Mix together the soy sauce, vinegar, and cornstarch with 2 tablespoons of the reserved mushroom liquid.

5 Stir the soy sauce and cornstarch mixture into the soup with the remaining mushroom liquid. Bring to a boil and season with salt and plenty of pepper. Simmer for 2 minutes.

6 Serve in warmed bowls with a few drops of sesame oil sprinkled over the top of each.

COOK'S TIP

If you use open-cup mushrooms instead of dried mushrooms, add an extra ⅔ cup vegetable stock or water to the soup, as these mushrooms do not need soaking.

Noodle & Mushroom Soup

This soup is very quickly and easily put together, and is cooked so that each ingredient can still be tasted in the finished dish.

NUTRITIONAL INFORMATION

Calories 74   Sugars 1g
Protein ....13g   Fat 3g
Carbohydrate ....9g   Saturates 0.4g

4 HOURS   10 MINS

SERVES 4

INGREDIENTS

¼ cup dried shiitake mushrooms or 1⅓ cups field or crimini mushrooms

4 cups hot Fresh Vegetable Stock (page 30)

4½ oz thread egg noodles

2 tsp sunflower oil

3 garlic cloves, minced

1 inch piece ginger, shredded finely

½ tsp mushroom catsup

1 tsp light soy sauce

2 cups mung bean sprouts

cilantro leaves, to garnish

1 Soak the dried shiitake mushrooms, if using, for at least 30 minutes in 1¼ cups of the hot vegetable stock. Remove the stalks and discard, then slice the mushrooms. Reserve the stock.

2 Cook the noodles for 2–3 minutes in boiling water. Drain, rinse and set aside until required.

3 Heat the oil over a high heat in a wok or large, heavy skillet. Add the garlic and ginger, stir and add the mushrooms. Stir over a high heat for 2 minutes.

4 Add the remaining vegetable stock with the reserved stock and bring to a boil. Add the mushroom catsup and soy sauce and mix well.

5 Stir in the bean sprouts and cook until tender. Serve over the noodles, garnished with cilantro leaves.

COOK'S TIP

Dried mushrooms are highly fragrant and add a special flavor to Chinese dishes. There are many different varieties but Shiitake are the best. Although not cheap, a small amount will go a long way and they will keep indefinitely in an airtight jar.

Sweet & Sour Cabbage Soup

This healthy soup is made with an unusual combination of fruits and vegetables, creating a tantalising flavor that will keep people guessing.

NUTRITIONAL INFORMATION

Calories 138	Sugars 27g	
Protein 3g	Fat 2g	
Carbohydrate ...28g	Saturates 0g	

🍳 25 MINS　　🕐 1¹/₄ HOURS

SERVES 4

I N G R E D I E N T S

1/2 cup golden raisins

1/2 cup orange juice

1 tbsp olive oil

1 large onion, chopped

3 cups shredded cabbage

2 apples, peeled and diced

½ cup apple juice

14 oz can peeled tomatoes in juice

1 cup tomato or vegetable juice

3 ½ oz pineapple flesh, finely chopped

5 cups water

2 tsp wine vinegar

salt and pepper

fresh mint leaves, to garnish

 Put the golden raisins in a bowl, pour the orange juice over and leave for 15 minutes.

 Heat the oil in a large saucepan over a medium heat, add the onion, cover, and cook for 3–4 minutes, stirring frequently, until it starts to soften. Add the cabbage and cook for a further 2 minutes; do not allow it to brown.

3 Add the apples and apple juice, cover and cook gently for 5 minutes.

4 Stir in the tomatoes, tomato juice, pineapple, and water. Season with salt and pepper and add the vinegar.

5 Add the golden raisins together with the orange juice soaking liquid. Bring to a boil, reduce the heat and simmer, partially covered, for about 1 hour until the fruit and vegetables are tender.

6 Allow the soup to cool slightly, then transfer to a blender or food processor and purée until smooth, working in batches if necessary. (If using a food processor, strain off the cooking liquid and reserve. Purée the soup solids with enough cooking liquid to moisten them, then combine with the remaining liquid.)

7 Return the soup to the saucepan and simmer gently for about 10 minutes to reheat. Ladle into warm bowls. Garnish with mint leaves and serve immediately.

Pepper & Chili Soup

This soup has a real Mediterranean flavor, using sweet red bell peppers, tomato, chili, and basil. It is great served with an olive bread.

NUTRITIONAL INFORMATION

Calories 55	Sugars 10g
Protein 2g	Fat 0.5g
Carbohydrate 11g	Saturates 0.1g

 10 MINS   25 MINS

SERVES 4

INGREDIENTS

8 oz red bell peppers, seeded and sliced

1 onion, sliced

2 garlic cloves, minced

1 green chili, chopped

1½ cups sieved tomatoes

2½ cups vegetable stock

2 tbsp chopped basil

basil sprigs, to garnish

1 Put the bell peppers in a large saucepan with the onion, garlic, and chili. Add the sieved tomatoes and vegetable stock and bring to a boil, stirring well.

VARIATION

This soup is also delicious served cold with ²/₃ cup of unsweetened yogurt swirled into it.

2 Reduce the heat to a simmer and cook for 20 minutes, or until the bell peppers have softened. Drain, reserving the liquid and vegetables separately.

3 Press the vegetables through a strainer with the back of a spoon. Alternatively, process in a food processor until smooth.

4 Return the vegetable purée to a clea saucepan with the reserved cookin liquid. Add the basil and heat throug until hot. Garnish the soup with fresh bas sprigs and serve immediately.

Mixed Vegetable Soup

Select 3 or 4 vegetables for this soup: the Chinese like to blend different colors, flavors, and textures to create harmony as well as contrast.

NUTRITIONAL INFORMATION

Calories 38	Sugars 3g	
Protein 3g	Fat 2g	
Carbohydrate 4g	Saturates 0.2g	

 3¹/₂ HOURS   5 MINS

SERVES 4

INGREDIENTS

1-2 oz each of
  mushrooms, carrots, asparagus, snow
  peas, bamboo shoots, baby corn,
  cucumber, tomatoes, spinach, lettuce,
  Chinese cabbage, bean curd etc.

2 ½ cups Chinese Stock
  (see page 14)

1 tbsp light soy sauce

a few drops sesame oil (optional)

salt and pepper

finely chopped scallions, to garnish

1 Preheat a wok or large heavy-bottomed skillet.

2 Using a sharp knife or cleaver, cut your selection of vegetables into roughly uniform shapes and sizes (slices, shreds, or cubes).

3 Pour the Chinese stock into the wok or skillet and bring to a rolling boil.

4 Add the vegetables, bearing in mind that some require a longer cooking time than others: add carrots and baby corn first, cook for 2 minutes, then add asparagus, mushrooms, Chinese cabbage, bean curd, and cook for another minute.

5 Spinach, lettuce, watercress, cucumber, and tomato are added last. Stir, and bring the soup back to a boil.

6 Add the soy sauce and the sesame oil, if wished, and adjust the seasoning to taste.

7 Transfer the mixed vegetable soup to warm serving bowls and serve hot, garnished with scallions.

COOK'S TIP

Sesame oil is a low-saturate oil widely used for its nutty, aromatic flavor. Made from toasted sesame seeds it is used as a seasoning, not as a cooking oil. Thick and dark, it burns easily, so it should be added at the last moment.

Chili & Watercress Soup

This delicious soup is a wonderful blend of colors and flavors. It is very hot, so if you prefer a milder taste, omit the seeds from the chilies.

NUTRITIONAL INFORMATION

Calories 90	Sugars 1g
Protein 7g	Fat 6g
Carbohydrate 2g	Saturates 1g

 10 MINS   🕐 15 MINS

SERVES 4

I N G R E D I E N T S

1 tbsp sunflower oil

9 oz smoked bean curd, sliced

1 cup shiitake mushrooms, sliced

2 tbsp chopped fresh cilantro

2 cups watercress

1 red chili, sliced finely, to garnish

S T O C K

1 tbsp tamarind pulp

2 dried red chilies, chopped

2 kaffir lime leaves, torn in half

1 inch piece ginger, chopped

2 inch piece galangal, chopped

1 stalk lemongrass, chopped

1 onion, quartered

4 cups cold water

1 Put all the ingredients for the stock into a saucepan and bring to a boil.

2 Simmer the stock for 5 minutes. Remove from the heat and strain, reserving the stock.

3 Heat the sunflower oil in a wok or large, heavy skillet and cook the bean curd over a high heat for about 2 minutes, stirring constantly so that the bean curd cooks evenly on both sides. Add the strained stock.

4 Add the mushrooms and cilantro, and boil for 3 minutes.

5 Add the watercress and boil for 1 minute.

6 Serve immediately, garnished with red chili slices.

VARIATION

You might like to try mixture of different types o mushroom. Oyster, button, an straw mushrooms are all suitable

Chili Fish Soup

Shiitake mushrooms add an intense flavor to this soup which is unique.
If they are unavailable, use open-cap mushrooms, sliced.

NUTRITIONAL INFORMATION

Calories ....166 Sugars 1g
Protein ....23g Fat 7g
Carbohydrate ....4g Saturates 1g

15 MINS   15 MINS

SERVES 4

I N G R E D I E N T S

½ oz Chinese dried mushrooms

2 tbsp sunflower oil

1 onion, sliced

1½ cups snow peas

1½ cups bamboo shoots

3 tbsp sweet chili sauce

5 cups fish or vegetable stock

3 tbsp light soy sauce

2 tbsp fresh cilantro, plus extra to garnish

1 lb cod fillet, skinned and cubed

COOK'S TIP

Cod is used in this recipe as it is a meaty white fish. For real luxury, use angler fish tail instead.

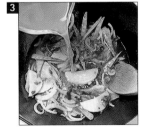

1 Place the mushrooms in a large bowl. Pour over enough boiling water to cover and leave to stand for 5 minutes. Drain the mushrooms thoroughly in a colander. Using a sharp knife, roughly chop the mushrooms.

2 Heat the sunflower oil in a preheated wok or large skillet. Add the sliced onion to the wok and stir-fry for 5 minutes, or until softened.

3 Add the snow peas, bamboo shoots, chili sauce, stock, and soy sauce to the wok and bring to a boil.

4 Add the cilantro and cod and leave to simmer for 5 minutes or until the fish is cooked through.

5 Transfer the soup to warm bowls, garnish with extra cilantro, if wished, and serve hot.

Fish & Vegetable Soup

A chunky fish soup with strips of vegetables, all flavored with ginger and lemon, makes a meal in itself.

NUTRITIONAL INFORMATION

Calories	.88	Sugars	.1g
Protein	.12g	Fat	.3g
Carbohydrate	.3g	Saturates	.0.5g

40 MINS   20 MINS

SERVES 4

I N G R E D I E N T S

9 oz white fish fillets (cod, halibut, haddock, sole etc)

½ tsp ground ginger

½ tsp salt

1 small leek, trimmed

2-4 crab sticks, defrosted if frozen (optional)

1 tbsp sunflower oil

1 large carrot, cut into julienne strips

8 canned water chestnuts, thinly sliced

5 cups fish or vegetable stock

1 tbsp lemon juice

1 tbsp light soy sauce

1 large zucchini, cut into julienne strips

black pepper

1 Remove any skin from the fish and cut into cubes, about 1 inch. Combine the ground ginger and salt and use to rub into the pieces of fish. Leave to marinate for at least 30 minutes.

2 Meanwhile, divide the green and white parts of the leek. Cut each part into 1 inch lengths and then into julienne strips down the length of each piece, keeping the two parts separate. Slice the crab sticks into ½ inch pieces.

3 Heat the oil in the wok, swirling it around so it is really hot. Add the white part of the leek and stir-fry for a couple of minutes, then add the carrots and water chestnuts and continue to cook for 1-2 minutes, stirring thoroughly.

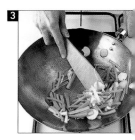

4 Add the stock and bring to a boil, then add the lemon juice and soy sauce and simmer for 2 minutes.

5 Add the fish and continue to cook for about 5 minutes until the fish begins to break up a little, then add the green part of the leek and the zucchini and simmer for about 1 minute. Add the sliced crab sticks, if using, and season to taste with black pepper. Simmer for a further minute or so and serve very hot.

COOK'S TIP

To skin fish, place the fillet skin-side down and insert a sharp, flexible knife at one end between the flesh and the skin. Hold the skin tightly at the end and push the knife along, keeping the blade flat against the skin.

Oriental Fish Soup

This is a deliciously different fish soup which can be made quickly and easily in a microwave.

NUTRITIONAL INFORMATION

Calories	105	Sugars	.........1g
Protein	........13g	Fat	..........5g
Carbohydrate	....1g	Saturates	.......1g

20 MINS   10 MINS

SERVES 4

INGREDIENTS

egg

tsp sesame seeds, toasted

celery stalk, chopped

carrot, cut into julienne strips

scallions, sliced on the diagonal

tbsp oil

½ cups fresh spinach

3½ cups hot vegetable stock

tsp light soy sauce

oz haddock, skinned and cut into small chunks

salt and pepper

VARIATION

Instead of topping the soup with omelet shreds, you could pour the beaten egg, without the sesame seeds, into the hot stock at the end of the cooking time. The egg will set in pretty strands to give a flowery look.

1 Beat the egg with the sesame seeds and seasoning. Lightly oil a plate and pour on the egg mixture. Cook on HIGH power for 1½ minutes until just setting in the center. Leave to stand for a few minutes then remove from the plate. Roll up the egg and shred thinly.

2 Mix together the celery, carrot, scallions, and oil. Cover and cook on HIGH power for 3 minutes.

3 Wash the spinach thoroughly under cold, running water. Cut off and discard any long stalks and drain well. Shred the spinach finely.

Add the hot stock, soy sauce, haddock, and spinach to the vegetable mixture. Cover and cook on HIGH power for 5 minutes. Stir the soup and season to taste. Serve in warmed bowls with the shredded egg scattered over.

Saffron Fish Soup

This elegant soup makes a good dinner party starter. To make planning easier, the saffron-flavored soup base can be made ahead.

NUTRITIONAL INFORMATION

Calories . . . . . . .364 Sugars 8g
Protein . . . . .20g Fat 18g
Carbohydrate . . .25g Saturates 11g

15 MINS   35 MINS

SERVES 4

INGREDIENTS

2 tsp butter

1 onion, finely chopped

1 leek, thinly sliced

1 carrot, thinly sliced

4 tbsp white rice

pinch of saffron threads

½ cup dry white wine

½ cup heavy cream

12 oz skinless white fish fillet, such as cod, haddock, or angler fish, cut into ½ inch cubes

4 cups fish stock

4 tomatoes, skinned, seeded, and chopped

3 tbsp snipped fresh chives, to garnish

salt and pepper

2 Add the saffron, rice, wine, and stock, bring just to the boil, and reduce the heat to low. Season with salt and pepper. Cover and simmer for 20 minutes, or until the rice and vegetables are soft.

3 Allow the soup to cool slightly, then transfer to a blender or food processor and purée until smooth, working in batches if necessary. (If using a food processor, strain off the cooking liquid and reserve. Purée the soup solids with enough cooking liquid to moisten them, then combine with the remaining liquid.)

4 Return the soup to the saucepan, stir in the cream and simmer over a low heat for a few minutes until heated through, stirring occasionally.

5 Season the fish and add, with the tomatoes, to the simmering soup. Cook for 3–5 minutes, or until the fish is just tender.

6 Stir in most of the chives. Taste the soup and adjust the seasoning, if necessary. Ladle into warm shallow bowls, sprinkle the remaining chilies on top and serve.

1 Heat the butter in a saucepan over a medium heat and add the onion, leek, and carrot. Cook for 3–4 minutes, stirring frequently, until the onion is soft.

Fish Soup with Won Tons

This soup is topped with small won tons filled with shrimp, making it both very tasty and satisfying.

10 MINS   15 MINS

SERVES 4

I N G R E D I E N T S

½ oz large, cooked, peeled shrimp

tsp chopped chives

small garlic clove, finely chopped

tbsp vegetable oil

2 won ton skins

small egg, beaten

¾ cups fish stock

oz white fish fillet, diced

ash of chili sauce

diced fresh red chili and chives, to garnish

1 Roughly chop a quarter of the shrimp and mix together with the chopped chives and garlic.

2 Heat the oil in a preheated wok or large skillet until it is really hot.

3 Stir-fry the shrimp mixture for 1–2 minutes. Remove from the heat and set aside to cool completely.

4 Spread out the won ton skins on a work counter. Spoon a little of the shrimp filling into the center of each skin. Brush the edges of the skins with beaten egg and press the edges together, scrunching them to form a 'moneybag' shape. Set aside while you are preparing the soup.

5 Pour the fish stock into a large saucepan and bring to a boil. Add the diced white fish and the remaining shrimp and cook for 5 minutes.

6 Season to taste with the chili sauce. Add the won tons and cook for a further 5 minutes.

7 Spoon into warmed serving bowls, garnish with sliced red chili and chives and serve immediately.

VARIATION

Replace the shrimp with cooked crabmeat for an alternative flavor.

Three-Flavor Soup

Ideally, use raw shrimp in this soup. If that is not possible, add ready-cooked ones at the very last stage.

NUTRITIONAL INFORMATION

Calories	117	Sugars	.........0g
Protein	........20g	Fat	...........3g
Carbohydrate	....2g	Saturates	.......1g

🍲 3¹/₂ HOURS   🕙 10 MINS

SERVES 4

I N G R E D I E N T S

4½ oz skinned, boned chicken breast

125 g/4½ oz raw peeled shrimp

salt

½ egg white, lightly beaten

2 tsp cornstarch paste (see page 15)

4½ oz honey-roast ham

3 cups Chinese Stock (see page 14)
   or water

finely chopped scallions, to garnish

1 Using a sharp knife or meat cleaver, thinly slice the chicken into small shreds. If the shrimp are large, cut each in half lengthways, otherwise leave them whole.

2 Place the chicken and shrimps in a bowl and mix with a pinch of salt, the egg white and cornstarch paste until well coated. Set aside until required.

3 Cut the honey-roast ham into small thin slices roughly the same size as the chicken pieces.

4 In a preheated wok or large, heavy skillet, bring the Chinese stock or water to a rolling boil and add the chicken, the raw shrimp and the ham.

5 Bring the soup back to a boil, and simmer for 1 minute.

6 Adjust the seasoning to taste, then pour the soup into four warmed individual serving bowls, garnish with the scallions and serve immediately.

COOK'S TI

Soups such as this a
improved enormously in flavor
you use a well-flavored stock. Eith
use a bouillon cube, or find time
make Chinese Stock–see the recipe c
page 28. Better still, mak
double quantities and free
some for future us

Thai Seafood Soup

As taste and tolerance for chilies varies, using chili paste offers more control of the heat.

NUTRITIONAL INFORMATION

Calories	92	Sugars	........0g
Protein	........17g	Fat	..........2g
Carbohydrate	....3g	Saturates	......0g

SERVES 4

INGREDIENTS

5 cups fish stock

1 lemongrass stalk, split lengthways

pared rind of ½ lime, or 1 lime leaf

1 inch piece fresh gingerroot, peeled and sliced

¼ tsp chili paste, or to taste

4–6 scallions, sliced

7 oz large of medium raw shrimp, peeled

9 oz scallops (16–20)

2 tbsp fresh cilantro leaves

salt

finely chopped red bell pepper, or red chili rings, to garnish

COOK'S TIP

If you have light chicken stock, but no fish stock, it will make an equally tasty though different version of this soup.

1 Put the stock in a saucepan with the lemongrass, lime rind or leaf, ginger, and chili paste. Bring just to a boil, reduce the heat, cover, and simmer for 10–15 minutes.

2 Cut the baby leek in half lengthways, then slice crossways very thinly. Cut the shrimp almost in half lengthways, keeping the tail intact.

3 Strain the stock, return to the saucepan and bring to a simmer, with bubbles rising at the edges and the surface trembling. Add the leek and cook for 2–3 minutes. Taste and season with salt, if needed, and stir in a little more chili paste if wished.

4 Add the scallops and shrimp and poach for about 1 minute until they turn opaque and the shrimp curl.

5 Drop in the fresh cilantro leaves, ladle the soup into warm bowls, dividing the shellfish evenly, and garnish with red bell pepper or chilies.

Seafood & Bean Curd Soup

Use shrimp, squid, or scallops, or a combination of all three in this healthy soup.

NUTRITIONAL INFORMATION

Calories ....97 Sugars 0g
Protein ....17g Fat 2g
Carbohydrate ....3g Saturates 0.4g

🍲 3¹/₂ HOURS   🕐 10 MINS

SERVES 4

I N G R E D I E N T S

9 oz seafood: peeled shrimp, squid, scallops, etc., defrosted if frozen

½ egg white, lightly beaten

1 tbsp cornstarch paste (see page 15)

1 cake bean curd

3 cups Chinese Stock (see page 14)

1 tbsp light soy sauce

salt and pepper

fresh cilantro leaves, to garnish (optional)

1 Small shrimp can be left whole; larger ones should be cut into smaller pieces; cut the squid and scallops into small pieces.

2 If raw, mix the shrimp and scallops with the egg white and cornstarch paste to prevent them from becoming tough when they are cooked. Cut the cake of bean curd into about 24 small cubes.

3 Bring the stock to a rolling boil. Add the bean curd and soy sauce, bring back to a boil and simmer for 1 minute.

4 Stir in the seafood, raw pieces first, pre-cooked ones last. Bring back to a boil and simmer for just 1 minute.

5 Adjust the seasoning to taste and serve, garnished with cilantro leaves if liked.

COOK'S TIP

Bean curd is made from puréed yellow soya beans, which are very high in protein. Although almost tasteless, it absorbs the flavors of other ingredients. It is widely available in supermarkets, and Oriental and health-food stores.

Shrimp Soup

This soup is an interesting mix of colors and textures. The egg may be made into a flat omelet and added as thin strips if preferred.

NUTRITIONAL INFORMATION

Calories	123	Sugars	.......0.2g
Protein	........13g	Fat	...........8g
Carbohydrate	....1g	Saturates	.......1g

5 MINS   20 MINS

SERVES 4

INGREDIENTS

2 tbsp sunflower oil

2 scallions, thinly sliced diagonally

1 carrot, coarsely grated

4½ oz large closed cup mushrooms, thinly sliced

4 cups fish or vegetable stock

½ tsp Chinese five-spice powder

1 tbsp light soy sauce

4½ oz large peeled shrimp or peeled jumbo shrimp, defrosted if frozen

½ bunch watercress, trimmed and roughly chopped

1 egg, well beaten

salt and pepper

4 large shrimp in shells, to garnish (optional)

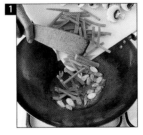 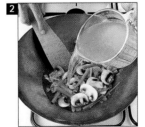 

1 Heat the oil in a wok, swirling it around until really hot. Add the scallions and stir-fry for a minute then add the carrots and mushrooms and continue to cook for about 2 minutes.

2 Add the stock and bring to a boil then season to taste with salt and pepper, five-spice powder, and soy sauce and simmer for 5 minutes.

3 If the shrimp are really large, cut them in half before adding to the wok and simmer for 3-4 minutes.

4 Add the watercress to the wok and mix well, then slowly pour in the beaten egg in a circular movement so that it cooks in threads in the soup. Adjust the seasoning and serve each portion topped with a whole shrimp.

COOK'S TIP

The large open mushrooms with black gills give the best flavor but they tend to spoil the color of the soup, making it very dark. Oyster mushrooms can also be used.

Spicy Shrimp Soup

Lime leaves are used as a flavoring in this soup to add tartness.

NUTRITIONAL INFORMATION

Calories 217   Sugars 16g
Protein . . . . .16g   Fat 4g
Carbohydrate . . .31g   Saturates 1g

 10 MINS   20 MINS

SERVES 4

I N G R E D I E N T S

2 tbsp tamarind paste

4 red chilies, very finely chopped

2 cloves garlic, minced

1 inch piece Thai ginger, peeled and very
   finely chopped

4 tbsp fish sauce

2 tbsp jaggery or superfine sugar

5 cups fish stock

8 lime leaves

3½ oz carrots, very thinly sliced

12 oz sweet potato, diced

1 cup baby-corn-on-th-cobs, halved

3 tbsp fresh cilantro, roughly chopped

3½ oz cherry tomatoes, halved

8 oz fan-tail shrimp

1 Place the tamarind paste, red chilies, garlic, ginger, fish sauce, sugar, and fish stock in a preheated wok or large, heavy skillet. Roughly tear the lime leaves and add to the wok. Bring to a boil, stirring constantly to blend the flavors.

2 Reduce the heat and add the carrot, sweet potato, and baby-corn-on-the-cobs to the mixture in the wok.

3 Leave the soup to simmer, uncovered for about 10 minutes, or until the vegetables are just tender.

4 Stir the cilantro, cherry tomatoes, and shrimp into the soup and heat through for 5 minutes.

5 Transfer the soup to a warm soup tureen or individual serving bowls and serve hot.

COOK'S TIP

Thai ginger or galangal
is a member of the ginger
family, but it is yellow in color
with pink sprouts. The flavor
is aromatic and less pungent
than ginger.

Crab & Ginger Soup

Two classic ingredients in Chinese cooking are blended together in this recipe for a special soup.

NUTRITIONAL INFORMATION

Calories ....32 Sugars 1g
Protein ....6g Fat 0.4g
Carbohydrate ....1g Saturates 0g

10 MINS   25 MINS

SERVES 4

INGREDIENTS

1 carrot

1 leek

1 bay leaf

3¾ cups fish stock

2 medium-sized cooked crabs

1-inch piece fresh gingerroot, grated

1 tsp light soy sauce

½ tsp ground star anise

salt and pepper

1 Using a sharp knife, chop the carrot and leek into small pieces and place in a large saucepan with the bay leaf and fish stock.

2 Bring the mixture in the saucepan to a boil.

3 Reduce the heat, cover, and leave to simmer for about 10 minutes, or until the vegetables are nearly tender.

4 Remove all of the meat from the cooked crabs. Break off and reserve the claws, break the joints and remove the meat, using a fork or skewer.

5 Add the crabmeat to the pan of fish stock, together with the ginger, soy sauce, and star anise and bring to a boil. Leave to simmer for about 10 minutes, or until the vegetables are tender and the crab is heated through.

6 Season the soup then ladle into a warmed soup tureen or individual serving bowls and garnish with crab claws. Serve immediately.

VARIATION

If fresh crabmeat is unavailable, use drained canned crabmeat or thawed frozen crabmeat instead.

Coconut & Crab Soup

Thai red curry paste is quite fiery, but adds a superb flavor to this dish. It is available in jars or packets from supermarkets.

NUTRITIONAL INFORMATION

Calories 122	Sugar 9g
Protein 11g	Fats 4g
Carbohydrates ...11g	Saturates 1g

5 MINS   10 MINS

SERVES 4

INGREDIENTS

1 tbsp groundnut oil

2 tbsp Thai red curry paste

1 red bell pepper, seeded and sliced

2½ cups coconut milk

2½ cups fish stock
  (see page 15)

2 tbsp fish sauce

8 oz canned or fresh white crab meat

8 oz fresh or frozen crab claws

2 tbsp chopped fresh cilantro

3 scallions, trimmed and sliced

COOK'S TIP

Clean the wok after use by washing it with water, using a mild detergent if necessary, and a soft cloth or brush. Do not scrub or use any abrasive cleaner as this will scratch the surface. Dry thoroughly then wipe the surface all over with a little oil to protect the surface.

1 Heat the oil in a large preheated wok.

2 Add the red curry paste and red bell pepper to the wok and stir-fry for 1 minute.

3 Add the coconut milk, fish stock and fish sauce and bring to a boil.

4 Add the crabmeat, crab claws, cilantro, and scallions to the wok.

5 Stir the mixture well and heat thoroughly for 2–3 minutes or until everything is warmed through.

6 Transfer the soup to warm bowls and serve hot.

Crab & Corn Soup

Crab and corn are classic ingredients in Chinese cookery. Here egg noodles are added for a filling dish.

NUTRITIONAL INFORMATION

Calories 324   Sugars 6g
Protein . . . . .27g   Fat 8g
Carbohydrate . . .39g   Saturates 2g

5 MINS   20 MINS

SERVES 4

INGREDIENTS

1 tbsp sunflower oil

1 tsp Chinese five-spice powder

8 oz carrots, cut into sticks

½ cup canned or frozen corn

¼ cup English peas

6 scallions, trimmed and sliced

1 red chili, seeded and very thinly sliced

2 x 7 oz can white crabmeat

6 oz egg noodles

7½ cups fish stock

3 tbsp soy sauce

1 Heat the sunflower oil in a large preheated wok or heavy-bottomed skillet.

2 Add the Chinese five-spice powder, carrots, corn, peas, scallions and red chili to the wok and cook for about 5 minutes, stirring constantly.

3 Add the crabmeat to the wok and stir-fry the mixture for 1 minute, distributing the crabmeat evenly.

4 Roughly break up the egg noodles and add to the wok.

5 Pour the fish stock and soy sauce into the mixture in the wok and bring to boil.

6 Cover the wok or skillet and leave the soup to simmer for 5 minutes.

7 Stir once more, then transfer the soup to a warm soup tureen or individual serving bowls and serve at once.

COOK'S TIP

Chinese five-spice powder is a mixture of star anise, fennel, cloves, cinnamon, and Szechuan pepper. It has an unmistakeable flavor. Use it sparingly, as it is very pungent.

Beef & Vegetable Noodle Soup

Thin strips of beef are marinated in soy sauce and garlic to form the basi of this tasty soup. Served with noodles, it is both filling and delicious.

NUTRITIONAL INFORMATION

Calories 186   Sugars 1g
Protein ....17g   Fat 5g
Carbohydrate ...20g   Saturates 1g

35 MINS   20 MINS

SERVES 4

INGREDIENTS

8 oz lean beef

1 garlic clove, minced

2 scallions, chopped

3 tbsp soy sauce

1 tsp sesame oil

8 oz egg noodles

3¾ cups beef stock

3 baby-corn-on-the-cobs, sliced

½ leek, shredded

4½ oz broccoli, cut into florets

pinch of chili powder

1 Using a sharp knife, cut the beef into thin strips and place in a bowl with the garlic, scallions, soy sauce, and sesame oil.

2 Mix together the ingredients in the bowl, turning the beef to coat. Cover and leave to marinate in the refrigerator for 30 minutes.

3 Cook the noodles in a saucepan of boiling water for 3–4 minutes. Drain the noodles thoroughly and set aside.

4 Put the beef stock in a large saucepan and bring to a boil. Add the beef, together with the marinade, the baby corn, leek, and broccoli. Cover and leave to simmer over a low heat for 7–10 minutes or until the beef and vegetables are tende and cooked through.

5 Stir in the noodles and chili powde and cook for a further 2–3 minutes.

6 Transfer the soup to bowls and serve immediately.

VARIATION

Vary the vegetables used, or use those to hand.

If preferred, use a few drops of chili sauce instead of chili powder, but remember it is very hot!

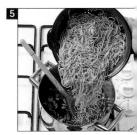

Chinese Potato & Pork Broth

In this recipe the pork is seasoned with traditional Chinese flavorings —soy sauce, rice-wine vinegar, and a dash of sesame oil.

NUTRITIONAL INFORMATION

Calories ....166 Sugars 2g
Protein ....10g Fat 5g
Carbohydrate ...26g Saturates 1g

5 MINS   20 MINS

SERVES 4

INGREDIENTS

½ cups chicken stock

large potatoes, diced

tbsp rice-wine vinegar

tbsp cornstarch

tbsp water

½ oz pork fillet, sliced

tbsp light soy sauce

tsp sesame oil

carrot, cut into very thin strips

tsp gingerroot, chopped

scallions, sliced thinly

red bell pepper, sliced

oz can bamboo shoots, drained

VARIATION

or extra heat,
dd 1 chopped red chili
r 1 tsp of chili powder to
he soup in step 5.

1 Add the chicken stock, diced potatoes, and 1 tbsp of the rice-wine vinegar to a saucepan and bring to a boil. Reduce the heat until the stock is just simmering.

2 Mix the cornstarch with the water then stir into the hot stock.

3 Bring the stock back to a boil, stirring until thickened, then reduce the heat until it is just simmering again.

4 Place the pork slices in a dish and season with the remaining rice-wine vinegar, the soy sauce, and sesame oil.

5 Add the pork slices, carrot strips, and ginger to the stock and cook for 10 minutes. Stir in the scallions, red bell pepper, and bamboo shoots. Cook for a further 5 minutes. Pour the soup into warmed bowls and serve immediately.

Pork & Vegetable Soup

Sold in cans, Szechuan preserved vegetable is pickled mustard root which is quite hot and salty, so rinse in water before use.

NUTRITIONAL INFORMATION

Calories	135	Sugars	.........1g
Protein	........14g	Fat	...........7g
Carbohydrate	....3g	Saturates	.......2g

 5 MINS   5 MINS

SERVES 4

INGREDIENTS

9 oz pork surloin

2 tsp cornstarch paste
(see page 15)

4½ oz Szechuan preserved vegetable

3 cups Chinese stock
(see page 14) or water

salt and pepper

a few drops sesame oil (optional)

2-3 scallions, sliced, to garnish

1 Preheat a wok or large, heavy-bottomed skillet.

2 Using a sharp knife, cut the pork across the grain into thin shreds.

3 Mix the pork with the cornstarch paste until the pork is completely coated in the mixture.

4 Thoroughly wash and rinse the Szechuan preserved vegetable, then pat dry on absorbent paper towels. Cut the Szechuan preserved vegetable into thin shreds the same size as the pork.

5 Pour the Chinese stock or water into the wok or skillet and bring to a rolling boil. Add the pork to the wok and

stir to separate the shreds. Return to a boil.

6 Add the shredded Szechuan preserved vegetable and bring back to a boil once more.

7 Adjust the seasoning to taste and sprinkle with sesame oil. Serve hot, garnished with scallions.

COOK'S TI

Szechuan preserve vegetable is actually musta green root, pickled in salt a chilies. Available in cans fro specialist Chinese supermarkets, gives a crunchy, spicy taste to dishe Rinse in cold water before use ar store in the refrigerato

Pork Chili Soup

This meaty chili tastes lighter than one made with beef. Good for informal entertaining, the recipe is easily doubled.

NUTRITIONAL INFORMATION

Calories	292	Sugar	.........11g
Protein	........41g	Fats	...........9g
Carbohydrates	...13g	Saturates	......0g

10 MINS   50 MINS

SERVES 4

INGREDIENTS

tsp olive oil

lb lean ground pork

onion, finely chopped

stalk celery, finely chopped

bell pepper, cored, seeded and finely
  chopped

–3 garlic cloves, finely chopped

tbsp tomato paste

4 oz can chopped tomatoes in juice

cups chicken or meat stock

/8 tsp ground coriander

/8 tsp ground cumin

/4 tsp dried oregano

tsp mild chili powder, or to taste

alt and pepper

hopped fresh cilantro leaves or parsley, to
  garnish

our cream, to serve

COOK'S TIP

or a festive presentation, pass
dditional accompaniments,
uch as grated cheese,
hopped scallion, and
uacamole.

1 Heat the oil in a large saucepan over a medium-high heat. Add the pork, season with salt and pepper, and cook until no longer pink, stirring frequently. Reduce the heat to medium and add the onion, celery, bell pepper, and garlic. Cover and continue cooking for 5 minutes, stirring occasionally, until the onion is softened.

2 Add the tomatoes, tomato paste and the stock. Add the coriander, cumin, oregano, and chili powder. Stir the ingredients in to combine well.

3 Bring just to a boil, reduce the heat to low, cover, and simmer for 30–40 minutes until all the vegetables are very tender. Taste and adjust the seasoning, adding more chili powder if you like it hotter.

4 Ladle the chili into warm bowls and sprinkle with cilantro or parsley. Pass the sour cream separately, or top each serving with a spoonful.

Pork Balls & Greens in Broth

Steaming the meatballs over the soup gives added flavor to the broth.

NUTRITIONAL INFORMATION

Calories ....98 Sugars 1g
Protein ....14g Fat 3g
Carbohydrate ....4g Saturates 0g

 15 MINS   20 MINS

SERVES 6

INGREDIENTS

2 quarts chicken stock

3 oz shiitake mushrooms, thinly sliced

6 oz pak choy or other oriental greens,
    sliced into thin ribbons

6 scallions, finely sliced

salt and pepper

PORK BALLS

8 oz lean ground pork

1 oz fresh spinach leaves, finely chopped

2 scallions, finely chopped

1 garlic clove, very finely chopped

pinch of oriental five-spice powder

1 tsp soy sauce

1 To make the pork balls, put the pork, spinach, scallions, and garlic in a bowl. Add the five-spice powder and soy sauce and mix until combined.

2 Shape the pork mixture into 24 balls. Place them in one layer in a steamer that will fit over the top of a saucepan.

3 Bring the stock just to a boil in a saucepan that will accommodate the steamer. Regulate the heat so that the liquid bubbles gently. Add the mushrooms to the stock and place the steamer, covered, on top of the pan. Steam for 10 minutes. Remove the steamer and set aside on a plate.

4 Add the pak choy and scallions to the pan and cook gently in the stock for 3-4 minutes, or until the leaves are wilted. Taste the soup and adjust the seasoning, if necessary.

5 Divide the pork balls evenly among 6 warm bowls and ladle the soup over them. Serve at once.

Lamb & Rice Soup

This is a very filling soup, as it contains rice and tender pieces of lamb. Serve before a light main course.

NUTRITIONAL INFORMATION

Calories . . . . .116 Sugars 0.2g
Protein . . . . .9g Fat 4g
Carbohydrate . . .12g Saturates 2g

5 MINS   35 MINS

SERVES 4

INGREDIENTS

½ oz lean lamb

¼ cup rice

3¾ cups lamb stock

leek, sliced

garlic clove, thinly sliced

tsp light soy sauce

tsp rice-wine vinegar

medium open-cap mushroom, thinly sliced

salt

1 Using a sharp knife, trim any fat from the lamb and cut the meat into thin strips. Set aside until required.

2 Bring a large pan of lightly salted water to a boil and add the rice. Bring back to a boil, stir once, reduce the heat and cook for 10–15 minutes, until tender.

3 Drain the rice, rinse under cold running water, drain again, and set aside until required.

4 Meanwhile, put the lamb stock in a large saucepan and bring to a boil.

5 Add the lamb strips, leek, garlic, soy sauce, and rice-wine vinegar to the stock in the pan. Reduce the heat, cover, and leave to simmer for 10 minutes, or until the lamb is tender and cooked through.

6 Add the mushroom slices and the rice to the pan and cook for a further 2–3 minutes, or until the mushroom is completely cooked through.

7 Ladle the soup into 4 individual warmed soup bowls and serve immediately.

VARIATION

Use a few dried shiitake mushrooms, rehydrated according to the packet directions and chopped, as an alternative to the open-cap mushroom. Add the shiitake mushrooms with the lamb in step 4.

Asian Lamb Soup

This soup needs a light stock. If using a bouillon cube, make it up to half strength, as it will gain flavor from the vegetables and herbs.

NUTRITIONAL INFORMATION

Calories 96	Sugar 2g	
Protein 10g	Fats 5g	
Carbohydrates 4g	Saturates 2g	

🍲 15 MINS   🕐 30 MINS

SERVES 4

INGREDIENTS

5½ oz lean tender lamb, such as neck fillet or leg steak

2 garlic cloves, very finely chopped

2 tbsp soy sauce

5 cups chicken stock

1 tbsp grated peeled fresh gingerroot

2 inch piece lemongrass, sliced into very thin rounds

¼ tsp chili paste, or to taste

6-8 cherry tomatoes, quartered

4 scallions, sliced finely

1 ¾ oz mung bean-sprouts, snapped in half

2 tbsp fresh cilantro leaves

1 tsp olive oil

1 Trim all visible fat from the lamb and slice the meat thinly. Cut the slices into bite-sized pieces. Spread the meat in one layer on a plate and sprinkle over the garlic and 1 tbsp of the soy sauce. Leave to marinate, covered, for at least 10 minutes or up to 1 hour.

2 Put the stock in a saucepan with the ginger, lemongrass, remaining soy sauce, and the chili paste. Bring just to a boil, reduce the heat, cover, and simmer for 10-15 minutes. Warm 4 ovenproof bowls in a low oven.

3 When ready to serve the soup, drop the tomatoes, scallions, bean-sprouts and fresh cilantro leaves into the simmering stock.

4 Heat the oil in a skillet and add the lamb with its marinade. Stir-fry the lamb just until it is no longer red and divide among the warm bowls.

5 Ladle over the hot stock and serve immediately.

COOK'S TIP

Substitute lean, tender pork or beef instead of lamb. If preferred, use spinach or Chinese basil, sliced into thin ribbons, in place of fresh cilantro leaves.

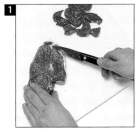  

Spicy Lamb Soup

This thick and hearty main course soup is bursting with exotic flavors and aromas.

NUTRITIONAL INFORMATION

Calories 306   Sugars 6g
Protein . . . . .26g   Fat 12g
Carbohydrate . . .25g   Saturates 1g

🥩 15 MINS   🕐 2 HOURS

SERVES 4

I N G R E D I E N T S

1-2 tbsp olive oil

1 lb lean boneless lamb, such as shoulder or neck fillet, trimmed of fat and cut into ½ inch cubes

1 onion, finely chopped

2-3 garlic cloves, minced

5 cups water

14 oz can chopped tomatoes in juice

1 bay leaf

½ tsp dried thyme

½ tsp dried oregano

⅛ tsp ground cinnamon

¼ tsp ground cumin

¼ tsp ground turmeric

1 tsp harissa, or more to taste

14 oz can garbanzo beans, rinsed and drained

1 carrot, diced

1 potato, diced

1 zucchini, quartered lengthways and sliced

3½ oz fresh or defrosted frozen English peas

chopped fresh mint or cilantro leaves, to garnish

1 Heat the oil in a large saucepan or cast-iron casserole over a medium-high heat. Add the lamb, in batches if necessary to avoid crowding the pan, and cook until evenly browned on all sides, adding a little more oil if needed. Remove the meat, with a draining spoon, when browned.

2 Reduce the heat and add the onion and garlic to the pan. Cook, stirring frequently, for 1–2 minutes.

3 Add the water and return all the meat to the pan. Bring just to a boil and skim off any foam that rises to the surface. Reduce the heat and stir in the tomatoes, bay leaf, thyme, oregano, cinnamon, cumin, turmeric, and harissa. Simmer for about 1 hour, or until the meat is very tender. Discard the bay leaf.

4 Stir in the garbanzo beans, carrot, and potato and simmer for 15 minutes. Add the zucchini and peas and continue simmering for 15–20 minutes, or until all the vegetables are tender.

5 Adjust the seasoning, adding more harissa, if desired. Ladle the soup into warm bowls, garnish with mint or cilantro.

Won Ton Soup

The recipe for the won ton skins makes 24 but the soup requires only half this quantity. The other half can be frozen ready for another time.

NUTRITIONAL INFORMATION

Calories ....278 Sugars 2g
Protein ....10g Fat 5g
Carbohydrate ...50g Saturates 1g

45 MINS   5 MINS

SERVES 4

INGREDIENTS

WON TON SKINS

1 egg

6 tbsp water

2 cups all-purpose flour, plus extra for dusting

FILLING

½ cup frozen chopped spinach, defrosted

1 tbsp pine nuts, toasted and chopped

¼ cup minced quorn (TVP)

salt

SOUP

2½ cups vegetable stock

1 tbsp dry sherry

1 tbsp light soy sauce

2 scallions, chopped

1 To make the won ton skins, beat the egg lightly in a bowl and mix with the water. Stir in the flour to form a stiff dough. Knead lightly, then cover with a damp cloth and leave to rest for 30 minutes.

2 Roll the dough out into a large sheet about ¼ inch thick. Cut out 24 x 3 inch squares. Dust each one lightly with flour. Only 12 squares are required

for the soup so freeze the remainder to use on another occasion.

3 To make the filling, squeeze out the excess water from the spinach. Mix the spinach with the pine nuts and quorn (TVP) until thoroughly combined. Season with salt.

4 Divide the mixture into 12 equal portions. Using a teaspoon, place one

portion in the center of each square. Seal the won tons by bringing the opposite corners of each square together and squeezing well.

5 To make the soup, bring the vegetable stock, sherry, and soy sauce to a boil, add the won tons and boil rapidly for 2–3 minutes. Add the scallions and serve in warmed bowls immediately.

Chicken, Noodle, & Corn

The vermicelli gives this Chinese-style soup an Italian twist, but you can use egg noodles if you prefer.

NUTRITIONAL INFORMATION

Calories 401   Sugars 6g
Protein . . . . .31g   Fat 24g
Carbohydrate . . .17g   Saturates 13g

5 MINS   25 MINS

SERVES 4

INGREDIENTS

lb boned chicken breasts, cut into strips

cups chicken stock

cup heavy cream

cup dried vermicelli

tbsp cornstarch

tbsp milk

oz corn kernels

alt and pepper

nely chopped scallions, to garnish (optional)

1 Put the chicken strips, chicken stock and heavy cream into a large saucepan and bring to a boil over a low heat.

2 Reduce the heat slightly and simmer for about 20 minutes. Season the soup with salt and black pepper to taste.

3 Meanwhile, cook the vermicelli in lightly salted boiling water for 10-12 minutes, until just tender. Drain the pasta and keep warm.

4 In a small bowl, mix together the cornstarch and milk to make a smooth paste. Stir the cornstarch into the soup until thickened.

5 Add the corn and vermicelli to the pan and heat through.

6 Transfer the soup to a warm tureen or individual soup bowls, garnish with scallions, if desired, and serve immediately.

VARIATION

For crab and corn soup, substitute 1 lb cooked crabmeat for the chicken breasts. Flake the crabmeat well before adding it to the saucepan and reduce the cooking time by 10 minutes.

Curried Chicken & Corn Soup

Tender cooked chicken strips and baby-corn-on-the-cobs are the main flavors in this delicious clear soup, with just a hint of ginger.

NUTRITIONAL INFORMATION

Calories	206	Sugars	........5g
Protein	........29g	Fat	..........5g
Carbohydrate	...13g	Saturates	.......1g

5 MINS   30 MINS

SERVES 4

INGREDIENTS

6 oz can corn, drained

3¾ cups chicken stock

12 oz cooked, lean chicken, cut into strips

16 baby-corn-on-the-cobs

1 tsp Chinese curry powder

½-inch piece fresh gingerroot, grated

3 tbsp light soy sauce

2 tbsp chopped chives

1 Place the canned corn in a food processor, together with ⅔ cup of the chicken stock and process until the mixture forms a smooth paste.

2 Pass the corn paste through a fine strainer, pressing with the back of a spoon to remove any husks.

3 Pour the remaining chicken stock into a large saucepan and add the strips of cooked chicken. Stir in the corn paste.

4 Add the baby-corn-on-the-cobs and bring the soup to a boil. Boil the soup for 10 minutes.

5 Add the Chinese curry powder, grated fresh gingerroot and light soy sauce and stir well to combine. Cook for a further 10–15 minutes.

6 Stir the chopped chives into the soup.

7 Transfer the curried chicken and corn soup to warm soup bowls and serve immediately.

COOK'S TI

Prepare the soup up to 2 hours in advance witho adding the chicken, cool, cove and store in the refrigerator. A the chicken and heat the so through thoroughly before servin

Chicken Soup with Almonds

This soup can also be made using pheasant breasts. For a really gamy flavor, make game stock from the carcass and use in the soup.

NUTRITIONAL INFORMATION

Calories 219   Sugars 2g
Protein . . . . .18g   Fat 15g
Carbohydrate . . . .2g   Saturates 2g

10 MINS   20 MINS

SERVES 4

INGREDIENTS

1 large or 2 small boneless skinned
   chicken breasts

1 tbsp sunflower oil

4 scallions, thinly sliced diagonally

1 carrot, cut into julienne strips

3 cups chicken stock

finely grated rind of ½ lemon

⅓ cup ground almonds

1 tbsp light soy sauce

1 tbsp lemon juice

¼ cup slivered almonds, toasted

salt and pepper

1 Cut each breast into 4 strips lengthways, then slice very thinly across the
grain to give shreds of chicken.

2 Heat the oil in a wok, swirling it
around until really hot.

3 Add the scallions and cook for 2
minutes, then add the chicken and
toss it for 3-4 minutes until sealed and
almost cooked through, stirring all the
time. Add the carrot strips and stir.

4 Add the stock to the wok and bring to
boil. Add the lemon rind, ground
almonds, soy sauce, lemon juice, and

plenty of seasoning. Bring back to a boil
and simmer, uncovered, for 5 minutes,
stirring from time to time.

5 Adjust the seasoning, add most of the
toasted almonds and continue to
cook for a further 1-2 minutes.

6 Serve the soup hot, in individual
bowls, sprinkled with the remaining
flaked almonds.

COOK'S TIP

To make game stock, break
up a pheasant carcass and place
in a pan with 2 quarts of water.
Bring to a boil slowly, skimming off
any scum. Add 1 bouquet garni, 1
peeled onion, and seasoning. Cover and
simmer gently for 1½ hours. Strain, and
skim any surface fat.

Chicken Won ton Soup

This Chinese-style soup is fiddly to make but is delicious as a starter to an oriental meal or as a light meal.

NUTRITIONAL INFORMATION

Calories 101   Sugars 0.3g
Protein . . . . .14g   Fat 4g
Carbohydrate . . . .3g   Saturates 1g

15 MINS   10 MINS

SERVES 4–6

I N G R E D I E N T S

FILLING

12 oz ground chicken

1 tbsp soy sauce

1 tsp grated, fresh gingerroot

1 garlic clove, minced

2 tsp sherry

2 scallions, chopped

1 tsp sesame oil

1 egg white

½ tsp cornstarch

½ tsp sugar

about 35 won ton skin

SOUP

6 cups chicken stock

1 tbsp light soy sauce

1 scallion, shredded

1 small carrot, cut into very thin slices

1 Place all the ingredients for the filling in a large bowl and mix until thoroughly combined.

2 Place a small spoonful of the filling in the center of each won ton skin.

3 Dampen the edges and gather up the won ton skin to form a small pouch enclosing the filling.

4 Cook the filled won tons in boiling water for 1 minute or until they float to the top. Remove with a draining spoon and set aside.

5 Bring the chicken stock to a boil. Add the soy sauce, scallion, and carrot.

6 Add the won tons to the soup and simmer gently for 2 minutes. Serve.

COOK'S TI

Make double quantities of wo
ton skins and freeze th
remainder. Place small squares o
baking parchment in betwee
each skin, then place in a freeze
bag and freeze. Defros
thoroughly before using

Clear Chicken & Egg Soup

This tasty chicken soup has the addition of poached eggs, making it both delicious and filling. Use fresh, home-made stock for a better flavor.

NUTRITIONAL INFORMATION

Calories 138	Sugars 1g	
Protein 16g	Fat 7g	
Carbohydrate 1g	Saturates 2g	

5 MINS   35 MINS

SERVES 4

INGREDIENTS

tsp salt

tbsp rice-wine vinegar

eggs

¾ cups chicken stock

leek, sliced

½ oz broccoli florets

cup shredded cooked chicken

open-cap mushrooms, sliced

tbsp dry sherry

ash of chili sauce

chili powder, to garnish

VARIATION

You could use 4 dried shiitake mushrooms, rehydrated according to the packet directions, instead of the open-cap mushrooms, if you prefer.

1 Bring a large saucepan of water to a boil and add the salt and rice-wine vinegar.

2 Reduce the heat so that it is just simmering and carefully break the eggs into the water, one at a time. Poach the eggs for 1 minute.

3 Remove the poached eggs with a draining spoon and set aside.

4 Bring the chicken stock to a boil in a separate pan and add the leek, broccoli, chicken, mushrooms, and sherry and season with chili sauce to taste. Cook for 10–15 minutes.

5 Add the poached eggs to the soup and cook for a further 2 minutes. Carefully transfer the soup and poached eggs to 4 soup bowls. Dust with a little chili powder and serve immediately.

Chicken & Corn Soup

A hint of chili and sherry flavor this soup while red bell pepper and tomato add color.

NUTRITIONAL INFORMATION

Calories ....199 Sugars 8g
Protein ....12g Fat 8g
Carbohydrate ...19g Saturates 1g

🍲 5 MINS 🕐 20 MINS

SERVES 4

INGREDIENTS

1 skinless, boneless chicken breast, about 6 oz

2 tbsp sunflower oil

2–3 scallions, thinly sliced diagonally

1 small or ½ large red bell pepper, thinly sliced

1 garlic clove, minced

4½ oz baby-corn-on-the-cob, thinly sliced

4 cups chicken stock

7 oz can of corn niblets, well drained

2 tbsp sherry

2–3 tsp bottled sweet chili sauce

2–3 tsp cornstarch

2 tomatoes, quartered and seeded, then sliced

salt and pepper

chopped fresh cilantro or parsley, to garnish

1 Cut the chicken breast into 4 strips lengthways, then cut each strip into narrow slices across the grain.

2 Heat the oil in a wok or skillet, swirling it around until it is really hot.

3 Add the chicken and stir-fry for 3–4 minutes, moving it around the wok until it is well sealed all over and almost cooked through.

4 Add the scallions, bell pepper, and garlic, and stir-fry for 2–3 minutes. Add the corn and stock and bring to boil.

5 Add the corn niblets, sherry, sweet chili sauce, and salt to taste, and simmer for 5 minutes, stirring from time to time.

6 Blend the cornstarch with a little cold water. Add to the soup and bring to a boil, stirring until the sauce is thickened. Add the tomato slices, season to taste, and simmer for 1–2 minutes.

7 Serve the chicken and corn soup hot, sprinkled with chopped cilantro or parsley.

Chicken Noodle Soup

Quick to make, this hot and spicy soup is hearty and warming. If you like your food really fiery, add a chopped dried or fresh chili with its seeds.

NUTRITIONAL INFORMATION

Calories	196	Sugars	........4g
Protein	........16g	Fat	...........11g
Carbohydrate	....8g	Saturates	.......2g

10 MINS   25 MINS

SERVES 4-6

INGREDIENTS

sheet of dried egg noodles
 from a 9 oz pack

tbsp oil

4 skinless, boneless
 chicken thighs, diced

bunch scallions, sliced

2 garlic cloves, chopped

¾ inch piece fresh gingerroot, finely
 chopped

3¾ cups chicken stock

scant 1 cup coconut milk

3 tsp red curry paste

3 tbsp peanut butter

2 tbsp light soy sauce

small red bell pepper, chopped

½ cup frozen English peas

salt and pepper

1 Put the noodles in a shallow dish and soak in boiling water as the packet directs.

2 Heat the oil in a large preheated saucepan or wok.

3 Add the diced chicken to the pan or wok and fry for 5 minutes, stirring until lightly browned.

4 Add the white part of the scallions, the garlic, and ginger and fry for 2 minutes, stirring.

5 Stir in the chicken stock, coconut milk, red curry paste, peanut butter, and soy sauce.

6 Season with salt and pepper to taste. Bring to a boil, stirring, then simmer for 8 minutes, stirring occasionally.

7 Add the red bell pepper, peas, and green scallion tops and cook for 2 minutes.

8 Add the drained noodles and heat through. Spoon the chicken noodle soup into warmed bowls and serve with a spoon and fork.

VARIATION

Green curry paste can be used instead of red curry paste for a less fiery flavor.

Spicy Chicken Noodle Soup

This filling soup is filled with spicy flavors and bright colors for a really attractive and hearty dish.

NUTRITIONAL INFORMATION

Calories	286	Sugars	........21g
Protein	........22g	Fat	...........6g
Carbohydrate	...37g	Saturates	.......1g

15 MINS   20 MINS

SERVES 4

INGREDIENTS

2 tbsp tamarind paste

4 red chilies, finely chopped

2 cloves garlic, minced

1-inch piece Thai ginger, peeled and very finely chopped

4 tbsp fish sauce

2 tbsp jaggery or superfine sugar

8 lime leaves, roughly torn

5 cups chicken stock

12 oz boneless chicken breast

3½ oz carrots, very thinly sliced

12 oz sweet potato, diced

3½ oz baby-corn-on-the-cobs, halved

3 tbsp fresh cilantro, roughly chopped

3½ oz cherry tomatoes, halved

5½ oz flat rice noodles

fresh cilantro, chopped,to garnish

1 Preheat a large wok or skillet. Place the tamarind paste, chilies, garlic, ginger, fish sauce, sugar, lime leaves, and chicken stock in the wok and bring to a boil, stirring constantly. Reduce the heat and cook for about 5 minutes.

2 Using a sharp knife, thinly slice the chicken. Add the chicken to the wok and cook for a further 5 minutes, stirring the mixture well.

3 Reduce the heat and add the carrots, sweet potato, and baby-corn-on-the-cobs to the wok. Leave to simmer, uncovered, for 5 minutes, or until the vegetables are just tender and the chicken is completely cooked through.

4 Stir in the chopped fresh cilantro, cherry tomatoes, and flat rice noodles.

5 Leave the soup to simmer for about 5 minutes, or until the noodles are tender.

6 Garnish the spicy chicken noodle soup with chopped fresh cilantro and serve hot.

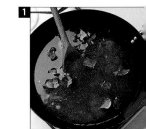

Peking Duck Soup

This is a hearty and robustly flavored soup, containing pieces of duck and vegetables cooked in a rich stock.

NUTRITIONAL INFORMATION

Calories	92	Sugars	. . . . .3g
Protein	. . . . .8g	Fat	. . . . .5g
Carbohydrate	. . . .3g	Saturates	. . . . . . .1g

5 MINS   35 MINS

SERVES 4

I N G R E D I E N T S

4½ oz lean duck breast meat

3 oz Chinese cabbage

3¾ cups chicken or duck stock

1 tbsp dry sherry or rice wine

1 tbsp light soy sauce

2 garlic cloves, minced

pinch of ground star anise

1 tbsp sesame seeds

1 tsp sesame oil

1 tbsp chopped fresh parsley

1 Remove the skin from the duck breast and finely dice the flesh.

2 Using a sharp knife, shred the Chinese cabbage.

3 Put the stock in a large saucepan and bring to boil. Add the sherry or rice wine, soy sauce, diced duck meat, and shredded Chinese cabbage and stir to mix thoroughly. Reduce the heat and leave to simmer gently for 15 minutes.

4 Stir in the garlic and star anise and cook over a low heat for a further 10–15 minutes, or until the duck is tender.

5 Meanwhile, dry-fry the sesame seeds in a preheated, heavy-bottomed skillet or wok, stirring constantly.

6 Remove the sesame seeds from the pan and stir them into the soup, together with the sesame oil and chopped fresh parsley.

7 Spoon the soup into warm bowls and serve immediately.

VARIATION

If Chinese cabbage is unavailable, use leafy green cabbage instead. You may wish to adjust the quantity to taste, as Western cabbage has a stronger flavor and odor than Chinese cabbage.

Chicken & Coconut Soup

This fragrant soup combines citrus flavours with coconut and a hint of piquancy from chilies.

NUTRITIONAL INFORMATION

Calories 345	Sugars 2g
Protein 28g	Fat 24g
Carbohydrate 5g	Saturates 18g

2¼ HOURS   15 MINS

SERVES 4

INGREDIENTS

1¾ cups cooked, skinned chicken breast

1⅓ cups unsweetened crushed coconut

2 cups boiling water

2 cups Fresh Chicken Stock
(see page 14)

4 scallions, white and green parts, sliced thinly

2 stalks lemongrass

1 lime

1 tsp grated gingerroot

1 tbsp light soy sauce

2 tsp ground coriander

2 large fresh red chilies

1 tbsp chopped fresh cilantro

1 tbsp cornstarch, mixed with 2 tbsp cold water

salt and white pepper

chopped red chili, to garnish

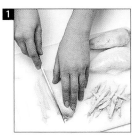

1 Using a sharp knife, slice the chicken into thin strips.

2 Place the coconut in a heatproof bowl and pour over the boiling water. Work the coconut mixture through a strainer. Pour the coconut water into a large saucepan and add the stock.

3 Add the scallions to the saucepan. Slice the base of each lemongrass and discard damaged leaves. Bruise the stalks and add to the saucepan.

4 Peel the rind from the lime in large strips. Extract the juice and add to the pan with the lime strips, ginger, soy sauce, and coriander. Bruise the chilies with a fork then add to the pan. Heat the pan to just below boiling point.

5 Add the chicken and fresh cilantro t the saucepan, bring to a boil, the simmer for 10 minutes.

6 Discard the lemongrass, lime rind, an red chilies. Pour the blende cornstarch mixture into the saucepan an stir until slightly thickened. Season wit salt and white pepper to taste and serv immediately, garnished with chopped re chili.

Thai-Style Chicken Soup

Make this soup when you want a change from traditional chicken soup.
Use a generous amount of fresh cilantro leaves to garnish.

NUTRITIONAL INFORMATION

Calories 81	Sugars 3g
Protein 14g	Fat 1g
Carbohydrate 4g	Saturates 0g

10 MINS   40 MINS

SERVES 4

INGREDIENTS

cups chicken stock

oz skinless boned chicken

fresh chili, split lengthways and seeded

inch piece lemongrass, split lengthways

-4 lime leaves

inch piece fresh gingerroot, peeled and
 sliced

cup coconut milk

-8 scallions, sliced diagonally

tsp chili paste, or to taste

alt

esh cilantro leaves, to garnish

1 Put the stock in a pan with the chicken, chili, lemon grass, lime leaves, and ginger. Bring almost to a boil, reduce the heat, cover and simmer for 20–25 minutes, or until the chicken is cooked through and firm to the touch.

2 Remove the chicken and strain the stock. When the chicken is cool, slice thinly or shred into bite-sized pieces.

3 Return the stock to the saucepan and heat to simmering. Stir in the coconut milk and scallions. Add the chicken and continue simmering for about 10 minutes, until the soup is heated through and the flavors have mingled.

4 Stir in the chili paste. Season to taste with salt and, if wished, add a little more chili paste.

5 Ladle into warm bowls and float fresh cilantro leaves on top to serve.

COOK'S TIP

nce the stock is flavored
nd the chicken cooked, this
oup is very quick to finish. If you
ish, poach the chicken and strain
e stock ahead of time. Store in the
frigerator separately.

Hot & Sour Soup

This well-known soup from Peking is unusual in that it is thickened. The 'hot' flavor is achieved by the addition of plenty of black pepper.

NUTRITIONAL INFORMATION

Calories ....124 Sugars 1g
Protein ....5g Fat 8g
Carbohydrate ....8g Saturates 1g

3½ HOURS   25 MINS

SERVES 4

I N G R E D I E N T S

2 tbsp cornstarch

4 tbsp water

2 tbsp light soy sauce

3 tbsp rice-wine vinegar

½ tsp ground black pepper

1 small fresh red chili, finely chopped

1 egg

2 tbsp vegetable oil

1 onion, chopped

3¾ cups chicken or beef consommé

1 open-cap mushroom, sliced

1¾ oz skinless chicken breast, cut into very thin strips

1 tsp sesame oil

1 In a mixing bowl, blend the cornstarch with the water to form a smooth paste.

2 Add the soy sauce, rice-wine vinegar and black pepper.

3 Finely chop the red chili and add to the ingredients in the bowl. Mix well.

4 Break the egg into a separate bowl and beat well. Set aside while you cook the other ingredients.

5 Heat the oil in a preheated wok and fry the onion for 1–2 minutes until softened.

6 Stir in the consommé, mushroom, and chicken and bring to a boil. Cook for about 15 minutes or until the chicken is tender.

7 Gradually pour the cornstarch mixture into the soup and cook,

stirring constantly, until it thickens.

8 As you are stirring, gradually drizz the egg into the soup, to creat threads of egg.

9 Pour the hot and sour soup into warm tureen or individual servin bowls, sprinkle with the sesame oil an serve immediately.

Chicken Soup with Stars

How delicious a simple, fresh soup can be. Chicken wings are good to use for making the stock, as the meat is very sweet and doesn't dry out.

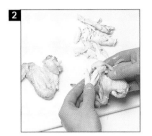

NUTRITIONAL INFORMATION

Calories	551	Sugar	.........5g
Protein	........45g	Fats	..........35g
Carbohydrates	...15g	Saturates	......9g

15 MINS   3 HOURS

SERVES 4

INGREDIENTS

¾ oz small pasta stars, or other very small shapes

chopped fresh parsley

CHICKEN STOCK

2 lb 8 oz chicken pieces, such as wings or legs

2½ quarts water

1 celery stalk, sliced

1 large carrot, sliced

1 onion, sliced

1 leek, sliced

2 garlic cloves, minced

8 peppercorns

4 allspice berries

3–4 parsley stems

2–3 fresh thyme sprigs

1 bay leaf

½ tsp salt

pepper

1 Put the chicken in a large 4 quart pot with the water, celery, carrot, onion, leek, garlic, peppercorns, allspice, herbs, and salt. Bring just to a boil and skim off the foam that rises to the surface. Reduce the heat and simmer, partially covered, for 2 hours.

2 Remove the chicken from the stock and set aside to cool. Continue simmering the stock, uncovered, for about 30 minutes. When the chicken is cool enough to handle, remove the meat from the bones and, if necessary, cut into bite-sized pieces.

3 Strain the stock and remove as much fat as possible. Discard the vegetables and flavorings. (There should be about 7½ cups of chicken stock.)

4 Bring the stock to a boil in a clean saucepan. Add the pasta and regulate the heat so that the stock boils very gently. Cook for about 10 minutes, or until the pasta is tender.

5 Stir in the chicken meat. Taste the soup and adjust the seasoning. Ladle into warm bowls and serve sprinkled with parsley.

Chicken & Rice Soup

Any kind of rice is suitable for this soup—white or brown long-grain rice, or even wild rice. Leftover cooked rice is a handy addition for soups.

NUTRITIONAL INFORMATION

Calories 100	Sugar 4g	
Protein 4g	Fats 2g	
Carbohydrates . . .19g	Saturates 0g	

 10 MINS   25 MINS

SERVES 4

I N G R E D I E N T S

6¼ cups chicken stock (see Cook's Tip)

2 small carrots, very thinly sliced

1 stalk celery, finely diced

1 baby leek, halved lengthways and thinly sliced

4 oz English peas, defrosted if frozen

1 cup cooked rice

5½ oz cooked chicken meat, sliced

2 tsp chopped fresh tarragon

1 tbsp chopped fresh parsley

salt and pepper

fresh parsley sprigs, to garnish

1 Put the stock in a large saucepan and add the carrots, celery, and leek. Bring to a boil, reduce the heat to low, and simmer gently, partially covered, for 10 minutes.

2 Stir in the peas, rice, and chicken meat and continue cooking for a further 10–15 minutes, or until the vegetables are tender.

3 Add the chopped tarragon and parsley, then taste and adjust the seasoning, adding salt and pepper as needed.

4 Ladle the soup into warm bowls, garnish with parsley and serve.

COOK'S TIP

If the stock you are using is a little weak, or if you have used a bouillon cube, add the herbs at the beginning, so that they can flavor the stock for a longer time.

Oriental Duck Broth

This soup combines delicate flavors with a satisfying meaty taste.

NUTRITIONAL INFORMATION

Calories	76	Sugar	.........5g
Protein	.........6g	Fats	...........2g
Carbohydrates	....9g	Saturates	......1g

  15 MINS   1³/₄ HOURS

SERVES 4

INGREDIENTS

2 duck leg quarters, skinned

4 cups water

2½ cups chicken stock

1 inch piece fresh gingerroot, peeled and
  sliced

1 large carrot, sliced

1 onion, sliced

1 leek, sliced

3 garlic cloves, minced

I tsp black peppercorns

2 tbsp soy sauce, or to taste

I small carrot, cut into thin strips or slivers

I small leek, cut into thin strips or slivers

3½ oz shiitake mushrooms, thinly sliced

1 oz watercress leaves

salt and pepper

1 Put the duck in a large saucepan with the water. Bring just to a boil and skim off the foam that rises to the surface. Add the stock, ginger, carrot, onion, leek, garlic, peppercorns, and soy sauce. Reduce the heat and simmer, partially covered, for 1½ hours.

2 Remove the duck from the stock and set aside. When the duck is cool enough to handle, remove the meat from the bones and slice thinly or shred into bite-sized pieces, discarding any fat.

3 Strain the stock and press with the back of a spoon to extract all the liquid. Remove as much fat as possible. Discard the vegetables and herbs.

4 Bring the stock just to a boil in a clean saucepan and add the strips of carrot and leek and the mushrooms together with the duck meat. Reduce the heat and cook gently for 5 minutes, or until the carrot is just tender.

5 Stir in the watercress and continue simmering for 1–2 minutes until it is wilted. Taste the soup and adjust the seasoning if needed, adding a little more soy sauce if wished. Ladle the soup into warm bowls and serve at once.

European
Soups

Soups are an important part of Mediterranean cuisine and
vary in content from hearty bean concoctions suitable for
the coldest winter's day to creamy Vichyssoise and meaty

stews. In this chapter there are nourishing
lentil soup recipes, variations on
Minestrone soup and thick fish soups.
Dishes are also included from France,
including Provence and Brittany, Hungary,

and a delicious lemony-flavored Greek bean soup. Many of
these soups are suitable for a main-course meal when
combined with delicious freshly baked bread.

Tomato & Pasta Soup

Plum tomatoes are ideal for making soups and sauces
as they have denser, less watery flesh than rounder varieties.

NUTRITIONAL INFORMATION

Calories 503   Sugars 16g
Protein . . . . .9g   Fat 28g
Carbohydrate . . .59g   Saturates 17g

🕑 5 MINS   🕐 50–55 MINS

SERVES 4

I N G R E D I E N T S

4 tbsp unsalted butter

1 large onion, chopped

2 ½ cups vegetable stock

2 lb Italian plum tomatoes, skinned
and roughly chopped

pinch of baking soda

2 cups dried fusilli

1 tbsp superfine sugar

⅔ cup heavy cream

salt and pepper

fresh basil leaves, to garnish

1 Melt the butter in a large pan, add the
onion and fry for 3 minutes, stirring.
Add 1¼ cups of vegetable stock to the
pan, with the chopped tomatoes and
baking soda. Bring the soup to a boil and

VARIATION

To make orange and tomato
soup, simply use half the
quantity of vegetable stock,
topped up with the same amount
of fresh orange juice and garnish
the soup with orange rind.

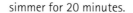

simmer for 20 minutes.

2 Remove the pan from the heat and
set aside to cool. Purée the soup in
a blender or food processor and pour
through a fine strainer back into
the saucepan.

3 Add the remaining vegetable stock
and the fusilli to the pan, and season
to taste with salt and pepper.

4 Add the sugar to the pan, bring to
boil, then lower the heat and simme
for about 15 minutes.

5 Pour the soup into a warm tureer
swirl the heavy cream around th
surface of the soup and garnish with fres
basil leaves. Serve immediately.

Gazpacho

This Spanish soup is full of chopped and grated vegetables with a puréed tomato base. It requires chilling, so prepare well in advance.

NUTRITIONAL INFORMATION

Calories . . . . . . .140 Sugars 12g
Protein . . . . .3g Fat 9g
Carbohydrate . . .13g Saturates 1g

 6½ HOURS   ⊙ 0 MINS

SERVES 4

I N G R E D I E N T S

½ small cucumber

½ small green bell pepper, seeded and
   very finely chopped

1 lb ripe tomatoes, peeled or
   14 oz can chopped tomatoes

½ onion, coarsely chopped

2–3 garlic cloves, minced

3 tbsp olive oil

4 tbsp white wine vinegar

1–2 tbsp lemon or lime juice

1 tbsp tomato paste

scant 2 cups tomato juice

salt and pepper

T O   S E R V E

chopped green bell pepper

thinly sliced onion rings

garlic croûtons

1 Coarsely grate the cucumber into a large bowl and add the chopped green bell pepper.

2 Process the tomatoes, onion, and garlic in a food processor or blender, then add the oil, vinegar, lemon or lime juice, and tomato paste and process until smooth. Alternatively, finely chop the tomatoes and finely grate the onion, then mix both with the garlic, oil, vinegar, lemon or lime juice, and tomato paste.

3 Add the tomato mixture to the bowl and mix well, then add the tomato juice and mix again.

4 Season to taste, cover the bowl with plastic wrap and chill thoroughly–for at least 6 hours and preferably longer so that the flavors have time to meld together.

5 Prepare the side dishes of green bell pepper, onion rings, and garlic croûtons, and arrange in individual serving bowls.

6 Ladle the soup into bowls, preferably from a soup tureen set on the table with the side dishes placed around it. Hand the dishes around to allow the guests to help themselves.

Thick Onion Soup

A delicious creamy soup with grated carrot and parsley for texture and color. Serve with crusty cheese biscuits for a hearty lunch.

NUTRITIONAL INFORMATION

Calories 277	Sugars 12g
Protein 6g	Fat 20g
Carbohydrate ...19g	Saturates 8g

20 MINS   1HR 10 MINS

SERVES 6

INGREDIENTS

5 tbsp butter

1 lb onions, finely chopped

1 garlic clove, minced

6 tbsp all-purpose flour

2½ cups vegetable stock

2½ cups milk

2–3 tsp lemon or lime juice

good pinch of ground allspice

1 bay leaf

1 carrot, coarsely grated

4–6 tbsp heavy cream

2 tbsp chopped parsley

salt and pepper

CHEESE BISCUITS

2 cups malted wheat or whole wheat flour

2 tsp baking powder

¼ cup butter

4 tbsp grated Parmesan cheese

1 egg, beaten

about ⅓ cup milk

1 Melt the butter in a saucepan and fry the onions and garlic over a low heat, stirring frequently, for 10–15 minutes, until soft, but not colored. Stir in the flour and cook, stirring, for 1 minute, then gradually stir in the stock and bring to a boil, stirring frequently. Add the milk, then bring back to a boil.

2 Season to taste with salt and pepper and add 2 teaspoons of the lemon or lime juice, the allspice, and bay leaf. Cover and simmer for about 25 minutes until the vegetables are tender. Discard the bay leaf.

3 Meanwhile, make the biscuits. Combine the flour, baking powder, and seasoning and rub in the butter until the mixture resembles fine breadcrumbs. Stir in 3 tablespoons of the cheese, the egg and enough milk to mix to a soft dough.

4 Shape into a bar about ¾ inch thick. Place on a floured baking sheet and score into slices. Sprinkle with the remaining cheese and bake in a preheated oven, 425°F/, for about 20 minutes, until risen and golden brown.

5 Stir the carrot into the soup and simmer for 2–3 minutes. Add more lemon or lime juice, if necessary. Stir in the cream and reheat. Garnish and serve with the warm biscuits.

Potato & Pesto Soup

Fresh pesto is a treat to the taste buds and very different in flavor from that available from supermarkets. Store fresh pesto in the refrigerator.

NUTRITIONAL INFORMATION

Calories	548	Sugars	.........0g
Protein	........11g	Fat	..........52g
Carbohydrate	...10g	Saturates	......18g

5–10 MINS   50 MINS

SERVES 4

INGREDIENTS

slices rindless, smoked, fatty bacon

lb mealy potatoes

lb onions

tbsp olive oil

tbsp butter

½ cups chicken stock

½ cups milk

cup dried conchigliette

cup heavy cream

opped fresh parsley

lt and pepper

eshly grated Parmesan cheese and garlic

bread, to serve

PESTO SAUCE

cup finely chopped fresh parsley

garlic cloves, minced

cup pine kernels, minced

tbsp chopped fresh basil leaves

cup freshly grated Parmesan cheese

hite pepper

cup olive oil

1 To make the pesto sauce, put all of the ingredients in a blender or food processor and process for 2 minutes, or blend by hand using a mortar and pestle.

2 Finely chop the bacon, potatoes, and onions. Fry the bacon in a large skillet over a medium heat for 4 minutes. Add the butter, potatoes, and onions and cook for 12 minutes, stirring constantly.

3 Add the stock and milk to the pan, bring to a boil and simmer for 10 minutes. Add the conchigliette and simmer for a further 10-12 minutes.

4 Blend in the cream and simmer for 5 minutes. Add the parsley, salt and pepper, and 2 tbsp pesto sauce. Transfer the soup to serving bowls and serve with Parmesan cheese and fresh garlic bread.

Broccoli & Potato Soup

This creamy soup has a delightful pale green coloring and rich flavor from the blend of tender broccoli and blue cheese.

NUTRITIONAL INFORMATION

Calories 452   Sugars 4g
Protein . . . . .14g   Fat 35g
Carbohydrate . . .20g   Saturates 19g

 5-10 MINS   40 MINS

SERVES 4

INGREDIENTS

2 tbsp olive oil

2 potatoes, diced

1 onion, diced

8 oz broccoli florets

4½ oz blue cheese, crumbled

4½ cups vegetable stock

⅔ cup heavy cream

pinch of paprika

salt and pepper

1 Heat the oil in a large saucepan. Add the potatoes and onion. Sauté, stirring constantly, for 5 minutes.

2 Reserve a few broccoli florets for the garnish and add the remaining broccoli to the pan. Add the cheese and vegetable stock.

3 Bring to a boil, then reduce the heat, cover the pan and simmer for 25 minutes, until the potatoes are tender.

4 Transfer the soup to a food processor or blender in batches and process until the mixture is smooth. Alternatively, press the vegetables through a strainer with the back of a wooden spoon.

5 Return the purée to a clean saucepan and stir in the heavy cream and a

pinch of paprika. Season to taste with sa and pepper.

6 Blanch the reserved broccoli florets a little boiling water for abo 2 minutes, then lift them out of the pa with a draining spoon.

7 Pour the soup into warmed individu bowls and garnish with the brocco florets and a sprinkling of paprik Serve immediately.

COOK'S TIP

This soup freezes very successfully. Follow the method described here up to step 4, and freeze the soup after it has been puréed. Add the cream and paprika just before serving. Garnish and serve.

Artichoke Soup

This refreshing chilled soup is ideal for *al fresco* dining. Bear in mind that this soup needs to be chilled for 3-4 hours, so allow plenty of time.

NUTRITIONAL INFORMATION

Calories	159	Sugars	.........2g
Protein	.........2g	Fat	15
Carbohydrate	....5g	Saturates	.......6g

5 MINS   15 MINS

SERVES 4

INGREDIENTS

tbsp olive oil

onion, chopped

garlic clove, minced

x 14 oz can artichoke hearts, drained

½ cups hot vegetable stock

cup light cream

tbsp fresh thyme, stalks removed

sun-dried tomatoes, cut into strips

esh, crusty bread, to serve

1 Heat the oil in a large saucepan and fry the chopped onion and crushed arlic, stirring, for 2–3 minutes or until st softened.

2 Using a sharp knife, roughly chop the artichoke hearts. Add the artichoke eces to the onion and garlic mixture in e pan. Pour in the hot vegetable stock, rring well.

3 Bring the mixture to a boil, then reduce the heat and leave to simmer, vered, for about 3 minutes.

4 Place the mixture into a food processor and blend until smooth. ternatively, push the mixture through a rainer to remove any lumps.

5 Return the soup to the saucepan. Stir the light cream and fresh thyme into the soup.

6 Transfer the soup to a large bowl, cover, and leave to chill in the refrigerator for about 3–4 hours.

7 Transfer the chilled soup to individual soup bowls and garnish with strips of sun-dried tomato. Serve with crusty bread.

VARIATION

Try adding 2 tablespoons of dry vermouth, such as Martini, to the soup in step 5, if you wish.

Cream of Artichoke Soup

A creamy soup with the unique, subtle flavoring of Jerusalem artichokes and a garnish of grated carrots for extra crunch.

NUTRITIONAL INFORMATION

Calories 19   Sugars 0g
Protein . . . . .0.4g   Fat 2g
Carbohydrate . . .0.7g   Saturates 0.7g

10–15 MINS   55–60 MINS

SERVES 6

INGREDIENTS

1 lb 10 oz Jerusalem artichokes

1 lemon, sliced thickly

¼ cup butter or margarine

2 onions, chopped

1 garlic clove, minced

5½ cups chicken or vegetable stock

2 bay leaves

¼ tsp ground mace or ground nutmeg

1 tbsp lemon juice

⅔ cup light cream or unsweetened fromage
    blanc

salt and pepper

TO GARNISH

coarsely grated carrot

chopped fresh parsley or cilantro

1 Peel and slice the artichokes. Put into a bowl of water with the lemon slices.

2 Melt the butter or margarine in a large saucepan. Add the onions and garlic and fry gently for 3–4 minutes until soft but not colored.

3 Drain the artichokes (discarding the lemon) and add to the pan. Mix well and cook gently for 2–3 minutes without allowing to color.

4 Add the stock, seasoning, bay leaves, mace or nutmeg and, lemon juice. Bring slowly to a boil, then cover and simmer gently for about 30 minutes until the vegetables are very tender.

5 Discard the bay leaves. Cool the soup slightly then press through a strainer or blend in a food processor until smooth. If liked, a little of the soup may be only partially puréed and added to the rest of the puréed soup, to give extra texture.

6 Pour into a clean pan and bring to a boil. Adjust the seasoning and stir in the cream or fromage blanc. Reheat gently without boiling. Garnish with grated carrot and chopped parsley or cilantro.

Roasted Vegetable Soup

Roasting the vegetables gives this soup its intense, rich flavor, reminiscent of ratatouille.

NUTRITIONAL INFORMATION

Calories	153	Sugar	........13g
Protein	.........5g	Fats	...........9g
Carbohydrates	...15g	Saturates	......3g

15 MINS   1¼ HOURS

SERVES 6

INGREDIENTS

-3 tbsp olive oil

lb 9 oz ripe tomatoes, skinned, cored, and halved

large yellow bell peppers, halved, cored, and seeded

zucchini, halved lengthways

small eggplant, halved lengthways

garlic cloves, halved

onions, cut into eighths

nch of dried thyme

cups chicken, vegetable or meat stock

cup light cream

lt and pepper

redded basil leaves, to garnish

Brush a large shallow baking dish with olive oil. Laying them cut-side own, arrange the tomatoes, bell peppers, cchini, and eggplant in one layer (use o dishes, if necessary). Tuck the garlic oves and onion pieces into the gaps and izzle the vegetables with olive oil. ason lightly with salt and pepper and rinkle with the thyme.

Place in a preheated oven at 375°C and bake, uncovered, for 30–35 nutes, or until soft and browned around the edges. Leave to cool, then scrape out the eggplant flesh and remove the skin from the bell peppers.

3 Working in batches, put the eggplant and bell pepper flesh, together with the zucchini, into a food processor and chop to the consistency of salsa or pickle; do not purée. Alternatively, place in a bowl and chop together with a knife.

4 Combine the stock and chopped vegetable mixture in a saucepan and simmer over a medium heat for between 20–30 minutes until all the vegetables are tender and the flavors have completely blended.

5 Stir in the cream and simmer over a low heat for about 5 minutes, stirring occasionally until hot. Taste and adjust the seasoning, if necessary. Ladle the soup into warm bowls, garnish with basil and serve.

Vegetable with Pesto Soup

This soup takes advantage of summer vegetables bursting with flavor.

NUTRITIONAL INFORMATION

Calories	262	Sugar	.........6g
Protein	........14g	Fats	..........15g
Carbohydrates	...20g	Saturates	......4g

🕐 15 MINS   🕐 55 MINS

SERVES 6

INGREDIENTS

1 tbsp olive oil

1 onion, finely chopped

1 large leek, split and thinly sliced

1 stalk celery, thinly sliced

1 carrot, quartered and thinly sliced

1 garlic clove, finely chopped

1½ quarts water

1 potato, diced

1 parsnip, finely diced

1 small kohlrabi or turnip, diced

5½ oz dwarf beans, cut in small pieces

5½ oz fresh or frozen English peas

2 small zucchini, quartered lengthways and sliced

14 oz can small navy beans, drained and rinsed

3½ oz spinach leaves, cut into thin ribbons

salt and pepper

PESTO:

1 large garlic clove, very finely chopped

½ oz basil leaves

2¾ oz Parmesan cheese, grated

4 tbsp extra-virgin olive oil

1 Heat the olive oil in a large saucepan over a medium-low heat. Add the onion and leek and cook for 5 minutes, stirring occasionally, until the onion softens. Add the celery, carrot, and garlic and cook, covered, for a further 5 minutes, stirring frequently.

2 Add the water, potato, parsnip, kohlrabi or turnip, and dwarf beans. Bring to a boil, reduce the heat to low, and simmer, covered, for 5 minutes.

3 Add the peas, zucchini and small navy beans, and season generously with salt and pepper. Cover again and simmer

for about 25 minutes until all th vegetables are tender.

4 Meanwhile, make the pesto. Put th garlic, basil, and cheese in a foo processor with the olive oil and proce until smooth, scraping down the sides necessary. Alternatively, pound togeth using a mortar and pestle.

5 Add the spinach to the soup ar simmer for a further 5 minutes. Tas and adjust the seasoning and stir about table-spoon of the pesto into the sou Ladle into warm bowls and pass th remaining pesto separately.

Vichyssoise

This is a classic creamy soup made from potatoes and leeks. To achieve the delicate pale color, be sure to use only the white parts of the leeks.

NUTRITIONAL INFORMATION

Calories	208	Sugars	.........5g
Protein	.........5g	Fat	..........12g
Carbohydrate	...20g	Saturates	.......6g

10 MINS   40 MINS

SERVES 6

I N G R E D I E N T S

large leeks

tbsp butter or margarine

onion, thinly sliced

lb potatoes, chopped

cups vegetable stock

tsp lemon juice

nch of ground nutmeg

tsp ground coriander

bay leaf

egg yolk

cup light cream

lt and white pepper

TO GARNISH

shly snipped chives

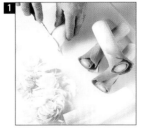

1 Trim the leeks and remove most of the green part. Slice the white part of the leeks very finely.

2 Melt the butter or margarine in a saucepan. Add the leeks and onion and fry, stirring occasionally, for about minutes without browning.

3 Add the potatoes, vegetable stock, lemon juice, nutmeg, coriander, and bay leaf to the pan, season to taste with salt and pepper and bring to a boil. Cover and simmer for about 30 minutes, until all the vegetables are very soft.

4 Cool the soup a little, remove and discard the bay leaf and then press through a strainer or process in a food processor or blender until smooth. Pour into a clean pan.

5 Blend the egg yolk into the cream, add a little of the soup to the mixture and then whisk it all back into the soup and reheat gently, without boiling. Adjust the seasoning to taste. Cool and then chill thoroughly in the refrigerator.

6 Serve the soup sprinkled with freshly snipped chives.

Tuscan Onion Soup

This soup is best made with white onions, which have a mild flavor. If you cannot get hold of them, try using large Spanish onions instead.

NUTRITIONAL INFORMATION

Calories	390	Sugars	.........0g
Protein	.........9g	Fat	..........33g
Carbohydrate	...15g	Saturates	......14g

5–10 MINS   40–45 MINS

SERVES 4

I N G R E D I E N T S

1¾ oz pancetta ham, diced

1 tbsp olive oil

4 large white onions, sliced thinly into rings

3 garlic cloves, chopped

3½ cups hot chicken or ham stock

4 slices ciabatta or other Italian bread

3 tbsp butter

2¾ oz Gruyère or Cheddar

salt and pepper

1 Dry fry the pancetta in a large saucepan for 3–4 minutes until it begins to brown. Remove the pancetta from the pan and set aside until required.

2 Add the oil to the pan and cook the onions and garlic over a high heat for

4 minutes. Reduce the heat, cover, and cook for 15 minutes or until the onions are lightly caramelized.

3 Add the stock to the saucepan and bring to a boil. Reduce the heat and leave the mixture to simmer, covered, for about 10 minutes.

4 Toast the slices of ciabatta on both sides, under a preheated broiler, for

2–3 minutes or until golden. Spread the ciabatta with butter and top with the Gruyère or Cheddar cheese. Cut the bread into bite-size pieces.

5 Add the reserved pancetta to the soup and season with salt and pepper to taste.

6 Pour into 4 soup bowls and top with the toasted bread.

COOK'S TIP

Pancetta is similar to bacon, but it is air- and salt-cured for about 6 months. Pancetta is available from most delicatessens and some large supermarkets. If you cannot obtain pancetta use unsmoked bacon instead.

ish Soup

There are many varieties of fish soup in Italy, some including shellfish. This one, from Tuscany, is more like a chowder.

NUTRITIONAL INFORMATION

Calories .... .305 Sugars 3g
Protein .... .47g Fat 7g
Carbohydrate ....11g Saturates 1g

5–10 MINS   1 HOUR

SERVES 6

N G R E D I E N T S

lb assorted prepared fish (including mixed fish fillets, squid, etc.)

onions, sliced thinly

celery stalks, sliced thinly

few sprigs of parsley

bay leaves

cup white wine

cups water

tbsp olive oil

garlic clove, minced

carrot, chopped finely

4 oz can peeled tomatoes, puréed

potatoes, chopped

tbsp tomato paste

tsp chopped fresh oregano or ½ tsp dried oregano

2 oz fresh mussels

oz peeled shrimp

tbsp chopped fresh parsley

lt and pepper

usty bread, to serve

Cut the fish into slices and put into a pan with half the onion and celery, the rsley, bay leaves, wine, and water. Bring a boil, cover and simmer for 25 minutes.

2 Strain the fish stock and discard the vegetables. Skin the fish, remove any bones and reserve.

3 Heat the oil in a pan. Fry the remaining onion and celery with the garlic and carrot until soft but not colored, stirring occasionally. Add the puréed canned tomatoes, potatoes, tomato paste, oregano, reserved stock, and seasoning. Bring to a boil and simmer for about 15 minutes or until the potato is almost tender.

4 Meanwhile, thoroughly scrub the mussels. Add the mussels to the pan with the shrimp and leave to simmer for about 5 minutes or until the mussels have opened (discard any that remain closed).

5 Return the fish to the soup with the chopped parsley, bring back to a boil and simmer for 5 minutes. Adjust the seasoning.

6 Serve the soup in warmed bowls with chunks of fresh crusty bread, or put a toasted slice of crusty bread in the bottom of each bowl before adding the soup. If possible, remove a few half shells from the mussels before serving.

Italian Fish Stew

This robust stew is full of Mediterranean flavors. If you do not want to prepare the fish yourself, ask your local fishstore to do it for you.

NUTRITIONAL INFORMATION

Calories	236	Sugars	.........4g
Protein	........20g	Fat	...........7g
Carbohydrate	...25g	Saturates	.......1g

5–10 MINS   25 MINS

SERVES 4

I N G R E D I E N T S

2 tbsp olive oil

2 red onions, finely chopped

1 garlic clove, minced

2 zucchini, sliced

14 oz can chopped tomatoes

3 ½ cups fish or vegetable stock

3 oz dried pasta shapes

12 oz firm white fish, such as cod, haddock
   or hake

1 tbsp chopped fresh basil or oregano or
   1 tsp dried oregano

1 tsp grated lemon rind

1 tbsp cornstarch

1 tbsp water

salt and pepper

sprigs of fresh basil or oregano, to garnish

1 Heat the oil in a large saucepan and fry the onions and garlic for 5 minutes. Add the zucchini and cook for 2–3 minutes, stirring often.

2 Add the tomatoes and stock to the saucepan and bring to a boil. Add the pasta, cover, and reduce the heat. Simmer for 5 minutes.

3 Skin and bone the fish, then cut it into chunks. Add to the saucepan with the basil or oregano and lemon rind and cook gently for 5 minutes until the fish is opaque and flakes easily (take care not to overcook it).

4 Blend the cornstarch with the wat and stir into the stew. Cook gently 2 minutes, stirring, until thickened. Seas with salt and pepper to taste and la into 4 warmed soup bowls. Garnish w basil or oregano sprigs and serve at once

Provençal Fish Soup

For the best results, you need to use flavorful fish, such as cod or haddock, for this recipe.

NUTRITIONAL INFORMATION

Calories . . . . .109 Sugars 3g
Protein . . . . .12g Fat 3g
Carbohydrate . . . .4g Saturates 0g

15 MINS 1 HOUR 20 MINS

SERVES 4

I N G R E D I E N T S

tbsp olive oil
onions, finely chopped
small leek, thinly sliced
small carrot, finely chopped
stalk celery, finely chopped
small fennel bulb, finely chopped (optional)
garlic cloves, finely chopped
cup dry white wine
cups water
4 oz can tomatoes in juice
bay leaf
inch of fennel seeds
strips orange rind
tsp saffron threads
2 oz skinless white fish fillets
alt and pepper
arlic croûtons, to serve

1 Heat the oil in a large saucepan over a medium heat. Add the onions and cook for about 5 minutes, stirring frequently, until softened. Add the leek, carrot, celery, fennel, and garlic and continue cooking for 4–5 minutes until the leek is wilted.

2 Add the wine and let it bubble for a minute. Add the tomatoes, bay leaf, fennel seeds, orange rind, saffron, and water. Bring just to a boil, reduce the heat, cover, and cook gently, stirring occasionally, for 30 minutes.

3 Add the fish and cook for a further 20–30 minutes until it is very soft and flaky. Remove the bay leaf and orange rind if possible.

4 Allow the soup to cool slightly, then transfer to a blender or food processor and purée until smooth, working in batches if necessary. (If using a food processor, strain off the cooking liquid and reserve. Purée the soup solids with enough cooking liquid to moisten them, then combine with the remaining liquid.)

5 Return the soup to the saucepan. Taste and adjust the seasoning, if necessary, and simmer for 5–10 minutes until heated through. Ladle the soup into warm bowls and sprinkle with croûtons.

Garlic Fish Soup

The delicate color of this soup belies its heady flavors. The recipe has been adapted from a classic French recipe.

NUTRITIONAL INFORMATION

Calories . . . . .200 Sugars 4g
Protein . . . . .19g Fat 7g
Carbohydrate . . .14g Saturates 3g

15 MINS   40 MINS

SERVES 4

I N G R E D I E N T S

2 tsp olive oil

1 large onion, chopped

1 small fennel bulb, chopped

1 leek, sliced

3–4 large garlic cloves, thinly sliced

½ cup dry white wine

5 cups fish stock

4 tbsp white rice

1 strip pared lemon rind

1 bay leaf

1 lb skinless white fish fillets, cut into
   1½ inch pieces

¼ cup heavy cream

2 tbsp chopped fresh parsley

salt and pepper

1 Heat the oil in a large saucepan over a medium-low heat. Add the onion, fennel, leek, and garlic and cook for 4–5 minutes, stirring frequently, until the onion is softened.

2 Add the wine and bubble briefly. Add the stock, rice, lemon rind, and bay leaf. Bring to a boil, reduce the heat to medium-low and simmer for 20–25 minutes, or until the rice and vegetables are soft. Remove the lemon rind and bay leaf.

3 Allow the soup to cool slightly, then transfer to a blender or food processor and purée until smooth, working in batches if necessary. (If using a food processor, strain off the cooking liquid and reserve. Purée the soup solids with enough cooking liquid to moisten them, then combine with the remaining liquid.)

4 Return the soup to the saucepan and bring to a simmer. Add the fish to the soup, cover and continue simmering gently, stirring occasionally, for 4–5 minutes, or until the fish is cooked and begins to flake.

5 Stir in the cream. Taste and adjust the seasoning, adding salt, if needed, and pepper. Ladle into warm bowls and serve sprinkled with parsley.

Breton Fish Soup

Fishermen's soups are inevitably variable, depending on the season and the catch.

NUTRITIONAL INFORMATION

Calories 436   Sugars 8g
Protein . . . . .19g   Fat 28g
Carbohydrate . . .27g   Saturates 17g

 15 MINS   35 MINS

SERVES 4

I N G R E D I E N T S

2 tsp butter

1 large leek, thinly sliced

2 shallots, finely chopped

½ cup hard cider

1¼ cups fish stock

9 oz potatoes, diced

1 bay leaf

1 tbsp all-purpose flour

¾ cup milk

¼ cup heavy cream

2 oz fresh sorrel leaves

12 oz skinless angler fish or cod fillet, cut into 1 inch pieces

salt and pepper

COOK'S TIP

Be careful not to overcook the fish, otherwise tender fish, such as cod, break up into smaller and smaller flakes and firm fish, like angler fish, can become tough.

1 Melt the butter in a large saucepan over a medium-low heat. Add the leek and shallots and cook for about 5 minutes, stirring frequently, until they start to soften. Add the cider and bring to a boil.

2 Stir in the stock, potatoes and bay leaf with a large pinch of salt (unless stock is salty) and bring back to a boil. Reduce the heat, cover, and cook gently for 10 minutes.

3 Put the flour in a small bowl and very slowly whisk in a few tablespoons of the milk to make a thick paste. Stir in a little more to make a smooth liquid.

4 Adjust the heat so the soup bubbles gently. Stir in the flour mixture and cook, stirring frequently, for 5 minutes. Add the remaining milk and half the cream. Continue cooking for about 10 minutes until the potatoes are tender.

5 Chop the sorrel finely and combine with the remaining cream. (If using a food processor, add the sorrel and chop, then add the cream and process briefly.)

6 Stir the sorrel cream into the soup and add the fish. Continue cooking, stirring occasionally, for about 3 minutes, until the angler fish stiffens or the cod just begins to flake. Taste the soup and adjust the seasoning, if needed. Ladle into warm bowls and serve.

Mussel, Potato, & Parsley
This soup can be made in stages, so is suitable for entertaining.

NUTRITIONAL INFORMATION

Calories 538   Sugars 11g
Protein . . . . .22g   Fat 34g
Carbohydrate . . .38g   Saturates 20g

15 MINS   50 MINS

SERVES 4

INGREDIENTS

2 lb mussels

10½ oz potatoes

3 tbsp all-purpose flour

2½ cups milk

1¼ cups whipping cream

1–2 garlic cloves, finely chopped

6 cups curly parsley leaves (1 large bunch)

salt and pepper

1 Discard any broken mussels and those with open shells that do not close when tapped. Rinse under cold running water, pull off any 'beards' and scrape off barnacles with a knife. Put the mussels in a large heavy-bottomed saucepan. Cover tightly and cook over a high heat for about 4 minutes, or until the mussels open.

2 When cool enough to handle, remove the mussels from the shells, adding any additional juices to the cooking liquid. Strain the cooking liquid into a bowl through a cheesecloth-lined strainer and put aside.

3 Boil the potatoes, in their skins, in salted water for about 15 minutes until tender. When cool enough to handle, peel and cut into small dice.

4 Put the flour in a mixing bowl and very slowly whisk in a few tablespoons of the milk to make a thick paste. Stir in a little more to make a smooth liquid.

5 Put the remaining milk, cream, and garlic in a saucepan and bring to a boil. Whisk in the flour mixture. Reduce the heat to medium-low and simmer for about 15 minutes until the garlic is tender and the liquid has thickened slightly. Drop in the parsley leaves and cook for about 2–3 minutes until bright green and wilted.

6 Allow the soup base to cool slightly, then transfer to a blender or food processor and purée until smooth, working in batches if necessary. (If using a food processor, strain off the cooking liquid and reserve. Purée the soup solids with enough cooking liquid to moisten, then combine with the remaining liquid.)

7 Return the purée to the saucepan and stir in the mussel cooking liquid and the potatoes. Season to taste with salt, if needed, and pepper. Simmer the soup gently for 5–7 minutes until reheated. Add the mussels and continue cooking for about 2 minutes until the soup is steaming and the mussels are hot. Ladle the soup into warm bowls and serve.

Italian Seafood Soup

This colorful mixed seafood soup would be superbly complemented by a dry white wine.

NUTRITIONAL INFORMATION

Calories	668	Sugars	.........3g
Protein	........48g	Fat	..........43g
Carbohydrate	...21g	Saturates	......25g

5 MINS   55 MINS

SERVES 4

INGREDIENTS

tbsp butter

lb assorted fish fillets, such as red mullet and snapper

lb prepared seafood, such as squid and shrimp

oz fresh crabmeat

large onion, sliced

cup all-purpose flour

cups fish stock

cup dried pasta shapes, such as ditalini or elbow macaroni

tbsp anchovy extract

grated rind and juice of 1 orange

cup dry sherry

cups heavy cream

salt and pepper

crusty brown bread, to serve

1 Melt the butter in a large saucepan, add the fish fillets, seafood, crabmeat, and onion and cook gently over a low heat for 6 minutes.

2 Add the flour to the seafood mixture, stirring thoroughly to avoid any lumps from forming.

3 Gradually add the stock, stirring, until the soup comes to a boil. Reduce the heat and simmer for 30 minutes.

4 Add the pasta to the pan and cook for a further 10 minutes.

5 Stir in the anchovy extract, orange rind, orange juice, sherry, and heavy cream. Season to taste with salt and pepper.

6 Heat the soup until completely warmed through.

7 Transfer the soup to a tureen or to warm soup bowls and serve with crusty brown bread.

Tuscan Veal Broth

Veal plays an important role in Italian cuisine and there are dozens of recipes for all cuts of this meat.

NUTRITIONAL INFORMATION

Calories 420	Sugars 5g	
Protein 54g	Fat 7g	
Carbohydrate ...37g	Saturates 2g	

2¼ HOURS   4¾ HOURS

SERVES 4

INGREDIENTS

⅓ cup dried peas, soaked for
   2 hours and drained

2 lb boned neck of veal, diced

5 cups beef or brown stock
   (see Cook's Tip)

2½ cups water

⅓ cup barley, washed

1 large carrot, diced

1 small turnip (about 6 oz), diced

1 large leek, thinly sliced

1 red onion, finely chopped

3½ oz chopped tomatoes

1 fresh basil sprig

¾ cup dried vermicelli

salt and white pepper

1 Put the peas, veal, stock, and water into a large pan and bring to a boil over a low heat. Using a draining spoon, skim off any scum that rises to the surface.

2 When all of the scum has been removed, add the barley and a pinch of salt to the mixture. Simmer gently over a low heat for 25 minutes.

3 Add the carrot, turnip, leek, onion, tomatoes, and basil to the pan, and season with salt and pepper to taste. Leave to simmer for about 2 hours, skimming the surface from time to time to remove any scum. Remove the pan from the heat and set aside for 2 hours.

4 Set the pan over a medium heat and bring to a boil. Add the vermicelli and cook for 12 minutes. Season with salt and pepper to taste; remove and discard the basil. Ladle into soup bowls and serve immediately.

COOK'S TI

The best brown stock
made with veal bones and sh
of beef roasted with drippings
the oven for 4
minutes. Transfer the bones to a pa
and add sliced leeks, onion, celery, ar
carrots, a bouquet garni, white wir
vinegar, and a thyme sprig and cov
with cold water. Simmer over a ve
low heat for 3 hours; strain before us

Veal & Mushroom Soup

Delicately scented with lemon, this luscious soup features the classic combination of tender veal with mushrooms and cream.

NUTRITIONAL INFORMATION

Calories 383	Sugars 6g	
Protein 23g	Fat 19g	
Carbohydrate ...31g	Saturates 11g	

15 MINS   1½ HOURS

SERVES 4

INGREDIENTS

2 oz boneless veal, cut into ½ inch pieces

cups chicken stock

onion, quartered

carrots, thinly sliced

garlic cloves, halved

pared strip lemon rind

bay leaf

tbsp butter

2 oz small button mushrooms, quartered

tbsp cornstarch

cup heavy cream

eshly grated nutmeg

esh lemon juice, to taste (optional)

-2 tbsp chopped fresh parsley

alt and pepper

1 Put the veal in a large saucepan and add the stock. Bring just to a boil nd skim off any foam that rises o the surface.

2 Add the onion, carrots, garlic, lemon rind, and bay leaf. Season with salt and pepper. Reduce the heat and simmer, partially covered, for about 45 minutes, stirring occasionally, until the veal is very tender.

3 Remove the veal and carrots with a draining spoon and reserve, covered. Strain the stock into a clean saucepan. Discard the onion and garlic, lemon rind, and bay leaf.

4 Melt the butter in a skillet over a medium-high heat. Add the mushrooms, season, and fry gently until lightly golden. Reserve with the veal and carrots.

5 Mix together the cornstarch and cream. Bring the cooking liquid just to a boil and whisk in the cream mixture. Boil very gently for 2-3 minutes until it thickens, whisking almost constantly.

6 Add the reserved meat and vegetables to the soup and simmer over a low heat for about 5 minutes until heated through. Taste and adjust the seasoning, adding nutmeg and a squeeze of lemon juice, if wished. Stir in the parsley, then ladle into warm bowls and serve.

Veal & Wild Mushroom

Wild mushrooms are available commercially and an increasing range of cultivated varieties is now to be found in many supermarkets.

NUTRITIONAL INFORMATION

Calories 413   Sugars 3g
Protein . . . . .28g   Fat 22g
Carbohydrate . . .28g   Saturates 12g

🕐 5 MINS   🕐 3¼ HOURS

SERVES 4

INGREDIENTS

1 lb veal, thinly sliced

1 lb veal bones

5 cups water

1 small onion

6 peppercorns

1 tsp cloves

pinch of mace

5 oz oyster and shiitake mushrooms,
   roughly chopped

⅔ cup heavy cream

¾ cup dried vermicelli

1 tbsp cornstarch

3 tbsp milk

salt and pepper

1 Put the veal, bones, and water into a large saucepan. Bring to a boil and lower the heat. Add the onion, peppercorns, cloves, and mace and simmer for about 3 hours, until the veal stock is reduced by one-third.

2 Strain the stock, skim off any fat on the surface, with a draining spoon, and pour the stock into a clean saucepan. Add the veal meat to the pan.

3 Add the mushrooms and cream, bring to a boil over a low heat and then leave to simmer for 12 minute stirring occasionally.

4 Meanwhile, cook the vermicelli lightly salted boiling water for 1 minutes or until tender, but still firm the bite. Drain and keep warm.

5 Mix the cornstarch and milk to form smooth paste. Stir into the soup thicken. Season to taste with salt ar pepper and just before serving, add th vermicelli. Transfer the soup to a war tureen and serve immediately.

COOK'S TIP

You can make this soup with the more inexpensive cuts of veal, such as breast or neck slices. These are lean and the long cooking time ensures that the meat is really tender.

Veal & Ham Soup

Veal and ham is a classic combination, complemented here with the addition of sherry to create a richly-flavored Italian soup.

NUTRITIONAL INFORMATION

Calories . . . . .501 Sugars 10g
Protein . . . . .38g Fat 18g
Carbohydrate . . .28g Saturates 10g

5 MINS   3¼ HOURS

SERVES 4

INGREDIENTS

tbsp butter

onion, diced

carrot, diced

celery stalk, diced

lb veal, very thinly sliced

lb ham, thinly sliced

cup all-purpose flour

⅜ cups beef stock

bay leaf

black peppercorns

inch of salt

tbsp redcurrant jelly

cup cream sherry

cup dried vermicelli

garlic croûtons (see Cook's Tip), to serve

1 Melt the butter in a large pan. Add the onions, carrot, celery, veal, and ham and cook over a low heat for 6 minutes.

2 Sprinkle over the flour and cook, stirring constantly, for a further 2 minutes. Gradually stir in the stock, then add the bay leaf, peppercorns, and salt. Bring to a boil and simmer for 1 hour.

3 Remove the pan from the heat and add the redcurrant jelly and cream sherry, stirring to combine. Set aside for about 4 hours.

4 Remove the bay leaf from the pan and discard. Reheat the soup over a very low heat until warmed through.

5 Meanwhile, cook the vermicelli in a saucepan of lightly salted boiling water for 10-12 minutes. Stir the vermicelli into the soup and transfer to soup bowls. Serve with garlic croûtons.

COOK'S TIP

To make garlic croûtons, remove the crusts from 3 slices of day-old white bread. Cut the bread into ¼ inch cubes. Heat 3 tbsp oil over a low heat and stir-fry 1–2 chopped garlic cloves for 1–2 minutes. Remove the garlic and add the bread. Cook, stirring frequently, until golden. Remove with a draining spoon and drain.

Chicken & Bean Soup

This hearty and nourishing soup, combining garbanzo beans and chicken, is an ideal starter for a family supper.

NUTRITIONAL INFORMATION

Calories 347   Sugars 2g
Protein ....28g   Fat 11g
Carbohydrate ...37g   Saturates 4g

5 MINS   1¾ HOURS

SERVES 4

INGREDIENTS

2 tbsp butter

3 scallions, chopped

2 garlic cloves, minced

1 fresh marjoram sprig, finely chopped

12 oz boned chicken breasts, diced

5 cups chicken stock

12 oz can garbanzo beans, drained

1 bouquet garni

1 red bell pepper, diced

1 green bell pepper, diced

1 cup small dried pasta shapes,
    such as elbow macaroni

salt and white pepper

croûtons, to serve

COOK'S TIP

If you prefer, you can use dried garbanzo beans. Cover with cold water and set aside to soak for 5–8 hours. Drain and add the beans to the soup, according to the recipe, and allow an additional 30 minutes– 1 hour cooking time.

1 Melt the butter in a large saucepan. Add the scallions, garlic, sprig of fresh marjoram, and the diced chicken and cook, stirring frequently, over a medium heat for 5 minutes.

2 Add the chicken stock, garbanzo beans and bouquet garni and season with salt and white pepper.

3 Bring the soup to a boil, lower the heat and simmer for about 2 hours.

4 Add the diced bell peppers and past to the pan, then simmer for a furthe 20 minutes.

5 Transfer the soup to a warm tureer To serve, ladle the soup into individua serving bowls and serve immediately garnished with the croûtons.

Chicken & Pasta Broth

This satisfying soup makes a good lunch or supper dish and you can use any vegetables you like. Children will love the tiny pasta shapes.

NUTRITIONAL INFORMATION

Calories 185	Sugars 5g	
Protein 17g	Fat 5g	
Carbohydrate ...20g	Saturates 1g	

5 MINS   15-20 MINS

SERVES 6

INGREDIENTS

2 oz boneless chicken breasts

tbsp sunflower oil

medium onion, diced

½ cups carrots, diced

oz cauliflower florets

¾ cups chicken stock

tsp dried mixed herbs

½ oz small pasta shapes

alt and pepper

armesan cheese (optional) and crusty
bread, to serve

1 Using a sharp knife, finely dice the chicken, discarding any skin.

2 Heat the oil in a large saucepan and quickly sauté the chicken, onion, carrots, and cauliflower until they are lightly colored.

3 Stir in the chicken stock and dried mixed herbs and bring to a boil.

4 Add the pasta shapes to the pan and return to a boil. Cover the pan and leave the broth to simmer for 10 minutes, stirring occasionally to prevent the pasta shapes from sticking together.

5 Season the broth with salt and pepper to taste and sprinkle with Parmesan cheese, if using. Serve the broth with fresh crusty bread.

COOK'S TIP

You can use any small pasta shapes for this soup—try conchigliette or ditali or even spaghetti broken up into small pieces. To make a fun soup for children you could add animal-shaped or alphabet pasta.

Lemon & Chicken Soup

This delicately flavored summer soup is surprisingly easy to make, and tastes delicious.

NUTRITIONAL INFORMATION

Calories 506	Sugars 4g	
Protein 19g	Fat 31g	
Carbohydrate ...41g	Saturates 19g	

5–10 MINS   1¼ HOURS

SERVES 4

INGREDIENTS

4 tbsp butter

8 shallots, thinly sliced

2 carrots, thinly sliced

2 celery stalks, thinly sliced

8 oz boned chicken breasts,
    finely chopped

3 lemons

5 cups chicken stock

8 oz dried spaghetti, broken into
    small pieces

⅝ cup heavy cream

salt and white pepper

TO GARNISH

fresh parsley sprig

3 lemon slices, halved

COOK'S TIP

You can prepare this soup up to the end of step 3 in advance, so that all you need do before serving is heat it through before adding the pasta and the finishing touches.

1 Melt the butter in a large saucepan. Add the shallots, carrots, celery, and chicken and cook over a low heat, stirring occasionally, for 8 minutes.

2 Thinly pare the lemons and blanch the lemon rind in boiling water for 3 minutes. Squeeze the juice from the lemons.

3 Add the lemon rind and juice to the pan, together with the chicken stock. Bring slowly to a boil over a low heat and simmer for 40 minute stirring occasionally.

4 Add the spaghetti to the pan and co for 15 minutes. Season to taste wi salt and white pepper and add the crea Heat through, but do not allow the so to boil or it will curdle.

5 Pour the soup into a ture or individual bowls, garnish wi the parsley, and half slices of lemon a serve immediately.

Ravioli in Tarragon Broth

Making filled pasta requires a bit of time and effort but the results are worth it. Homemade stock is essential.

NUTRITIONAL INFORMATION

Calories ....278 Sugar 1g
Protein ....14g Fats 17g
Carbohydrates ...17g Saturates 9g

🍳 20 MINS 🕐 35 MINS

SERVES 6

I N G R E D I E N T S

cups chicken stock

tbsp finely chopped fresh
tarragon leaves

HOMEMADE PASTA

cup all-purpose flour, plus extra if needed

tbsp fresh tarragon leaves, with stems
removed

egg

egg, separated

tsp extra-virgin olive oil

-3 tbsp water

FILLING:

oz cooked chicken, coarsely chopped

tsp grated lemon rind

tbsp chopped mixed fresh tarragon,
chives and parsley

tbsp whipping cream

t and pepper

To make the pasta, combine the flour, tarragon, and salt in a food processor. Beat together the egg, egg yolk, oil, and 2 tablespoons of the water. With the machine running, pour in the egg mixture and process until it forms a ball, leaving the sides of the bowl virtually clean. If the dough is crumbly, add the remaining

water; if the dough is sticky, add 1–2 tablespoons flour and continue kneading in the food processor until a ball forms. Wrap and chill for at least 30 minutes. Reserve the egg white.

2 To make the filling, put the chicken, lemon rind and mixed herbs in a food processor and season with salt and pepper. Chop finely, by pulsing; do not overprocess. Scrape into a bowl and stir in the cream. Taste and adjust the seasoning, if necessary.

3 Divide the pasta dough in half. Cover one half and roll the other half on a floured surface as thinly as possible, less than 1/16 inch. Cut out rectangles about 4 x 2 inches.

4 Place rounded teaspoons of filling on one half of the dough pieces. Brush around the edges with egg white and fold

in half. Press the edges gently but firmly to seal. Arrange the ravioli in one layer on a baking sheet, dusted generously with flour. Repeat with the remaining dough. Allow the ravioli to dry in a cool place for about 15 minutes or chill for 1–2 hours.

5 Bring a large quantity of salted water to a boil. Drop in half the ravioli and cook for 12–15 minutes until just tender. Drain on a clean dish cloth while cooking the remainder.

6 Meanwhile, put the stock and tarragon in a large saucepan. Bring to a boil and reduce the heat to bubble very gently. Cover and simmer for about 15 minutes, to infuse. Add the cooked ravioli to the stock and simmer for about 5 minutes until reheated. Ladle into warm soup plates to serve.

Provençal Turkey Soup

Pre-packed turkey, such as boneless breast or stir-fry meat, makes this a year-round favorite.

NUTRITIONAL INFORMATION

Calories ....175 Sugars 12g
Protein ....16g Fat 5g
Carbohydrate ...13g Saturates 1g

10 MINS   50 MINS

SERVES 4

INGREDIENTS

1 tbsp olive oil

2 red, yellow or green bell peppers, cored, seeded and finely chopped

1 stalk celery, thinly sliced

1 large onion, finely chopped

½ cup dry white wine

14 oz can plum tomatoes in juice

3-4 garlic cloves, finely chopped

4 cups turkey or chicken stock

¼ tsp dried thyme

1 bay leaf

2 zucchini, finely diced

12 oz cooked cubed turkey

salt and pepper

fresh basil leaves, to garnish

COOK'S TIP

A large turkey leg can be used to make this soup. Put in a pan, add water to cover generously, and add 1 each carrot, celery stalk, leek, and onion, coarsely chopped, and a little salt; poach for 3 hours. Reserve the meat, discard the skin, bone, and vegetables and remove the fat from the stock before making the soup.

1 Heat the oil in a large saucepan over a medium heat. Add the bell peppers, celery, and onion and cook for about 8 minutes until softened and just beginning to color.

2 Add the wine and bubble for 1 minute. Add the tomatoes and garlic.

3 Stir in the stock. Add the thyme and bay leaf, season with salt and pepper and bring to a boil. Reduce the heat, cover

and simmer for about 25 minutes until t vegetables are tender.

4 Add the zucchini and turkey. Contin cooking for another 10-15 minut until the zucchini are completely tender.

5 Taste the soup and adjust t seasoning. Ladle into warm bow garnish with basil leaves and serve.

Beef Goulash Soup

This aromatic dish originates from Hungary, where goulash soups are often served with dumplings. Noodles are a tasty and quick alternative.

NUTRITIONAL INFORMATION

Calories 320   Sugars 10g
Protein . . . . .27g   Fat 13g
Carbohydrate . . .27g   Saturates 5g

15 MINS   2.15 HOURS

SERVES 6

INGREDIENTS

tbsp oil

lb lean ground beef

onions, finely chopped

garlic cloves, finely chopped

tbsp all-purpose flour

cup water

oz can chopped tomatoes in juice

carrot, finely chopped

oz red bell pepper, roasted, peeled, seeded, and chopped

tsp Hungarian paprika

tsp caraway seeds

nch of dried oregano

cups beef stock

oz tagliatelle, broken into small pieces

lt and pepper

ur cream and cilantro to garnish

1 Heat the oil in a large wide saucepan over a medium-high heat. Add the beef and sprinkle with salt and pepper. Fry until lightly browned.

2 Reduce the heat and add the onions and garlic. Cook for about 3 minutes, stirring frequently, until the onions are soft. Stir in the flour and continue cooking for 1 minute.

3 Add the water and stir to combine well, scraping the bottom of the pan to mix in the flour. Stir in the tomatoes, carrot, pepper, paprika, caraway seeds, oregano, and stock.

4 Bring just to a boil. Reduce the heat, cover, and simmer gently for about 40 minutes, stirring occasionally, until all the vegetables are tender.

5 Add the noodles to the soup and simmer for a further 20 minutes, or until the noodles are cooked.

6 Taste the soup and adjust the seasoning, if necessary. Ladle into warm bowls and top each with a tablespoonful of sour cream. Garnish with cilantro.

Squid & Tomato Soup

This soup is full of interesting flavors. The chorizo gives it appealing spicy undertones that marry well with the meaty squid.

NUTRITIONAL INFORMATION

Calories 165	Sugar 5g	
Protein 18g	Fats 8g	
Carbohydrates 7g	Saturates 3g	

15 MINS   1 HOUR

SERVES 6

INGREDIENTS

1 lb cleaned squid

5 ½ oz lean chorizo, peeled and very finely diced

1 onion, finely chopped

1 stalk celery, thinly sliced

1 carrot, thinly sliced

2 garlic cloves, finely chopped or minced

14 oz can chopped tomatoes in juice

5 cups fish stock

½ tsp ground cumin

pinch of saffron

1 bay leaf

salt and pepper

chili paste (optional)

fresh parsley, chopped

1 Cut off the squid tentacles and cut into bite-sized pieces. Slice the bodies into rings.

2 Place a large saucepan over a medium-low heat and add the chorizo. Cook for 5–10 minutes, stirring frequently, until it renders most of its fat. Remove with a draining spoon and drain on paper towels.

3 Pour off all the fat from the pan and add the onion, celery, carrot, and garlic. Cover and cook for 3–4 minutes until the onion is slightly soft.

4 Stir in the tomatoes, fish stock, cumin, saffron, bay leaf, and chorizo.

5 Add the squid to the soup. Bring almost to a boil, reduce the heat, cover, and cook gently for 40–45 minutes, or until the squid and carrot are tender, stirring occasionally.

6 Taste the soup and stir in a little chili paste for a spicier flavor, if wished. Season with salt and pepper. Ladle into warm bowls, sprinkle with parsley and serve.

COOK'S TIP

Chorizo varies in the amount of fat and the degree of spiciness. A lean style is best for this soup.

Bean Soup

Pinto beans feature in Mexican cooking, and here they are used to give an exotic variation to other beans. They require soaking overnight.

NUTRITIONAL INFORMATION

Calories	188	Sugars	.........9g
Protein	........13g	Fat	...........1g
Carbohydrate	...33g	Saturates	.....0.3g

20 MINS   3 HOURS

SERVES 4

INGREDIENTS

oz pinto beans

¼ pints water

–8 oz carrots, finely chopped

large onion, finely chopped

–3 garlic cloves, minced

–1 chili, seeded and finely chopped

¾ pints vegetable stock

tomatoes, peeled and finely chopped

celery storks, very thinly sliced

alt and pepper

tbsp chopped cilantro (optional)

CROUTONS

slices white bread, crusts removed

il, for deep-frying

–2 garlic cloves, minced

1 Soak the beans overnight in cold water; drain and place in a pan with the water. Bring to a boil and boil vigorously for 10 minutes. Lower the heat, cover and simmer for 2 hours, or until the beans are tender.

2 Add the carrots, onion, garlic, chili, and stock and bring back to a boil. Cover and simmer for a further 30 minutes, until very tender.

3 Remove half the beans and vegetables with the cooking juices and press through a strainer or process in a food processor or blender until smooth.

4 Return the bean purée to the saucepan and add the tomatoes and celery. Simmer for 10–15 minutes, or until the celery is just tender, adding a little more stock or water if necessary.

5 Meanwhile, make the croûtons. Dice the bread. Heat the oil with the garlic in a small skillet and fry the croûtons until golden brown. Drain on paper towels.

6 Season the soup and stir in the chopped cilantro, if using. Transfer to a warm tureen and serve immediately with the croûtons.

VARIATION

nto beans are widely vailable, but if you cannot nd them or you wish to vary e recipe, you can use cannellini eans or black-eyed peas as an ternative.

White Bean Soup

In this elegant soup, the pungent green olive paste provides a pleasant counterpoint to the natural sweetness of the beans.

NUTRITIONAL INFORMATION

Calories ....257 Sugars 5g
Protein ....11g Fat 13g
Carbohydrate ...27g Saturates 2g

20 MINS   2 HOURS

SERVES 8

INGREDIENTS

12 oz dried green string beans

1 tbsp olive oil

1 large onion, finely chopped

1 large leek (white part only), thinly sliced

3 garlic cloves, finely chopped

2 stalk celery, finely chopped

2 small carrots, finely chopped

1 small fennel bulb, finely chopped

2 quarts water

¼ tsp dried thyme

¼ tsp dried marjoram

salt and pepper

TAPENADE:

1 garlic clove

1 small bunch fresh flat-leaf parsley, stems removed

8½ oz almond-stuffed green olives, drained

5 tbsp olive oil

1 Pick over the beans, cover generously with cold water and leave to soak for 6 hours or overnight. Drain the beans, put in a saucepan and add cold water to cover by 2 inches. Bring to a boil and boil for 10 minutes. Drain and rinse well.

2 Heat the oil in a large heavy-bottomed saucepan over a medium heat. Add the onion and leek, cover and cook for 3–4 minutes, stirring occasionally, until just softened. Add the garlic, celery, carrots, and fennel, and continue cooking for 2 minutes.

3 Add the water, drained beans, and the herbs. When the mixture begins to bubble, reduce the heat to low. Cover and simmer gently, stirring occasionally, for about 1½ hours until the beans are very tender.

4 Meanwhile make the tapenade. Put the garlic, parsley, and drained olives in a blender or food processor with the olive oil. Blend to a purée and scrape into a small serving bowl.

5 Allow the soup to cool slightly, then transfer to a blender or food processor and purée until smooth, working in batches if necessary. (If using a food processor, strain off the cooking liquid and reserve. Purée the soup solids with enough cooking liquid to moisten them, then combine with the remaining liquid.)

6 Return the puréed soup to the saucepan and thin with a little water, if necessary. Season with salt and pepper to taste, and simmer until heated through. Ladle into warm bowls and serve, stirring a generous teaspoon of the tapenade into each serving.

Mixed Bean Soup

This is a really hearty soup, filled with color, flavor, and goodness, which may be adapted to any vegetables that you have at hand.

NUTRITIONAL INFORMATION

Calories	190	Sugars	........9g
Protein	........10g	Fat	..........4g
Carbohydrate	...30g	Saturates	.....0.5g

  10 MINS 40 MINS

SERVES 4

INGREDIENTS

tbsp vegetable oil

red onion, halved and sliced

cup potato, diced

carrot, diced

leek, sliced

green chili, sliced

garlic cloves, minced

tsp ground coriander

tsp chili powder

cups vegetable stock

lb mixed canned beans,

  such as red kidney, borlotti, black eye

  or small navy, drained

alt and pepper

tbsp chopped cilantro,

  to garnish

1 Heat the vegetable oil in a large saucepan. Add the onion, potato, carrot, and leek and sauté, stirring constantly, for about 2 minutes, until the vegetables are slightly softened.

2 Add the sliced chili and minced garlic and cook for a further 1 minute.

3 Stir in the ground coriander, chili powder, and the vegetable stock.

4 Bring the soup to a boil, reduce the heat and cook for 20 minutes, or until the vegetables are tender.

5 Stir in the beans, season well with salt and pepper, and cook, stirring occasionally, for a further 10 minutes.

6 Transfer the soup to a warm tureen or individual bowls, garnish with chopped cilantro and serve.

COOK'S TIP

erve this soup with slices
 warm corn bread or a
eese loaf.

Tuscan Bean Soup

A thick and creamy soup that is based on a traditional Tuscan recipe. If you use dried beans, the preparation and cooking times will be longer.

NUTRITIONAL INFORMATION

Calories	250	Sugars	.........4g
Protein	........13g	Fat	..........10g
Carbohydrate	...29g	Saturates	.......2g

2 MINS   10 MINS

SERVES 4

I N G R E D I E N T S

8 oz dried lima beans, soaked overnight, or 2 x 14 oz can lima beans

1 tbsp olive oil

2 garlic cloves, minced

1 vegetable or chicken bouillon cube, crumbled

⅔ cup milk

2 tbsp chopped fresh oregano

salt and pepper

1 If you are using dried beans that have been soaked overnight, drain them thoroughly. Bring a large pan of water to a boil, add the beans and boil for 10 minutes. Cover the pan and simmer for a further 30 minutes or until tender. Drain the beans, reserving the cooking liquid. If you are using canned beans, drain them thoroughly and reserve the liquid.

2 Heat the oil in a large skillet and fry the garlic for 2–3 minutes or until just beginning to brown.

3 Add the beans and 1⅔ cup of the reserved liquid to the skillet, stirring. You may need to add a little water if there is insufficient liquid. Stir in the crumbled bouillon cube. Bring the mixture to a boil

and then remove the pan from the heat.

4 Place the bean mixture in a food processor and blend to form a smooth purée. Alternatively, mash the bean mixture to a smooth consistency. Season to taste with salt and pepper and stir in

the milk.

5 Pour the soup back into the pan and gently heat to just below boiling point. Stir in the chopped oregano just before serving.

Greek Bean Soup

This is based on a simple and variable bean soup typical in Greek home cooking.

NUTRITIONAL INFORMATION

Calories . . . . . . .186 Sugar 8g
Protein . . . . .10g Fats 3g
Carbohydrates . . .33g Saturates 0g

15 MINS   1 HOUR

SERVES 6

INGREDIENTS

| tbsp olive oil |
| large onion, finely chopped |
| large carrot, finely diced |
| stalks celery, finely chopped |
| tomatoes, skinned, seeded and chopped, or 9 oz drained canned tomatoes |
| garlic cloves, finely chopped |
| x 14 oz cans cannellini or small navy beans, drained and rinsed well |
| cups water |
| zucchini, finely diced |
| grated rind of ½ lemon |
| tbsp chopped fresh mint, or ¼ tsp dried mint |
| tsp chopped fresh thyme, or ⅛ tsp dried thyme |
| bay leaf |
| 4 oz can artichoke hearts |
| salt and pepper |

1 Heat 1 teaspoon of the olive oil in a large saucepan over a medium heat. Add the onion and cook for 3–4 minutes, stirring occasionally, until the onion softens. Add the carrot, celery, tomatoes, and garlic and continue cooking for a further 5 minutes, stirring frequently.

2 Add the beans and water. Bring to a boil, reduce the heat, cover, and cook gently for about 10 minutes.

3 Add the zucchini, lemon rind, mint, thyme, and bay leaf and season with salt and pepper. Cover and simmer about 40 minutes until all the vegetables are tender. Allow to cool slightly. Transfer 2 cups to a blender or food processor, purée until smooth and recombine.

4 Meanwhile, heat the remaining oil in a skillet over a medium heat, adding more if necessary to coat the bottom of the pan. Fry the artichokes, cut side down, until lightly browned. Turn over and fry long enough to heat through.

5 Ladle the soup into warm bowls and top each with an artichoke heart.

Vegetable & Bean Soup

This wonderful combination of cannellini beans, vegetables, and vermicel
is made even richer by the addition of pesto and dried mushrooms.

NUTRITIONAL INFORMATION

Calories 294   Sugars 2g
Protein . . . . .11g   Fat 16g
Carbohydrate . . .30g   Saturates 2g

30 MINS   30 MINS

SERVES 4

I N G R E D I E N T S

1 small eggplant

2 large tomatoes

1 potato, peeled

1 carrot, peeled

1 leek

15 oz can cannellini beans

3 ¾ cups hot vegetable or chicken stock

2 tsp dried basil

½ oz dried porcini mushrooms,
   soaked for 10 minutes in enough warm
   water to cover

¼ cup vermicelli

3 tbsp pesto (use store bought)

freshly grated Parmesan cheese, to serve
   (optional)

1 Slice the eggplant into rings about ½ inch thick, then cut each ring into 4.

2 Cut the tomatoes and potato into small dice. Cut the carrot into sticks, about 1 inch long and cut the leek into rings.

3 Place the cannellini beans and their liquid in a large saucepan. Add the

eggplant, tomatoes, potatoes, carrot, and leek, stirring to mix.

4 Add the stock to the pan and bring to a boil. Reduce the heat and leave to simmer for 15 minutes.

5 Add the basil, dried mushrooms and their soaking liquid, and the vermicelli and simmer for 5 minutes or until all of the vegetables are tender.

6 Remove the pan from the heat a▮ stir in the pesto.

7 Serve with freshly grated Parmes▮ cheese, if using.

Bean & Pasta Soup

A dish with proud Mediterranean origins, this soup is a winter warmer. Serve with warm, crusty bread and, if you like, a slice of cheese.

NUTRITIONAL INFORMATION

Calories	463	Sugars	.........5g
Protein	........13g	Fat	..........33g
Carbohydrate	...30g	Saturates	.......7g

5–10 MINS   1¼ HOURS

SERVES 4

INGREDIENTS

enerous 1 cup dried navy beans, soaked, drained, and rinsed

tbsp olive oil

large onions, sliced

garlic cloves, chopped

4 oz can chopped tomatoes

tsp dried oregano

tsp tomato paste

½ cups water

oz small pasta shapes, such as fusilli or conchigliette

½ oz sun-dried tomatoes, drained and sliced thinly

tbsp chopped cilantro, or flat-leaf parsley

tbsp freshly grated Parmesan

alt and pepper

1 Put the soaked beans into a large pan, cover with cold water and bring them a boil. Boil rapidly for 15 minutes to emove any harmful toxins. Drain the eans in a colander.

2 Heat the oil in a skillet over a medium heat and fry the onions until they are st beginning to change color. Stir in the arlic and cook for 1 further minute. Stir in the chopped tomatoes, oregano, and the tomato paste and pour on the water. Add the beans, bring to a boil and cover the pan. Simmer for 45 minutes or until the beans are almost tender.

3 Add the pasta, season the soup with salt and pepper to taste, and stir in the sun-dried tomatoes. Return the soup to a boil, partly cover the pan, and continue cooking for 10 minutes, or until the pasta is nearly tender.

4 Stir in the chopped cilantro or parsley. Taste the soup and adjust the seasoning if necessary. Transfer to a warmed soup tureen to serve. Sprinkle with the cheese and serve hot.

Garbanzo bean Soup

A thick vegetable soup which is a delicious meal in itself. Serve with Parmesan cheese and warm sun-dried tomato-flavored ciabatta bread.

NUTRITIONAL INFORMATION

Calories 297   Sugars 0g
Protein . . . . .11g   Fat 18g
Carbohydrate . . .24g   Saturates 2g

 5 MINS   15 MINS

SERVES 4

I N G R E D I E N T S

2 tbsp olive oil

2 leeks, sliced

2 zucchini, diced

2 garlic cloves, minced

2 x 14 oz cans chopped tomatoes

1 tbsp tomato paste

1 fresh bay leaf

3¾ cups chicken stock

14 oz can garbanzo beans,
  drained and rinsed

8 oz spinach

salt and pepper

T O S E R V E

Parmesan cheese

sun-dried tomato bread

1 Heat the oil in a large saucepan, add the leeks and zucchini and cook briskly for 5 minutes, stirring constantly.

2 Add the garlic, tomatoes, tomato paste, bay leaf, stock, and garbanzo beans. Bring to a boil and simmer for 5 minutes.

3 Shred the spinach finely, add to th soup and cook for 2 minutes. Season

4 Remove the bay leaf from the sou and discard.

5 Serve the soup with freshly grate Parmesan cheese and sun-drie tomato bread.

COOK'S TIP

Garbanzo beans are used extensively in North African cuisine and are also found in Italian, Spanish, Middle Eastern, and Indian cooking. They have a deliciously nutty flavor with a firm texture and are an excellent canned product.

Red Bean Soup

Beans feature widely in Italian soups, making them hearty and tasty. The beans need to be soaked overnight, so prepare well in advance.

NUTRITIONAL INFORMATION

Calories ....184 Sugars 5g
Protein ....4g Fat 11g
Carbohydrate ...19g Saturates 2g

5–10 MINS   3¾ HOURS

SERVES 6

I N G R E D I E N T S

scant 1 cup dried red kidney beans,
   soaked overnight

7½ cups water

1 large ham bone or bacon knuckle

2 carrots, chopped

1 large onion, chopped

2 celery stalks, sliced thinly

1 leek, trimmed, washed, and sliced

1–2 bay leaves

2 tbsp olive oil

2–3 tomatoes, peeled and chopped

1 garlic clove, minced

1 tbsp tomato paste

1½ tbsp arborio rice

4–6 oz green cabbage, shredded finely

salt and pepper

1 Drain the beans and place them in a saucepan with enough water to cover. Bring to a boil, then boil for 15 minutes to remove any harmful toxins. Reduce the heat and simmer for 45 minutes.

2 Drain the beans and put into a clean saucepan with the water, ham bone or knuckle, carrots, onion, celery, leek, bay leaves, and olive oil. Bring to a boil, then cover and simmer for 1 hour or until the beans are very tender.

3 Discard the bay leaves and bone, reserving any ham pieces from the bone. Remove a small cupful of the beans and reserve. Purée or liquidize the soup in a food processor or blender, or push through a coarse strainer, and return to a clean pan.

4 Add the tomatoes, garlic, tomato paste, rice, and season. Bring back to a boil and simmer for about 15 minutes or until the rice is tender.

5 Add the cabbage and reserved beans and ham, and continue to simmer for 5 minutes. Adjust the seasoning and serve very hot. If liked, a piece of toasted crusty bread may be put in the base of each soup bowl before ladling in the soup. If the soup is too thick, add a little boiling water or stock.

Brown Lentil & Pasta Soup

In Italy, this soup is called *Minestrade Lentiche*. A *minestra* is a soup cooked with pasta; here, farfalline, a small bow-shaped variety, is used.

NUTRITIONAL INFORMATION

Calories 225   Sugars 1g
Protein . . . . .13g   Fat 8g
Carbohydrate . . .27g   Saturates 3g

 5 MINS   25 MINS

SERVES 4

INGREDIENTS

4 rashers sliced bacon, cut into small squares

1 onion, chopped

2 garlic cloves, minced

2 stalks celery, chopped

¼ cup farfalline or spaghetti, broken into small pieces

1 x 14 oz can brown lentils, drained

5 cups hot ham or vegetable stock

2 tbsp chopped, fresh mint

1 Place the bacon in a large skillet together with the onions, garlic, and celery. Dry fry for 4–5 minutes, stirring, until the onion is tender and the bacon is just beginning to brown.

2 Add the pasta to the skillet and cook, stirring, for about 1 minute to coat the pasta in the oil.

3 Add the lentils and the stock and bring to a boil. Reduce the heat and leave to simmer for 12–15 minutes or until the pasta is tender.

4 Remove the skillet from the heat and stir in the chopped fresh mint.

5 Transfer the soup to warm soup bowls and serve immeditely.

COOK'S TIP

If you prefer to use dried lentils, add the stock before the pasta and cook for 1–1¼ hours until the lentils are tender. Add the pasta and cook for a further 12–15 minutes.

Ravioli alla Parmigiana

This soup is traditionally served at Easter and Christmas in the province of Parma.

NUTRITIONAL INFORMATION

Calories .... .554 Sugars 3g
Protein ....26g Fat .... .24g
Carbohydrate ...64g Saturates 9g

4½–5 HOURS 25 MINS

SERVES 4

I N G R E D I E N T S

oz Basic Pasta Dough

cups veal stock

eshly grated Parmesan cheese, to serve

F I L L I N G

cup brown sauce

cup freshly grated Parmesan cheese

⅔ cup fine white bread crumbs

eggs

small onion, finely chopped

tsp freshly grated nutmeg

1 Make the Basic Pasta Dough and the brown sauce.

2 Carefully roll out 2 sheets of the pasta dough and cover with a damp dish cloth while you make the filling for the ravioli.

3 To make the filling, place the freshly grated Parmesan cheese, fine white bread crumbs, eggs, brown sauce, finely chopped onion, and the freshly grated nutmeg in a large mixing bowl, and mix together well.

4 Place spoonfuls of the filling at regular intervals on 1 sheet of pasta dough. Cover with the second sheet of pasta dough, then cut into squares and seal the edges.

5 Bring the veal stock to a boil in a large saucepan.

6 Add the ravioli to the pan and cook for about 15 minutes.

7 Transfer the soup and ravioli to warm serving bowls and serve, generously sprinkled with Parmesan cheese.

OOK'S TIP

is advisable to prepare
e Basic Pasta Dough and
e brown sauce well in advance,
buy ready-made
uivalents if you are short of time.

Minestrone

Minestrone translates as 'big soup' in Italian. It is made all over Italy, but this version comes from Livorno, a port on the western coast.

NUTRITIONAL INFORMATION

Calories	311	Sugars	.........8g
Protein	........12g	Fat	..........19g
Carbohydrate	...26g	Saturates	.......5g

 10 MINS   30 MINS

SERVES 4

INGREDIENTS

1 tbsp olive oil

3 ½ oz pancetta ham, diced

2 medium onions, chopped

2 cloves garlic, minced

1 potato, peeled and cut into ½ inch cubes

1 carrot, peeled and cut into chunks

1 leek, sliced into rings

¼ green cabbage, shredded

1 celery stalk, chopped

1 lb can chopped tomatoes

7 oz can small navy beans,
   drained and rinsed

2 ½ cups hot ham or chicken stock,
   diluted with 2 ½ cups boiling water

bouquet garni

salt and pepper

freshly grated Parmesan cheese, to serve

1 Heat the olive oil in a large saucepan. Add the diced pancetta, chopped onions, and garlic and fry for about 5 minutes, stirring, or until the onions are soft and golden.

2 Add the prepared potato, carrot, leek, cabbage, and celery to the saucepan. Cook for a further 2 minutes, stirring frequently, to coat all of the vegetables in the oil.

3 Add the tomatoes, small navy bean, hot ham or chicken stock, a bouquet garni to the pan, stirring to m Leave the soup to simmer, covered, f 15–20 minutes or until all of t vegetables are just tender.

4 Remove the bouquet garni, seas with salt and pepper to taste, a serve with plenty of freshly grat Parmesan cheese.

Minestrone with Pesto

This version of minestrone contains cannellini beans–these need to be soaked overnight, so prepare in advance.

NUTRITIONAL INFORMATION

Calories	604	Sugars	.........3g
Protein	........26g	Fat	..........45g
Carbohydrate	...24g	Saturates	......11g

10-15 MINS   1¾ HOURS

SERVES 6

INGREDIENTS

scant 1 cup dried cannellini beans, soaked overnight

2 quarts water or stock

1 large onion, chopped

1 leek, trimmed and sliced thinly

2 celery stalks, sliced very thinly

2 carrots, chopped

2 tbsp olive oil

4 tomatoes, peeled and chopped roughly

2 zucchini, trimmed and sliced thinly

2 potatoes, diced

2 oz elbow macaroni

(or other small macaroni)

salt and pepper

4–6 tbsp freshly grated Parmesan, to serve

PESTO

1 tbsp pine nuts

2 tbsp olive oil

2 bunches basil, stems removed

4–6 garlic cloves, minced

½ cup Pecorino or Parmesan, grated

1 Drain the beans, rinse and put in a pan with the water or stock. Bring to a boil, cover and simmer for 1 hour.

2 Add the onion, leek, celery, carrots, and oil. Cover and simmer for 4–5 minutes.

3 Add the tomatoes, zucchini, potatoes, macaroni, and seasoning. Cover again and continue to simmer for about 30 minutes or until very tender.

4 Meanwhile, make the pesto. Fry the pine nuts in 1 tablespoon of the oil until pale brown, then drain. Put the basil into a food processor or blender with the nuts and garlic. Process until well chopped. Alternatively, chop finely by hand and pound with a mortar and pestle. Gradually add the remaining oil until smooth. Turn into a bowl, add the cheese and seasoning, and mix thoroughly.

5 Stir 1½ tablespoons of the pesto into the soup until well blended. Simmer for a further 5 minutes and adjust the seasoning. Serve very hot, sprinkled with the cheese.

Red Bell Pepper Soup

This soup has a real Mediterranean flavor, using sweet red bell peppers, tomato, chili, and basil. It is great served with a warm olive bread.

NUTRITIONAL INFORMATION

Calories 55   Sugar 10g

Protein . . . . .2g   Fats 0.5g

Carbohydrates . . .11g   Saturates 0.1g

5 MINS   25 MINS

SERVES 4

I N G R E D I E N T S

8 oz red bell peppers, seeded and sliced

1 onion, sliced

2 garlic cloves, minced

1 green chili, chopped

1½ cups sieved tomatoes

2½ cups vegetable stock

2 tbsp basil, chopped

fresh basil sprigs, to garnish

1 Put the bell peppers in a large saucepan with the onion, garlic, and chili. Add the sieved tomatoes and vegetable stock and bring to a boil, stirring well.

2 Reduce the heat to a simmer and cook for 20 minutes or until the bell peppers have softened. Drain, reserving the liquid and vegetables separately.

3 Sieve the vegetables by pressir through a strainer with the back of spoon. Alternatively, blend in a foc processor until smooth.

4 Return the vegetable paste to a clea saucepan with the reserved cookir liquid. Add the basil and heat throug until hot. Garnish the soup with fresh ba sprigs and serve.

VARIATION

This soup is also delicious served cold with ¼ cup of unsweetened yogurt swirled into it.

Tomato & Bell Pepper Soup

Sweet red bell peppers and tangy tomatoes are blended together in a smooth vegetable soup that makes a perfect starter or light lunch.

NUTRITIONAL INFORMATION

Calories ....52 Sugars 9g
Protein ....3g Fat 0.4g
Carbohydrate ...10g Saturates 0g

1¼ HOURS   35 MINS

SERVES 4

INGREDIENTS

large red bell peppers

large onion, chopped

celery stalks, trimmed and chopped

garlic clove, minced

½ cups Fresh Vegetable Stock
(see page 14)

bay leaves

x 14 oz cans plum tomatoes

salt and pepper

scallions, finely shredded, to garnish

crusty bread, to serve

1 Preheat the broiler to hot. Halve and seed the bell peppers, arrange them on the broiler rack and cook, turning occasionally, for 8–10 minutes until soft and charred.

2 Leave to cool slightly, then carefully peel off the charred skin. Reserving a small piece for garnish, chop the bell pepper flesh and place in a large saucepan.

3 Mix in the onion, celery, and garlic. Add the stock and the bay leaves. Bring to a boil, cover and simmer for 15 minutes. Remove from the heat.

4 Stir in the tomatoes and transfer to a blender. Process for a few seconds until smooth. Return to the saucepan.

5 Season to taste and heat for 3–4 minutes until very hot. Ladle into warm bowls and garnish with the reserved bell pepper cut into strips and the scallion. Serve with crusty bread.

COOK'S TIP

If you prefer a coarser, more robust soup, lightly mash the tomatoes with a wooden spoon and omit the blending process in step 4.

Spiced Fruit Soup

This delicately flavored apple and apricot soup is gently spiced with ginger and allspice, and finished with a swirl of sour cream.

NUTRITIONAL INFORMATION

Calories	147	Sugar	........28g
Protein	.........3g	Fats	.........0.4g
Carbohydrates	...29g	Saturates	......0g

 7³/₄ HOURS 25 MINS

SERVES 4–6

INGREDIENTS

⅔ cup dried apricots, soaked overnight or no-need-to-soak dried apricots

1 lb dessert apples, peeled, cored, and chopped

1 small onion, chopped

1 tbsp lemon or lime juice

3 cups fresh chicken stock (see page 14)

⅔ cup dry white wine

¼ tsp ground ginger

good pinch of ground allspice

salt and pepper

TO GARNISH

4–6 tbsp sour cream or unsweetened fromage blanc

little ground ginger or ground allspice

1 Drain the apricot, if necessary and chop.

2 Put in a saucepan and add the apples, onion, lemon or lime juice, and stock. Bring to a boil, cover, and simmer gently for about 20 minutes.

3 Leave the soup to cool a little, then press through a strainer or blend in a food processor or blender until smooth.

Pour the fruit soup into a clean pan.

4 Add the wine and spices and season to taste. Bring back to a boil, then leave to cool. If too thick, add a little more stock or water and then chill thoroughly.

5 Put a spoonful of sour cream or fromage blanc on top of each portion and lightly dust with ginger or allspice.

VARIATION

Other fruits can be combined with apples to make fruit soups–try raspberries, blackberries, blackcurrants, or cherries. If the fruits have a lot of seeds or pits, the soup should be strained after puréeing.

Spinach & Mascarpone

Spinach is the basis for this delicious soup, but use sorrel or watercress instead for a pleasant change.

NUTRITIONAL INFORMATION

Calories	537	Sugars	.........2g
Protein	.........6g	Fat	.........53g
Carbohydrate	....9g	Saturates	.....29g

5 MINS   35 MINS

SERVES 4

I N G R E D I E N T S

¼ cup butter

1 bunch scallions, trimmed and chopped

2 celery stalks, chopped

3 cups spinach or sorrel, or 3 bunches
   watercress

3½ cups vegetable stock

1 cup Mascarpone cheese

1 tbsp olive oil

2 slices thick-cut bread, cut into cubes

½ tsp caraway seeds

salt and pepper

sesame bread sticks, to serve

1 Melt half the butter in a very large saucepan. Add the scallions and celery and cook gently for about 5 minutes, or until soft.

2 Pack the spinach, sorrel, or watercress into the saucepan. Add the vegetable stock and bring to a boil; then reduce the heat and simmer, covered, for 15–20 minutes.

3 Transfer the soup to a blender or food processor and blend until smooth, or pass through a straner Return to the saucepan.

4 Add the Mascarpone cheese to the soup and heat gently, stirring, until smooth and blended. Taste and season with salt and pepper.

5 Heat the remaining butter with the oil in a skillet. Add the bread cubes and fry in the hot oil until golden brown, adding the caraway seeds towards the end of cooking, so that they do not burn.

6 Ladle the soup into 4 warmed bowls. Sprinkle with the croûtons and serve at once, accompanied by the sesame bread sticks.

VARIATIONS

Any leafy vegetable can be used to make this soup to give variations to the flavor. For anyone who grows their own vegetables, it is the perfect recipe for experimenting with a glut of produce. Try young beet leaves or surplus lettuces for a change.

International
Soups

Today people travel the world as a matter of course, and as
we have access to more culinary influences our tastes have
become more demanding. This chapter caters for that desire for

unusual recipes by featuring an international
range of modern-day soups, incorporating
unusual ingredients such as sweet potato
and arugula combined with curry and chili
flavorings. Recipes have been drawn from

Senegal, Eastern Europe, the Americas and the Caribbean; there
is something for the most discerning of palates to enjoy.

Squash & Sweet Potato Soup

When there's a chill in the air, this vivid soup is just the thing to serve –it's very warm and comforting.

NUTRITIONAL INFORMATION

Calories 128	Sugars 7g	
Protein 3g	Fat 4g	
Carbohydrate ...21g	Saturates 2g	

 15 MINS   1 HOUR 25 MINS

SERVES 6

INGREDIENTS

1 sweet potato, about 12 oz

1 acorn squash

4 shallots

olive oil

5–6 garlic cloves, unpeeled

3¾ cups chicken stock

½ cup light cream

salt and pepper

snipped chives, to garnish

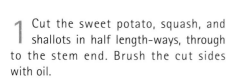

1 Cut the sweet potato, squash, and shallots in half length-ways, through to the stem end. Brush the cut sides with oil.

2 Put the vegetables, cut sides down, in a shallow roasting pan. Add the garlic cloves. Roast in a preheated oven at 375ºF for about 40 minutes until tender and light brown.

3 When cool, scoop the flesh from the potato and squash halves and put in a saucepan with the shallots. Remove the garlic peel and add the soft insides to the other vegetables.

4 Add the stock and a pinch of salt. Bring just to a boil, reduce the heat and simmer, partially covered, for about 30 minutes, stirring occasionally, until the vegetables are very tender.

5 Allow the soup to cool slightly, then transfer to a blender or food processor and purée until smooth, working in batches, if necessary. (If using a food processor, strain off the cooking liquid ar reserve. Purée the soup solids with enoug cooking liquid to moisten them, the combine with the remaining liquid.)

6 Return the soup to the saucepan ar stir in the cream. Season to tast then simmer for 5–10 minutes unt completely heated through. Ladle in warm bowls to serve.

Corn Soup with Chilies

This soup is rich and exotic but relatively simple to make. Ancho chilies have a distinct smoky flavour.

NUTRITIONAL INFORMATION

Calories	848	Sugars	........14g
Protein	........10g	Fat	..........75g
Carbohydrate	...37g	Saturates	.....46g

25 MINS   35 MINS

SERVES 4

INGREDIENTS

dried ancho chili

tbsp butter

lb defrosted frozen corn kernels

large onion, finely chopped

large garlic clove, finely chopped

red bell pepper, cored, seeded, and finely chopped

/4 cups chicken stock or water

/2 cups whipping cream

tsp ground cumin

lt

opped fresh cilantro or parsley, to garnish

pepper and cook for about 7–10 minutes, stirring frequently, until the onion is soft and the mixture starts to stick.

3 Transfer the mixture to a blender or food processor, add the stock and purée until smooth.

4 Put the cream in a large saucepan, stir in the puréed vegetables and bring almost to a boil. Add the cumin. Season with a little salt. Adjust the heat so the soup bubbles very gently and cook until the mixture is reduced by about one-quarter.

5 Remove the ancho chili from its liquid and discard the core and the seeds. (Wash hands well after touching chilies.) Put the chili into a blender or food processor with 4–5 tablespoons of the soaking water and purée until smooth. Stir 2–4 tablespoons of the purée into the soup, according to taste, and continue cooking for a further 5 minutes.

6 Taste the soup and adjust the seasoning, if necessary. Ladle the soup into warm bowls, garnish with cilantro or parsley and serve.

1 Put the chili in a bowl and cover with boiling water. Stand about 15 minutes o soften.

2 Melt the butter in a skillet over a medium-low heat. Add the corn and rn to coat. Cook for about 15 minutes, irring frequently, until it starts to brown ightly. Add the onion, garlic, and bell

Melon Gazpacho

Glass bowls are pretty for serving this soup, which makes a very light starter for warm days.

NUTRITIONAL INFORMATION

Calories 86   Sugar 17g
Protein ....2g   Fats 1g
Carbohydrates ...18g   Saturates 0g

 10 MINS   10 MINS

SERVES 4

INGREDIENTS

1 tsp oil

1 onion, finely chopped

1 large garlic clove, finely chopped

1 tsp chopped fresh chili

1 lb 9 oz seedless cantaloupe melon flesh, cubed

½ tsp raspberry vinegar, or 1 tsp lemon juice

pinch of salt

½ ripe green melon, (about 1 lb)

snipped chives, to garnish

1 Heat the oil in a small pan over a low heat. Add the onion, garlic, and chili, cover and cook for 6–7 minutes, stirring occasionally, until the onion is soft but not browned.

2 Put the cantaloupe melon flesh in a blender or food processor, add the onion, garlic, and chili and purée until smooth, stopping to scrape down the sides as needed. (You may need to work in batches.) Add the vinegar or lemon juice with the salt and process to combine.

3 Chill for about 30 minutes, or until the mixture is cold.

4 Remove the seeds from the green melon, then cut into balls with a melon baller. Or alternatively, cut into cubes with a sharp knife.

5 Divide the soup among 4 shallow bowls and top with the green melon balls. Sprinkle lightly with chives to garnish and serve.

COOK'S TIP

If you are wary of using fresh chili, omit it and add a few drops of shop-bought hot pepper sauce to taste, at the end of Step 2, to liven up the soup.

Tomato & Orange Soup

This soup is made from raw vegetables and fruit, so it is full of goodness as well as good taste and is wonderfully refreshing on a warm day.

NUTRITIONAL INFORMATION

Calories	107	Sugar	23g
Protein	3g	Fats	1g
Carbohydrates	24g	Saturates	0g

20 MINS   0 MINS

SERVES 4

I N G R E D I E N T S

large seedless oranges

ripe tomatoes

stalks celery, strings removed, chopped

carrots, grated

/₂ cups tomato juice

alt

abasco sauce (optional)

tbsp chopped fresh mint

esh mint sprigs, to garnish

1 Working over a bowl to catch the juices, peel the oranges. Cut down etween the membranes and drop the range segments into the bowl.

2 Put the tomatoes in a small bowl and pour over boiling water to cover. llow to stand for 10 seconds, then drain. eel off the skin and cut the tomatoes half crossways. Scoop out the seeds to a strainer set over a bowl; reserve e tomato juices.

3 Put the tomatoes, celery, and carrots in a blender or food processor. Add e orange segments and their juice and e juice saved from the tomatoes. Purée ntil smooth.

4 Scrape into a bowl and stir in the tomato juice. Cover and chill until cold.

5 Taste the soup and add salt, if needed, and a few drops of Tabasco sauce to heighten the flavor, if wished. Stir in the chopped mint, ladle into cold bowls and garnish with fresh mint sprigs.

COOK'S TIP

This soup really needs to be made in a blender for the best texture. A food processor can be used but the soup will not be completely smooth.

Avocado & Almond Soup

This rich-tasting cold soup has an inviting color and would make an appetizing start to a dinner party.

NUTRITIONAL INFORMATION

Calories	368	Sugar	.........5g
Protein	.........8g	Fats	..........34g
Carbohydrates	....9g	Saturates	......5g

20 MINS   35 MINS

SERVES 4

I N G R E D I E N T S

2½ cups water

1 onion, finely chopped

1 x celery, finely chopped

1 carrot, grated

4 garlic cloves, chopped or minced

1 bay leaf

½ tsp salt

¾ cup ground almonds

2 ripe avocados (about 1 lb)

3–4 tbsp fresh lemon juice

salt

snipped chives, to garnish

1 Combine the water, onion, celery, carrot, garlic, and bay leaf in a saucepan with the salt. Bring to a boil, reduce the heat, cover and simmer for about 30 minutes, or until the vegetables are very tender.

2 Strain the soup base, reserving the liquid and vegetables separately.

3 Put the vegetables into a blender or food processor. Add the almonds and a small amount of the liquid and purée until very smooth, scraping down the sides as necessary. Add as much of the remaining liquid as the capacity of the blender or processor permits and process to combine. Scrape into a bowl, stir in any remaining liquid and chill until cold.

4 Cut the avocados in half, discard the pits and scoop the flesh into the blender or food processor. Add the cold soup base and purée until smooth, scraping down the sides as necessary. For a thinner consistency, add a few spoonfuls of cold water.

5 Add the lemon juice and season with salt to taste. Ladle into chilled soup bowls and sprinkle each serving lightly with chives.

Chilled Borscht

There are innumerable versions of this soup of Eastern European origin. This refreshing vegetarian version is light and flavorful.

NUTRITIONAL INFORMATION

Calories	91	Sugars	. . . . .12g
Protein	. . . . .4g	Fat	. . . . .3g
Carbohydrate	. . .15g	Saturates	. . . . . .0g

15 MINS   1½ HOURS

SERVES 4

INGREDIENTS

medium cabbage, cored and coarsely chopped

tbsp vegetable oil

onion, finely chopped

leek, halved lengthways and sliced

oz can peeled tomatoes in juice

cups water, plus extra if needed

carrot, thinly sliced

small parsnip, finely chopped

beet (raw or cooked), peeled and cubed

bay leaf

½ cups tomato juice

-3 tbsp chopped fresh dill

esh lemon juice (optional)

lt and pepper

ur cream or yogurt, to garnish

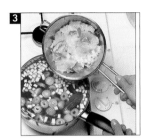

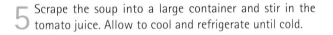

3 Add the tomatoes, water, carrot, parsnip, beet, and bay leaf. Stir in the blanched cabbage and add a large pinch of salt. Bring to a boil, reduce the heat and simmer for about 1¼ hours until all the vegetables are tender. Remove the bay leaf, if possible.

4 Allow the soup to cool slightly, then transfer to a blender or food processor and purée until smooth, working in batches if necessary. (If using a food processor, strain off the cooking liquid and reserve. Purée the soup solids with enough cooking liquid to moisten them, then combine with the remaining liquid.)

5 Scrape the soup into a large container and stir in the tomato juice. Allow to cool and refrigerate until cold.

6 Add the dill and stir. Thin the soup with more tomato juice or water, if wished. Season to taste with salt and pepper and, if you prefer it less sweet, add a few drops of lemon juice. Ladle into chilled soup bowls, top each with a spiral of sour cream or a dollop of yogurt.

1 Cover the cabbage generously with cold water in a pan. Bring to a boil, il for 3 minutes, then drain.

2 Heat the oil in a large saucepan over a medium-low heat. Add the onion and ek, cover and cook for about 5 minutes, irring occasionally, until the vegetables gin to soften.

Iced Salsa Soup

A chunky mix of colorful vegetables, highlighted with Mexican flavors, this cold soup makes a lively starter to any meal.

NUTRITIONAL INFORMATION

Calories	136	Sugar	........12g
Protein	.........4g	Fats	...........4g
Carbohydrates	...21g	Saturates	......1g

 15 MINS   🕐 20 MINS

SERVES 4

I N G R E D I E N T S

2 large corn-on-the-cobs, or 8 oz frozen corn kernels

1 tbsp olive oil

1 orange or red bell pepper, cored, seeded, and finely chopped

1 green bell pepper, cored, seeded, and finely chopped

1 onion, finely chopped

3 ripe tomatoes, skinned, seeded, and chopped

½ tsp chili powder, or to taste

½ cup water

2 cups tomato juice

chili paste (optional)

salt and pepper

TO GARNISH

3–4 scallions, finely chopped

fresh cilantro leaves

1 Cut the corn kernels from the cobs, or if using frozen corn, defrost and drain.

2 Heat the oil in a saucepan over a medium-high heat. Add the bell peppers and cook, stirring briskly, for 3 minutes. Add the onion and continue cooking for about 2 minutes, or until it starts to color slightly.

3 Add the tomatoes, corn and chili powder. Continue cooking, stirring frequently, for 1 minute. Pour in the water and when it bubbles, reduce the heat, cover and cook for a further 4–5 minutes, or until the bell peppers are just barely tender.

4 Transfer the mixture to a lar container and stir in the tomato jui Season with salt and pepper and add m chili powder if wished. Cover a refrigerate until cold.

5 Taste and adjust the seasoning. a more spicy soup, stir in a lit chili paste to taste. For a thinner soup, a a small amount of iced water. Ladle i chilled bowls and garnish with scalli and fresh cilantro leaves.

Sweet Potato & Apple Soup

This soup makes a marvelous late fall or winter starter.
It has a delicious texture and cheerful golden color.

NUTRITIONAL INFORMATION

Calories ....235 Sugar 20g
Protein ....3g Fats 10g
Carbohydrates ...36g Saturates 6g

  15 MINS   50 MINS

SERVES 4

INGREDIENTS

tbsp butter

leeks, thinly sliced

large carrot, thinly sliced

sweet potatoes, peeled and cubed

large tart eating apples, peeled and cubed

cups water

freshly grated nutmeg

cup apple juice

cup whipping or light cream

salt and pepper

snipped fresh chives or fresh cilantro
    leaves, to garnish

1 Melt the butter in a large saucepan over a medium-low heat. Add the leeks, cover and cook for 6–8 minutes, or until soft, stirring frequently.

2 Add the carrot, sweet potatoes, apples, and water. Season lightly with salt, pepper, and nutmeg. Bring to a boil, reduce the heat and simmer, covered, for about 20 minutes, stirring occasionally, until the vegetables are very tender.

3 Allow the soup to cool slightly, then transfer to a blender or food processor and purée until smooth, working in batches if necessary. (If using a food processor, strain off the cooking liquid and reserve. Purée the soup solids with enough cooking liquid to moisten them, then combine with the remaining liquid.)

4 Return the puréed soup to the saucepan and stir in the apple juice. Place over a low heat and simmer for about 10 minutes until heated through.

5 Stir in the cream and continue simmering for about 5 minutes, stirring frequently, until heated through. Taste and adjust the seasoning, adding more salt, pepper, and nutmeg, if necessary. Ladle the soup into warm bowls, garnish with chives or cilantro and serve.

Sweet Potato & Onion Soup

This simple recipe uses the sweet potato with its distinctive flavor and color, combined with a hint of orange and cilantro.

NUTRITIONAL INFORMATION

Calories ....320 Sugars 26g
Protein ....7g Fat 7g
Carbohydrate ...62g Saturates 1g

15 MINS   30 MINS

SERVES 4

INGREDIENTS

2 tbsp vegetable oil

2 lb sweet potatoes, diced

1 carrot, diced

2 onions, sliced

2 garlic cloves, minced

2½ cups vegetable stock

1¼ cups unsweetened orange juice

1 cup low-fat unsweetened yogurt

2 tbsp chopped fresh cilantro

salt and pepper

TO GARNISH

cilantro sprigs

orange rind

1 Heat the vegetable oil in a large saucepan and add the diced sweet potatoes and carrot, sliced onions, and garlic. Sauté the vegetables gently for 5 minutes, stirring constantly.

2 Pour in the vegetable stock and orange juice and bring them to a boil.

3 Reduce the heat to a simmer, cover the saucepan and cook the vegetables for 20 minutes or until the sweet potato and carrot cubes are tender.

4 Transfer the mixture to a food processor or blender in batches and process for 1 minute until puréed. Return the purée to the rinsed-out saucepan.

5 Stir in the unsweetened yogurt and chopped cilantro and season to taste.

6 Serve the soup in warm bowls and garnish with cilantro sprigs and orange rind.

VARIATION

This soup can be chilled before serving, if preferred. If chilling it, stir the yogurt into the dish just before serving. Serve in chilled bowls.

orn & Spinach Soup

resh corn retains a little crunch when cooked, adding a pleasing texture
o this soup.

NUTRITIONAL INFORMATION

Calories ....336 Sugars 11g
Protein ....9g Fat 18g
Carbohydrate ...36g Saturates 10g

🍲 15 MINS   🕐 40 MINS

SERVES 4

I N G R E D I E N T S

orn-on-the-cobs, cooked

sp butter

sp oil

arge onion, finely chopped

eek, thinly sliced

carrot, finely chopped

arge potato, diced

ups water

cup heavy cream

cup milk

shly grated nutmeg

z spinach leaves, finely chopped

t and pepper

---

1 Cut the kernels from the corn, without
cutting all the way down to the cob.
ng the back of a knife, scrape the cobs
extract the milky liquid; reserve.

OOK'S TIP

cut corn kernels off the
, lay on its side on a cutting
rd and slice lengthwise, rotating
il all kernels are removed. Then
nd on its stem and scrape down
extract the remaining pulp and juice.

---

2 Heat the butter and oil in a large saucepan over a
medium heat and add the onion and leek. Cover and
cook for 3–4 minutes, stirring frequently, until soft.

3 Add the carrot, potato, and water with a large pinch of
salt. Bring just to a boil and stir in the corn kernels and
the liquid scraped from the cobs. Reduce the heat to low,
cover and simmer for about 25 minutes, or until the carrot
and potato are tender.

4 Allow the soup to cool slightly, then transfer about
half of it to a blender or food processor and purée
until smooth.

5 Return the puréed soup to the saucepan, add the cream
and milk and stir to blend. Thin with a little more milk,
if preferred. Season with salt, pepper, and nutmeg. Simmer
over a low heat until reheated.

6 Add the spinach and cook for 4–5 minutes, stirring
frequently, just until the spinach is completely wilted.
Taste and adjust the seasoning, if necessary, then ladle the
soup into warm bowls. Serve at once.

Cheese & Vegetable Chowder

For this soup, the root vegetables should be cut into small dice so that they all cook in the same amount of time.

NUTRITIONAL INFORMATION

Calories........651	Sugar.........9g
Protein........25g	Fats..........48g
Carbohydrates...30g	Saturates.....30g

15 MINS   50 MINS

SERVES 4

INGREDIENTS

2 tbsp butter

1 large onion, finely chopped

1 large leek, split lengthways and thinly sliced

1–2 garlic cloves, minced

6 tbsp all-purpose flour

5 cups chicken or vegetable stock

3 carrots, finely diced

2 stalks celery, finely diced

1 turnip, finely diced

1 large potato, finely diced

3–4 sprigs fresh thyme, or ⅛ tsp dried thyme

1 bay leaf

1½ cups light cream

10½ oz hard Cheddar cheese, grated

2 tbsp chopped mixed fresh parsley, tarragon and chives

fresh chopped parsley, to garnish

salt and pepper

1 Melt the butter in a large heavy-bottomed saucepan over a medium-low heat. Add the onion, leek, and garlic. Cover and cook for about 5 minutes, stirring frequently, until the vegetables start to soften.

2 Stir the flour into the vegetables and continue cooking for 2 minutes. Add a little of the stock and stir well, scraping the bottom of the pan to mix in the flour. Bring to a boil, stirring frequently, and slowly stir in the rest of the stock.

3 Add the carrots, celery, turnip, potato, thyme, and bay leaf. Reduce the heat, cover and cook gently for about 35 minutes, stirring occasionally, until the vegetables are tender. Remove the bay leaf and the thyme branches.

4 Stir in the cream and simmer over a very low heat for 5 minutes. Add the cheese a handful at a time, stirring constantly for 1 minute after each addition, to make sure it is completely melted. Taste the soup and adjust the seasoning, adding salt if needed, and pepper to taste. Ladle immediately into warm bowls, sprinkle with fresh chopped parsley and serve.

Vegetable & Corn Chowder

This is a really filling soup, which should be served before a light main course. It is easy to prepare and filled with flavor.

NUTRITIONAL INFORMATION

Calories . . . . . . .378 Sugars 20g
Protein . . . . .16g Fat 13g
Carbohydrate . . .52g Saturates 6g

15 MINS   30 MINS

SERVES 4

I N G R E D I E N T S

tbsp vegetable oil

red onion, diced

red bell pepper, seeded and diced

garlic cloves, minced

large potato, diced

tbsp all-purpose flour

½ cups milk

¼ cups vegetable stock

¼ oz broccoli florets

cups canned corn, drained

cup Cheddar cheese, grated

lt and pepper

tbsp chopped cilantro,
to garnish

COOK'S TIP

getarian cheeses are made
th rennets of
n-animal origin, using
crobial or fungal enzymes.

1 Heat the oil in a large saucepan. Add the onion, bell pepper, garlic, and potato and sauté over a low heat, stirring frequently, for 2–3 minutes.

2 Stir in the flour and cook, stirring for 30 seconds. Gradually stir in the milk and stock.

3 Add the broccoli and corn. Bring the mixture to a boil, stirring constantly, then reduce the heat and simmer for about 20 minutes, or until all the vegetables are tender.

4 Stir in ½ cup of the cheese until it melts.

5 Season and spoon the chowder into a warm soup tureen. Garnish with the remaining cheese and the cilantro and serve.

Lettuce & Arugula Soup

Cooked lettuce tastes similar to sorrel, but lettuce is much easier to find and cheaper.

NUTRITIONAL INFORMATION

Calories 236   Sugars 7g
Protein ....3g   Fat 17g
Carbohydrate ...19g   Saturates 10g

15 MINS   55 MINS

SERVES 4

INGREDIENTS

1 tbsp butter

1 large sweet onion, halved and sliced

2 leeks, sliced

6¼ cups chicken stock

3 oz tbsp white rice

2 carrots, thinly sliced

3 garlic cloves

1 bay leaf

2 heads soft round lettuce (about
    1 lb), cored and chopped

¾ cup heavy cream

freshly grated nutmeg

3 oz arugula leaves, finely chopped

salt and pepper

1 Heat the butter in a large saucepan over a medium heat and add the onion and leeks. Cover and cook for 3-4 minutes, stirring frequently, until the vegetables begin to soften.

2 Add the stock, rice, carrots, garlic, and bay leaf with a large pinch of salt. Bring just to a boil. Reduce the heat, cover and simmer for 25-30 minutes, or until the rice and vegetables are tender. Remove the bay leaf.

3 Add the lettuce and cook for 10 minutes, until the leaves are soft, stirring occasionally.

4 Allow the soup to cool slightly, then transfer to a blender or food processor and purée until smooth, working in batches if necessary. (If using a food processor, strain off the cooking liquid and reserve. Purée the soup solids with enough cooking liquid to moisten them, then combine with the remaining liquid.)

5 Return the soup to the saucepan and place over a medium-low heat. Stir in the cream and a grating of nutmeg. Simmer for about 5 minutes, stirring occasionally, until the soup is reheated. Add more water or cream if you prefer a thinner soup.

6 Add the arugula and simmer for 2-3 minutes, stirring occasionally, until it is wilted. Adjust the seasoning and ladle the soup into warm bowls.

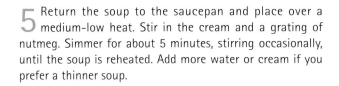

Curried Tuna Chowder

This tasty soup uses canned tuna and tomatoes, two store-cupboard favorites that you are likely to have on hand.

NUTRITIONAL INFORMATION

Calories ....265 Sugar 8g
Protein ....17g Fats 11g
Carbohydrates ...26g Saturates 7g

10 MINS   35 MINS

SERVES 4

INGREDIENTS

oz can light meat tuna packed in water

½ tbsp butter

onion, finely chopped

garlic clove, finely chopped

tbsp all purpose flour

tsp mild curry powder

4 oz can plum tomatoes in juice

tbsp white rice

zucchini, finely diced

cup single cream

alt and pepper

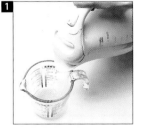

1 Drain the tuna over a measuring cup and add boiling water to make up to 2 cups.

2 Melt the butter in a large saucepan over a medium-low heat. Add the onion and garlic and cook for about 5 minutes until the onion is soft, stirring frequently.

3 Stir in the flour and curry powder. Continue cooking for 2 minutes.

4 Slowly add about half of the tuna juice and water mixture and stir well, scraping the bottom of the pan to mix in the flour. Pour in the remaining mixture and bring just to a boil, stirring frequently. Add the tomatoes and break up with a spoon. When the soup almost comes back to the boil, stir in the rice, reduce the heat, cover and simmer for 10 minutes.

5 Add the tuna and zucchini and continue cooking for about 15 minutes, or until the vegetables and rice are tender.

6 Stir in the cream, season with salt and pepper to taste and continue simmering for 3–4 minutes until heated through. Ladle into warm bowls and serve.

Caribbean Seafood Soup

This soup is traditionally made with the roots and leaves of local tuberous vegetables, but potato and spinach are a good alternative.

NUTRITIONAL INFORMATION

Calories	134	Sugars	........4g
Protein	........15g	Fat	..........4g
Carbohydrate	....11g	Saturates	......2g

🍲 15 MINS   🕐 50 MINS

SERVES 4

INGREDIENTS

5½ oz peeled medium shrimp

7 oz skinless firm white fish fillets, cubed

¾ tsp ground coriander

¼ tsp ground cumin

1 tsp chili paste, or to taste

3 tbsp fresh lemon juice, or to taste

1 tbsp butter

1 onion, halved and thinly sliced

2 large leeks, thinly sliced

3 garlic cloves, finely chopped

1 large potato, diced

5 cups chicken or vegetable stock

9 oz spinach leaves

½ cup coconut milk

salt and pepper

1 Put the shrimp and fish in a bowl with the coriander, cumin, chilli paste, and lemon juice and leave to marinate.

2 Melt the butter in a large saucepan over a medium heat. Add the onion and leeks, cover and cook for about 10 minutes, stirring occasionally, until they are soft. Add the garlic and cook for a further 3–4 minutes.

3 Add the potato and stock, together with a large pinch of salt, if using unsalted stock. Bring to a boil, reduce the heat, cover and cook gently for 15–20 minutes until the potato is tender. Stir in the spinach and continue cooking, uncovered, for about 3 minutes until it is just wilted.

4 Allow the soup to cool slightly, then transfer to a blender or food processor, working in batches if necessar Purée the soup until smooth. (If using food processor, strain off the cookin liquid and reserve. Purée the soup soli with enough cooking liquid to moiste them, then combine with the remainir liquid.)

5 Return the soup to the saucepan ar stir in the coconut milk. Add the fi and shrimp with their marinade. Simm over a medium-low heat for about minutes, stirring frequently, until the sou is heated through and the fish is cooke and flakes easily.

6 Taste and adjust the seasonin adding more chili paste and/or lemo juice if wished. Ladle into warm bowls ar serve.

COOK'S TIP

Add a handful of fresh cilantro leaves to the spinach.

Seafood Chowder

The proportions of fish and shrimp are flexible—use more or less as you wish.

NUTRITIONAL INFORMATION

Calories 310   Sugars 5g
Protein . . . . .29g   Fat 14g
Carbohydrate . . .17g   Saturates 8g

15 MINS   35 MINS

SERVES 4

INGREDIENTS

lb mussels

tbsp all-purpose flour

/4 cups fish stock

tbsp butter

large onion, finely chopped

2 oz skinless white fish fillets, such as cod, sole, or haddock

oz cooked or raw peeled shrimp

/4 cups whipping cream or heavy cream

lt and pepper

ipped fresh dill, to garnish

Discard any broken mussels and those with open shells that do not close hen tapped. Rinse, pull off any 'beards', d scrape off any barnacles with a knife nder cold running water. Put the mussels a large heavy-bottomed saucepan. over tightly and cook over a high heat r about 4 minutes, or until the mussels en, shaking the pan occasionally. When ey are cool enough to handle, remove e mussels from the shells, adding any dditional juices to the cooking liquid. train the cooking liquid through a eesecloth-lined strainer and reserve.

2 Put the flour in a mixing bowl and very slowly whisk in enough of the stock to make a thick paste. Whisk in a little more stock to make a smooth liquid.

3 Melt the butter in heavy-bottomed saucepan over a medium-low heat. Add the onion, cover, and cook for about 5 minutes, stirring frequently, until it softens.

4 Add the remaining fish stock and bring to a boil. Slowly whisk in the flour mixture until well combined and bring back to a boil, whisking constantly.

Add the mussel cooking liquid. Season with salt, if needed, and pepper. Reduce the heat and simmer, partially covered, for 15 minutes.

5 Add the fish and mussels and continue simmering, stirring occasionally, for about 5 minutes, or until the fish is cooked and begins to flake.

6 Stir in the shrimp and cream. Taste and adjust the seasoning. Simmer for a few minutes longer to heat through. Ladle into warm bowls, sprinkle with dill and serve.

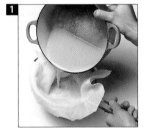

Shellfish & Tomato Soup

This soup is swimming with seafood. Depending on availability, you could substitute skinless, boneless white fish for the scallops or shrimp

NUTRITIONAL INFORMATION

Calories 316	Sugars 3g	
Protein 26g	Fat 14g	
Carbohydrate . . .21g	Saturates 8g	

 15 MINS   🕐 35 MINS

SERVES 4

I N G R E D I E N T S

2 lb mussels

2 tbsp butter

2 shallots, finely chopped

4 tbsp all-purpose flour

4 tbsp dry white wine

2½ cups fish stock

7 oz bay scallops

7 oz cooked shrimp

½ cup heavy cream

4 tomatoes, skinned, seeded and chopped

2 tbsp snipped fresh chives

2 tbsp chopped fresh parsley

salt and pepper

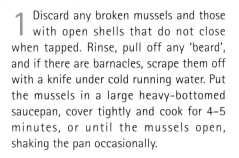

1 Discard any broken mussels and those with open shells that do not close when tapped. Rinse, pull off any 'beard', and if there are barnacles, scrape them off with a knife under cold running water. Put the mussels in a large heavy-bottomed saucepan, cover tightly and cook for 4–5 minutes, or until the mussels open, shaking the pan occasionally.

2 When they are cool enough to handle, remove the mussels from the shells, adding additional juices to the cooking liquid. Strain the liquid through a cheesecloth-lined strainer. Top it up with water to make 2 cups.

3 Melt the butter in a large saucepan over a medium-low heat. Add the shallots and cook for 3–4 minutes, stirring frequently, until soft. Stir in the flour and continue cooking for 2 minutes. Add the wine.

4 Slowly add the fish stock and stir well, scraping the bottom of the pan to mix in the flour. Pour in the remaining muss cooking liquid and water and bring just a boil, stirring frequently. Reduce the he cover and simmer for 10 minutes.

5 Add the scallops, shrimp, and musse and continue cooking for 1 minute.

6 Stir in the cream, tomatoes, chive lemon juice, and parsley. Seasc to taste with salt. Sprinkle with parsl and serve.

Fennel & Tomato Soup

This light and refreshing soup is also good served cold.

NUTRITIONAL INFORMATION

Calories 117   Sugars 9g
Protein . . . . .10g   Fat 2g
Carbohydrate . . .15g   Saturates 0g

10 MINS   45 MINS

SERVES 4

INGREDIENTS

tsp olive oil

large onion, halved and sliced

large fennel bulbs, halved and sliced

small potato, diced

/₄ cups water

/₃ cups tomato juice

bay leaf

/₂ oz cooked peeled small shrimp

tomatoes, skinned, seeded and chopped

tsp snipped fresh dill

lt and pepper

l sprigs or fennel fronds, to garnish

1 Heat the olive oil in a large saucepan over a medium heat. Add the onion and fennel and cook for 3–4 minutes, stirring occasionally, until the onion is just softened.

2 Add the potato, water, tomato juice, and bay leaf with a large pinch of salt. Reduce the heat, cover, and simmer for about 25 minutes, stirring once or twice, until the vegetables are soft.

3 Allow the soup to cool slightly, then transfer to a blender or food processor and purée until smooth, working in batches if necessary. (If using a food processor, strain off the cooking liquid and reserve. Purée the soup solids with enough cooking liquid to moisten them, then combine with the remaining liquid.)

4 Return the soup to the saucepan and add the shrimp. Simmer gently for about 10 minutes, to reheat the soup and allow it to absorb the shrimp flavor.

5 Stir in the tomatoes and dill. Taste and adjust the seasoning, adding salt, if needed, and pepper. Thin the soup with a little more tomato juice, if wished. Ladle into warm bowls, garnish with dill or fennel fronds and serve.

Scallops in Garlic Broth

This soup is both simple and very elegant. Its lightness makes it particularly suitable as a starter.

NUTRITIONAL INFORMATION

Calories 112	Sugars 4g	
Protein 16g	Fat 1g	
Carbohydrate 11g	Saturates 0g	

 10 MINS   50 MINS

SERVES 4

I N G R E D I E N T S

5 cups water

1 large garlic bulb (about 3½ oz), separated into unpeeled cloves

1 celery stalk, chopped

1 carrot, chopped

1 onion, chopped

10 peppercorns

5–6 parsley stems

1 tbsp oil

8 oz large sea scallops or bay scallops

salt and pepper

fresh cilantro leaves, to garnish

1 Combine the garlic cloves, celery, carrot, onion, peppercorns, parsley stems, and water in a saucepan with a good pinch of salt. Bring to a boil, reduce the heat and simmer, partially covered, for 30–45 minutes.

VARIATION

Use fish stock instead of water to make the garlic stock if you want a more fishy flavor, or add oriental fish sauce, such as nam pla, to taste.

2 Strain the stock into a clean saucepan. Taste and adjust the seasoning, and keep hot.

3 If using sea scallops, slice in half crossways to form 2 thinner rounds from each. (If the scallops are very large, slice them into 3 rounds.) Sprinkle with salt and pepper.

4 Heat the oil in a skillet over medium-high heat and cook the scallops on one side for 1–2 minutes until lightly browned and the flesh become opaque.

5 Divide the scallops between 4 war shallow bowls, arranging the browned-side up. Ladle the soup over the scallops, then float a few cilantro leave on top. Serve at once.

Clam & Corn Chowder

Fresh clams make this chowder that bit more special, but they can be expensive. Canned baby clams or razor shell clams can be used instead.

NUTRITIONAL INFORMATION

Calories . . . . . . .344 Sugar 11g
Protein . . . . .20g Fats 10g
Carbohydrates . . .45g Saturates 6g

  15 MINS   40 MINS

SERVES 4

I N G R E D I E N T S

1 lb 10 oz clams, or 10 oz can clams

4 tbsp dry white wine (if needed)

1 tsp butter

1 large onion, finely chopped

1 small carrot, finely diced

1 tbsp all-purpose flour

3/4 cups fish stock

1 cup water (if needed)

1 lb potatoes, diced

1 cup cooked or defrosted frozen corn

2 cups whole milk

salt and pepper

chopped fresh parsley, to garnish

1 If using fresh clams, put them into a heavy-bottomed saucepan with the wine. Cover tightly, set over a medium-high heat and cook for 2–4 minutes, or until they open, shaking the pan occasionally. Remove the clams from the shells and strain the cooking liquid through a very fine strainer; reserve both. If using canned clams, drain and rinse well.

2 Melt the butter in a large saucepan over a medium-low heat. Add the onion and carrot and cook for 3–4 minutes, stirring frequently, until the onion is soft. Stir in the flour and continue cooking for 2 minutes.

3 Slowly add about half the stock and stir well, scraping the bottom of the pan to mix in the flour. Pour in the remaining stock and the reserved clam cooking liquid, or the water if using canned clams, and bring just to a boil, stirring.

4 Add the potatoes, corn and milk and stir to combine. Reduce the heat and simmer gently, partially covered, for about 20 minutes, stirring occasionally, until all the vegetables are tender.

5 Chop the clams, if large. Stir in the clams and continue cooking for about 5 minutes until heated through. Taste and adjust the seasoning, if needed.

6 Ladle the soup into bowls and sprinkle with parsley.

Mexican Beef & Rice Soup

For this tasty and unusual soup, boneless leg is a good cut of beef to use, as it is generally lean and any fat is easily trimmed off.

NUTRITIONAL INFORMATION

Calories 501   Sugars 14g
Protein . . . . .45g   Fat 18g
Carbohydrate . . .36g   Saturates 5g

 15 MINS   2 HOURS

SERVES 4

INGREDIENTS

3 tbsp olive oil

1 lb boneless stewing beef, cut into 1 inch pieces

²⁄₃ cup red wine

1 onion, finely chopped

1 green bell pepper, cored, seeded and finely chopped

1 small fresh red chili, seeded and finely chopped

2 garlic cloves, finely chopped

1 carrot, finely chopped

¼ tsp ground coriander

¼ tsp ground cumin

⅛ tsp ground cinnamon

¼ tsp dried oregano

1 bay leaf

grated rind of ½ orange

14 oz can chopped tomatoes

5 cups beef stock

¼ cup long-grain white rice

3 tbsp raisins

½ oz plain semi-sweet chocolate, melted

chopped fresh cilantro, to garnish

1 Heat half the oil in a large skillet over a medium-high heat. Add the meat in one layer and cook until well browned, turning to color all sides. Remove the skillet from the heat and pour in the wine.

2 Heat the remaining oil in a large saucepan over a medium heat. Add the onion, cover and cook for about 3 minutes, stirring occasionally, until just soft. Add the green bell pepper, chili, garlic, and carrot, and continue cooking, covered, for 3 minutes.

3 Add the coriander, cumin, cinnamon, oregano, bay leaf, and orange rind. Stir in the tomatoes and stock, along with the beef and wine. Bring almost to a boil and when the mixture begins to bubble, reduce the heat to low. Cover and simmer gently, stirring occasionally, for about 1 hour until the meat is tender.

4 Stir in the rice, raisins, and chocolate, and continue cooking, stirring occasionally, for about 30 minutes until the rice is tender.

5 Ladle into warm bowls and garnish with cilantro.

Cabbage Soup with Sausage

Spicy or smoky sausages add substance to this soup, which makes a hearty and warming supper, served with crusty bread and green salad.

NUTRITIONAL INFORMATION

Calories	160	Sugar	.........7g
Protein	........10g	Fats	...........8g
Carbohydrates	...12g	Saturates	......2g

10 MINS   1¼ HOURS

SERVES 4

INGREDIENTS

2 oz lean sausages, preferably highly
  seasoned

1 tsp oil

1 onion, finely chopped

1 leek, halved lengthways and thinly sliced

2 carrots, halved and thinly sliced

14 oz can chopped tomatoes

12 oz young green cabbage, cored and
  coarsely shredded

1-2 garlic cloves, finely chopped

pinch dried thyme

4¼ cups chicken or meat stock

salt and pepper

freshly grated Parmesan cheese, to serve

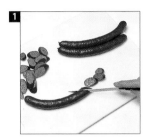

1 Put the sausages in water to cover generously and bring to a boil. Reduce the heat and simmer until firm. Drain the sausages and, when cool enough to handle, remove the skin, if you wish, and slice thinly.

2 Heat the oil in a large saucepan over a medium heat, add the onion, leek and carrots and cook for 3–4 minutes, stirring frequently, until the onion starts to soften.

3 Add the tomatoes, cabbage, garlic, thyme, stock, and sausages. Bring to a boil, reduce the heat to low and cook gently, partially covered, for about 40 minutes until the vegetables are tender.

4 Taste the soup and adjust the seasoning, if necessary. Ladle into warm bowls and serve with Parmesan cheese.

VARIATION

If you don't have fresh stock available, use water instead, with 1 bouillon cube only dissolved in it. Add a little more onion and garlic, plus a bouquet garni (remove it before serving).

Hunter's Soup

This soup is perfect for the sweet meat of rabbit, which is traditionally paired with tomatoes and mushrooms.

NUTRITIONAL INFORMATION

Calories 358	Sugar 10g	
Protein 35g	Fats 17g	
Carbohydrates ...12g	Saturates 6g	

🍲 25 MINS   🕐 1½ HOURS

SERVES 4

I N G R E D I E N T S

1-2 tbsp olive oil

2 lb rabbit, jointed

1 onion, finely chopped

2-3 garlic cloves, finely chopped or minced

3½ oz lean smoked back bacon, finely chopped

½ cup white wine

5 cups chicken stock

2 cups tomato juice

2 tbsp tomato paste

2 carrots, halved lengthways and sliced

1 bay leaf

¼ tsp dried thyme

¼ tsp dried oregano

1 tbsp butter

10½ oz mushrooms, quartered if small or sliced

chopped fresh parsley, to garnish

1 Heat the oil in a large saucepan or flameproof casserole over a medium-high heat. Add the rabbit, in batches if necessary to avoid crowding, and cook until lightly browned on all sides, adding a little more oil if needed. Remove the pieces when browned.

2 Reduce the heat a little and add the onion, garlic, and bacon to the pan. Cook, stirring frequently, for a further 2 minutes.

3 Add the wine and bubble for 1 minute. Add the stock and return the rabbit to the pan with any juices. Bring to a boil and skim off any foam that rises to the surface. Reduce the heat and stir in the tomato juice, tomato paste, carrots, bay leaf, thyme, and oregano. Season with salt and pepper. Cover and simmer gently for 1 hour, or until very tender.

4 Remove the rabbit pieces with a draining spoon and, when cool enough to handle, remove the meat from the bones. Discard any fat or gristle, along with the bones. Cut the meat into bite-sized pieces and return to the soup.

5 Melt the butter in a skillet over a medium-high heat. Add the mushrooms and season with salt and pepper. Fry gently until lightly golden, then add to the soup. Simmer for 10-15 minutes to blend. Season to taste and serve sprinkled with parsley.

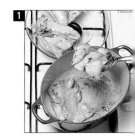

Chicken, Corn, & Bean Soup

This soup is especially tasty using fresh corn kernels
cut from 3 or 4 corn-on-the-cobs.

NUTRITIONAL INFORMATION

Calories 256   Sugars 6g
Protein . . . . .19g   Fat 7g
Carbohydrate . . .32g   Saturates 3g

10 MINS   45 MINS

SERVES 4

INGREDIENTS

½ tbsp butter

large onion, finely chopped

garlic clove, finely chopped

tbsp all-purpose flour

½ cups water

cups chicken stock

carrot, quartered and thinly sliced

oz dwarf beans, trimmed
and cut into short pieces

4 oz can lima beans, drained and rinsed

2 oz cooked corn or frozen corn kernels

oz cooked chicken meat

lt and pepper

VARIATION

Replace the lima beans with
½ oz cooked fresh fava
ans, peeled if wished. You
uld also substitute sliced
nner beans for the dwarf beans.

1 Melt the butter in a large saucepan over a medium-low heat. Add the onion and garlic and cook, stirring frequently, for 3–4 minutes until just softened.

2 Stir in the flour and continue cooking for 2 minutes, stirring occasionally.

3 Gradually pour in the water, stirring constantly and scraping the bottom of the pan to mix in the flour. Bring to a boil, stirring frequently, and cook for 2 minutes. Add the stock and stir until smooth.

4 Add the carrot, dwarf beans, lima beans, corn, and chicken meat. Season with salt and pepper. Bring back to a boil, reduce the heat to medium-low, cover and simmer for about 35 minutes until the vegetables are tender.

5 Taste the soup and adjust the seasoning, adding salt, if needed, and plenty of pepper.

6 Ladle the soup into warm, deep bowls and serve.

Senegalese Soup

This delicately curried chicken soup requires a flavorful stock. Its velvety texture makes it an elegant starter.

NUTRITIONAL INFORMATION

Calories 428	Sugars 6g	
Protein 16g	Fat 26g	
Carbohydrate ...34g	Saturates 15g	

15 MINS   40 MINS

SERVES 4

INGREDIENTS

5 cups chicken stock

1 small onion, thinly sliced

1 small carrot, finely chopped

1 celery stalk, finely chopped

½ small eating apple, peeled, cored, and chopped

1–2 garlic cloves, halved

1 tsp mild curry powder

7 oz skinless, boneless chicken breast

2 egg yolks

4 tbsp cornstarch

1 cup whipping cream

freshly grated nutmeg

salt and white pepper

toasted coconut strips or pecans, to garnish

1 Heat the stock in a large saucepan. Add the onion, carrot, celery, apple, garlic, and curry powder with a large pinch of salt, if the stock is unsalted. Bring to a boil, reduce the heat, and simmer, covered, for 20 minutes.

2 Trim any fat from the chicken. Add the chicken to the stock and continue

simmering for 10 minutes, or until the chicken is tender. Remove the chicken with a draining spoon.

3 Strain the stock and discard the stock vegetables. Spoon off any fat. When cool enough to handle, cut the chicken into thin slivers.

4 Put the strained stock in a large heavy-bottomed saucepan and put over a medium heat. When starting to bubble around the edge, adjust the heat so it continues to bubble gently at the edge but remains still in the center.

5 Put the egg yolks in a bowl. Add the cornstarch and cream and whisk until smooth. Whisk one-quarter of the hot stock into the cream mixture, then pour it all back into the saucepan, whisking constantly. With a wooden spoon, stir constantly for 10 minutes until the soup thickens slightly. Do not allow it to boil or the soup may curdle. If you see the soup beginning to boil, take the pan off the heat and stir more quickly until it cools down.

6 Stir in the chicken and reduce the heat to low. Season the soup with salt, pepper, and nutmeg. Ladle into warm soup bowls, garnish with toasted coconut strips or pecans and serve.

Chicken Gumbo

This soup contains okra, an essential ingredient in a gumbo. It helps thicken the soup

NUTRITIONAL INFORMATION

Calories 242   Sugars 5g
Protein ....17g   Fat 10g
Carbohydrate ...23g   Saturates 2g

15 MINS   60 MINS

SERVES 4

INGREDIENTS

tbsp olive oil

tbsp all-purpose flour

onion, finely chopped

small green bell pepper, cored, seeded, and finely chopped

celery stalk, finely chopped

cups chicken stock

oz can chopped tomatoes in juice

garlic cloves, finely chopped or minced

½ oz okra, stems removed, cut into ¼ inch thick slices

tbsp white rice

oz cooked chicken, cubed

oz cooked garlic sausage, sliced or cubed

Heat the oil in a large heavy-bottomed saucepan over a medium-low heat and stir in the flour. Cook for about 15 minutes, stirring occasionally, until the mixture is a rich golden brown (see Cook's Tip).

Add the onion, green bell pepper and celery and continue cooking for about minutes until the onion softens.

Slowly pour in the stock and bring to a boil, stirring well and scraping the bottom of the pan to mix in the flour. Remove the pan from the heat.

4 Add the tomatoes and garlic. Stir in the okra and rice and season. Reduce the heat, cover and simmer for 20 minutes, or until the okra is tender.

5 Add the chicken and sausage and continue simmering for about 10 minutes. Taste and adjust the seasoning, if necessary, and ladle into warm bowls to serve.

COOK'S TIP

Keep a watchful eye on the roux (flour and oil) as it begins to darken. The soup gains a lot of flavor from this traditional Cajun base, but if it burns the soup will be bitter. If you prefer, omit it and start by cooking the onion, green bell pepper and celery in the oil, adding the flour when they are softened.

Turkey & Mushrooms Soup

This is a warming wintery soup, substantial enough to serve as a main course, with lots of crusty bread.

NUTRITIONAL INFORMATION

Calories	465	Sugar	.........3g
Protein	........18g	Fats	..........30g
Carbohydrates	...33g	Saturates	.....18g

🥄 15 MINS 🕐 60 MINS

SERVES 4

INGREDIENTS

3 tbsp butter

1 onion, finely chopped

1 celery stalk, finely chopped

25 large fresh sage leaves, finely chopped

4 tbsp all-purpose flour

5 cups turkey or chicken stock

²⁄₃ cup brown rice

9 oz mushrooms, sliced

7 oz cooked turkey

¾ cup heavy cream

freshly grated Parmesan cheese, to serve

1 Melt half the butter in a large saucepan over a medium-low heat. Add the onion, celery, and sage and cook for 3-4 minutes until the onion is soft, stirring frequently. Stir in the flour and continue cooking for 2 minutes.

2 Slowly add about one quarter of the stock and stir well, scraping the bottom of the pan to mix in the flour. Pour in the remaining stock, stirring to combine completely, and bring just to a boil.

3 Stir in the rice and season with salt and pepper. Reduce the heat and simmer gently, partially covered, for about 30 minutes until the rice is just tender, stirring occasionally.

4 Meanwhile, melt the remaining butter in a large skillet over a medium heat. Add the mushrooms and season with salt and pepper. Cook for about 8 minutes until they are golden brown, stirring occasionally at first, then more often aft they start to color. Add the mushrooms the soup.

5 Add the turkey to the soup and stir the cream. Continue simmering f about 10 minutes until heated throug Taste and adjust the seasoning, necessary. Ladle into warm bowls a serve with Parmesan cheese.

Confetti Bean Soup

This soup uses the colorful dried bean mixes available that include a variety of different beans.

NUTRITIONAL INFORMATION

Calories . . . . .241 Sugar 6g
Protein . . . . .16g Fats 2g
Carbohydrates . . .41g Saturates 0g

15 MINS   1³/₄ HOURS

SERVES 4

INGREDIENTS

b mixed dried beans

bsp olive oil

onions, finely chopped

yellow or orange bell pepper, cored, seeded and finely chopped

garlic cloves, finely chopped or minced

carrots, cubed

parsnip, cubed

celery stalks, halved lengthways and cut into ¼ inch pieces

½ oz lean smoked gammon or ham, cubed

quarts water

bsp tomato paste

tsp dried thyme

bay leaf

potato, finely diced

bsp chopped fresh marjoram

bsp chopped fresh parsley

t and pepper

Pick over the beans, cover generously with cold water, and leave to soak for hours or overnight. Drain the beans, put a saucepan, and add enough cold water cover by 2 inches. Bring to a boil and boil for 10 minutes, skimming off the foam as it accumulates. Drain and rinse well.

2 Heat the oil in a large saucepan over a medium heat. Add the onions and bell pepper, cover, and cook for 3–4 minutes, stirring occasionally, until the onion is just softened. Add the garlic, carrots, parsnip, celery, and gammon or ham and continue cooking for 2–3 minutes, or until the onion begins to color.

3 Add the water, drained beans, tomato paste, thyme, and bay leaf. Bring just to a boil, cover, and simmer, occasionally stirring, for 1¼ hours, or until the beans and vegetables are tender.

4 Put the potato in a small saucepan and ladle over just enough of the bean cooking liquid to cover the potatoes. Bring to a boil, cover the pan, reduce the heat, and boil gently for about 12 minutes or until the potato is very tender.

5 Put the potato and its cooking liquid into a blender or food processor, then add 3 ladlefuls of the beans with a small amount of their liquid and purée until completely smooth.

6 Scrape the purée into the saucepan, add the marjoram and parsley and stir to blend. Season the soup to taste, adding salt and pepper generously. Reheat gently over a medium-low heat until hot and ladle the soup into warm bowls.

Black Bean & Pumpkin Soup

Pumpkin, a greatly underrated vegetable, balances the spicy heat in this soup and gives it a splash of color, too.

NUTRITIONAL INFORMATION

Calories	174	Sugar	.........7g
Protein	........10g	Fats	...........2g
Carbohydrates	...30g	Saturates	......0g

 10 MINS 2¹/₂ HOURS

SERVES 4

I N G R E D I E N T S

9 oz dried kidney beans

1 tbsp olive oil

2 onions, finely chopped

4 garlic cloves, finely chopped

1 celery stalk, thinly sliced

1 carrot, halved and thinly sliced

2 tsp tomato paste

¹/₈ tsp dried thyme

¹/₈ tsp dried oregano

¹/₈ tsp ground cumin

5 cups water

1 bay leaf

14 oz can chopped tomatoes in juice

9 oz peeled pumpkin flesh, diced

¹/₄ tsp chili paste, or to taste

salt and pepper

fresh cilantro leaves, to garnish

2 Heat the oil in a large saucepan over a medium heat. Add the onions and cook, covered, for 3–4 minutes until they are just soft, stirring occasionally. Add the garlic, celery, and carrot, and continue cooking for 2 minutes.

3 Add the water, drained beans, tomato paste, thyme, oregano, cumin, water, and bay leaf. When the mixture begins to bubble, reduce the heat to low. Cover, and simmer gently for 1 hour, stirring occasionally.

4 Stir in the tomatoes, pumpkin, a▮ chili paste and continue simmering f about 1 hour more, or until the beans a▮ pumpkin are tender, stirring from time time.

5 Taste and season the soup, stir in little more chili paste if liked. Lad▮ the soup into bowls, garnish with cilant▮ and serve.

1 Pick over the beans, cover generously with cold water and leave to soak for 6 hours or overnight. Drain the beans, put in a saucepan and add enough cold water to cover by 2 inches. Bring to a boil and boil for 10 minutes. Drain and rinse well.

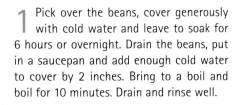

Rice & Black-Eye Pea Soup

This soup is satisfying and very healthy. Brown rice gives a pleasing chewy texture, but white rice could be used instead.

NUTRITIONAL INFORMATION

Calories 260   Sugar 8g
Protein . . . . .15g   Fats 4g
Carbohydrates . . .44g   Saturates 1g

15 MINS   1¹/₄ HOURS

SERVES 4

I N G R E D I E N T S

oz dried black-eye peas

tbsp olive oil

large onion, finely chopped

garlic cloves, finely chopped or minced

carrots, finely chopped

celery stalks, finely chopped

small red bell pepper, seeded and finely chopped

oz lean smoked ham, finely diced

tsp fresh thyme leaves, or ¹/₈ tsp dried thyme

bay leaf

cups chicken or vegetable stock

¹/₂ cups water

cup brown rice

opped fresh parsley or chives, to garnish

Pick over the beans, cover generously with cold water and leave to soak for least 6 hours or overnight. Drain the ans, put in a saucepan and add enough ld water to cover by 2 inches. Bring to a il and boil for 10 minutes. Drain and se well.

Heat the oil in a large heavy-bottomed saucepan over a medium heat. Add the onion, cover, and cook for 3–4 minutes, stirring frequently, until just softened. Add the garlic, carrots, celery, and bell pepper, stir well and cook for a further 2 minutes.

3 Add the drained beans, ham, thyme, bay leaf, stock, and water. Bring to a boil, reduce the heat, cover, and simmer gently, stirring occasionally, for 1 hour, or until the beans are just tender.

4 Stir in the rice and season the soup with salt, if needed, and pepper. Continue cooking for 30 minutes, or until the rice and beans are tender.

5 Taste the soup and adjust the seasoning, if necessary. Ladle into warm bowls and serve garnished with parsley or chives.

Traditional Soups

The range of soups found in this chapter is guaranteed to provide good old-fashioned nourishment and are perfect served as a main course accompanied by a hearty chunk of

fresh bread or perhaps a salad or a hunk of strong-tasting cheese. Wholesome treats include the traditional Scots recipe for Partan Bree, lentil and ham soup, and delicious fresh mushroom soup. To make

the most of these soups, remember that they are only as good as their ingredients, so be sure to pick good quality produce.

Celeriac, Leek, & Potato

It is hard to imagine that celeriac, a coarse, knobbly vegetable, can taste so sweet. It makes a wonderfully flavorful soup.

NUTRITIONAL INFORMATION

Calories ....123 Sugars 8g
Protein ....4g Fat 4g
Carbohydrate ...17g Saturates 2g

 15 MINS   35 MINS

SERVES 4

INGREDIENTS

1 tbsp butter

1 onion, chopped

2 large leeks, halved lengthways and sliced

1 large celeriac (about 1 lb 10 oz), peeled and cubed

1 potato, cubed

1 carrot, quartered and thinly sliced

5 cups water

⅛ tsp dried marjoram

1 bay leaf

freshly grated nutmeg

salt and pepper

celery leaves, to garnish

1 Melt the butter in a large saucepan over a medium-low heat. Add the onion and leeks and cook for about 4 minutes, stirring frequently, until just softened; do not allow to color.

2 Add the celeriac, potato, carrot, water, marjoram, and bay leaf, with a large pinch of salt. Bring to a boil, reduce the heat, cover and simmer for about 25 minutes until the vegetables are tender. Remove the bay leaf.

3 Allow the soup to cool slightly. Transfer to a blender or food processor and purée until smooth. (If using food processor, strain off cooking liquid and reserve. Purée the soup solids with enough cooking liquid to moisten them, then combine with remaining liquid.)

4 Return the puréed soup to the saucepan and stir to blend. Season with salt, pepper, and nutmeg. Simmer over a medium-low heat until reheated.

5 Ladle the soup into warm bowls garnish with celery leaves and serve.

Baked Leek & Cabbage Soup

A flavorful stock is important for this delicious and filling soup, which is a typical peasant-style bread soup, perfect for supper.

NUTRITIONAL INFORMATION

Calories 448	Sugar 7g	
Protein 23g	Fats 29g	
Carbohydrates ...26g	Saturates 17g	

🍲 15 MINS 🕐 1 HOUR 25 MINS

SERVES 4

I N G R E D I E N T S

tbsp butter

large leeks, halved lengthways and thinly sliced

large onion, halved and thinly sliced

garlic cloves, finely chopped

oz finely shredded green cabbage

cups chicken or meat stock

slices firm bread, cut in half, or 8 slices baguette

oz grated Gruyère cheese

1 Melt the butter in a large saucepan over a medium heat. Add the leeks and onion and cook for 4–5 minutes, stirring frequently, until just softened.

COOK'S TIP

A large soufflé dish or earthenware casserole at least 4 inches deep, or an enameled cast-iron casserole, is good for baking the soup. If the soup fills the dish to the top, put a baking sheet with a rim underneath to catch any overflow.

2 Add the garlic and cabbage, stir to combine and continue cooking for about 5 minutes until the cabbage is wilted.

3 Stir in the stock and simmer for 10 minutes. Taste and season with salt and pepper.

4 Arrange the bread in the base of a large deep 3 quart ovenproof dish. Sprinkle about half the cheese over the bread.

5 Ladle over the soup and top with the remaining cheese. Bake in a preheated oven at 350°F for 1 hour. Serve at once.

Leek, Potato, & Carrot Soup

A quick chunky soup, ideal for a snack or a quick lunch. The leftovers can be puréed to make one portion of creamed soup for the next day.

NUTRITIONAL INFORMATION

Calories 156	Sugars 7g
Protein 4g	Fat 6g
Carbohydrate ...22g	Saturates 0.7g

 10 MINS   25 MINS

SERVES 2

INGREDIENTS

1 leek, about 6 oz

1 tbsp sunflower oil

1 garlic clove, minced

3 cups vegetable stock

1 bay leaf

¼ tsp ground cumin

1 cup potatoes, diced

1 cup coarsely grated carrot

salt and pepper

chopped parsley, to garnish

PUREED SOUP

5–6 tbsp milk

1–2 tbsp heavy cream, crème
    fraîche or sour cream

1 Trim off and discard some of the coarse green part of the leek, then slice thinly and rinse thoroughly in cold water. Drain well.

2 Heat the sunflower oil in a heavy-bottomed saucepan. Add the leek and garlic, and fry over a low heat for about 2–3 minutes, until soft, but barely colored. Add the vegetable stock, bay leaf, and cumin and season to taste with salt and pepper. Bring the mixture to a boil, stirring constantly.

3 Add the diced potato to the saucepan, cover and simmer over a low heat for 10–15 minutes until the potato is just tender, but not broken up.

4 Add the grated carrot and simmer for a further 2–3 minutes. Adjust the seasoning, discard the bay leaf and serve sprinkled liberally with chopped parsley.

5 To make a puréed soup, first proce the leftovers (about half the origin soup) in a blender or food processor press through a strainer until smooth a then return to a clean saucepan with t milk. Bring to a boil and simmer f 2–3 minutes. Adjust the seasoning and s in the cream or crème fraîche befo serving sprinkled with chopped parsley.

Cauliflower & Cider Soup

This was inspired by a visit to Normandy, France where cider and cream are plentiful, and are used in many local specialties.

NUTRITIONAL INFORMATION

Calories	.312	Sugars	.13g
Protein	.7g	Fat	.21g
Carbohydrate	.15g	Saturates	.13g

15 MINS   60 MINS

SERVES 4

INGREDIENTS

tbsp butter

onion, finely chopped

garlic clove, minced

carrot, thinly sliced

lb cauliflower florets (from 1 medium head)

¹/₂ cups hard cider

eshly grated nutmeg

½ cup milk

² cup heavy cream

alt and pepper

nipped chives, to garnish

1 Melt the butter in a saucepan over a medium heat. Add the onion and garlic and cook for about 5 minutes, stirring occasionally, until just softened.

2 Add the carrot and cauliflower to the pan and pour over the cider. Season with salt, pepper, and a generous grating of nutmeg. Bring to a boil, then reduce the heat to low. Cover and cook gently for about 50 minutes until the vegetables are very soft.

3 Allow the soup to cool slightly, then transfer to a blender or food processor and purée until smooth, working in batches if necessary. (If using a food processor, strain off the cooking liquid and reserve. Purée the soup solids with enough cooking liquid to moisten them, then combine with the remaining liquid.)

4 Return the soup to the saucepan and stir in the milk and cream. Taste and adjust the seasoning, if necessary. Simmer the soup over a low heat, stirring occasionally, until heated through.

5 Ladle the soup into warm bowls, garnish with chives and serve.

OOK'S TIP

you don't have hard cider, ıbstitute ¹/₂ cup each white ine, apple juice, and water.

Cauliflower & Broccoli Soup

Full of flavor, this creamy cauliflower and broccoli soup is simple to make and absolutely delicious to eat.

NUTRITIONAL INFORMATION

Calories	378	Sugars	........14g
Protein	........18g	Fat	..........26g
Carbohydrate	...20g	Saturates	.......7g

10 MINS   35 MINS

SERVES 4

INGREDIENTS

3 tbsp vegetable oil

1 red onion, chopped

2 garlic cloves, minced

10½ oz cauliflower florets

10½ oz broccoli florets

1 tbsp all-purpose flour

2½ cups milk

1¼ cups vegetable stock

¾ cup Gruyère cheese, grated

pinch of paprika

⅔ cup light cream

paprika and Gruyère cheese shavings,
    to garnish

1 Heat the oil in a large, heavy-bottomed saucepan. Add the onion, garlic, cauliflower florets, and broccoli florets and sauté over a low heat, stirring constantly, for 3–4 minutes. Add the flour and cook, stirring constantly for a further 1 minute.

2 Gradually stir in the milk and stock and bring to a boil, stirring constantly. Reduce the heat and simmer for 20 minutes.

3 Remove about a quarter of the vegetables with a draining spoon and set aside. Put the remaining soup in a food processor or blender and process for about 30 seconds, until smooth. Alternatively, press the vegetables through a strainer with the back of a wooden spoon. Transfer the soup to a clean saucepan.

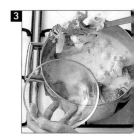

4 Return the reserved vegetable pieces to the soup. Stir in the grated cheese, paprika and light cream and heat through over a low heat, without boiling, for 2–3 minutes, or until the cheese starts to melt.

5 Transfer to warmed individual serving bowls, garnish with shavings of Gruyère and dust with paprika and serve immediately.

COOK'S TIP

The soup must not start to boil after the cream has been added, otherwise it will curdle. Use unsweetened yogurt instead of the cream if preferred, but again do not allow it to boil.

Asparagus Soup

Fresh asparagus is now available for most of the year, so this soup can be made at any time. It can also be made using canned asparagus.

NUTRITIONAL INFORMATION

Calories 196	Sugars 7g
Protein 7g	Fat 12g
Carbohydrate ...15g	Saturates 4g

🍲 5-10 MINS   🕐 55 MINS

SERVES 6

I N G R E D I E N T S

bunch asparagus, about 12 oz, or

2 packs mini asparagus,
  about 5½ oz each

cups vegetable stock

cup butter or margarine

onion, chopped

tbsp all-purpose flour

tsp ground coriander

tbsp lemon juice

cups milk

-6 tbsp heavy or light cream

lt and pepper

1 Wash and trim the asparagus, discarding the woody part of the stem. Cut the remainder into short lengths, keeping a few tips for garnish. Mini asparagus does not need to be trimmed.

2 Cook the tips in the minimum of boiling salted water for 5–10 minutes. Drain and set aside.

3 Put the asparagus in a saucepan with the stock, bring to a boil, cover, and simmer for about 20 minutes, until soft. Drain and reserve the stock.

4 Melt the butter or margarine in a saucepan. Add the onion and fry over a low heat until soft, but only barely colored. Stir in the flour and cook for 1 minute, then gradually whisk in the reserved stock and bring to a boil.

5 Simmer for 2–3 minutes, until thickened, then stir in the cooked asparagus, seasoning, coriander, and lemon juice. Simmer for 10 minutes, then cool a little and either press through a strainer or process in a blender or food processor until smooth.

6 Pour into a clean pan, add the milk and reserved asparagus tips and bring to a boil. Simmer for 2 minutes. Stir in the cream, reheat gently, and serve.

OOK'S TIP

using canned asparagus,
ain off the liquid and use as
rt of the measured stock.
move a few small asparagus
s for garnish and chop the
mainder. Continue as above.

Mushroom & Barley Soup

This old-fashioned soup is nourishing and warming, with distinctive flavors and a nice chewy texture.

NUTRITIONAL INFORMATION

Calories ....128 Sugar 5g
Protein ....4g Fats 4g
Carbohydrates ...19g Saturates 2g

15 MINS   1¼ HOURS

SERVES 4

INGREDIENTS

⅓ cup pearl barley

6¼ cups chicken or vegetable stock

1 bay leaf

1 tbsp butter

12 oz mushrooms, thinly sliced

1 tsp olive oil

1 onion, finely chopped

2 carrots, thinly sliced

1 tbsp chopped fresh tarragon

1 tbsp chopped fresh parsley or tarragon, to garnish

1 Rinse the barley and drain. Bring 2 cups of the stock to the boil in a small saucepan. Add the bay leaf and, if the stock is unsalted, add a large pinch of salt. Stir in the barley, reduce the heat, cover, and simmer for 40 minutes.

2 Melt the butter in a large skillet over a medium heat. Add the mushrooms and season with salt and pepper. Cook for about 8 minutes until they are golden brown, stirring occasionally at first, then more often after they start to color. Remove the mushrooms from the heat.

3 Heat the oil in a large saucepan over a medium heat and add the onion and carrots. Cover and cook for about 3 minutes, stirring frequently, until the onion is softened.

4 Add the remaining stock and bring to a boil. Stir in the barley with its cooking liquid and add the mushrooms. Reduce the heat, cover and simmer gently for about 20 minutes, or until the carrots are tender, stirring occasionally.

5 Stir in the tarragon and parsley. Taste and adjust the seasoning, if necessary. Ladle into warm bowls, garnish with fresh parsley or tarragon and serve.

COOK'S TIP

The barley will continue to absorb liquid if the soup is stored, so if making ahead, you may need to add a little more stock or water when reheating.

Fresh Mushroom Soup

When you see mushrooms at a special price in your local supermarket, bare this recipe in mind!

NUTRITIONAL INFORMATION

Calories 225   Sugars 5g
Protein . . . . .6g   Fat 17g
Carbohydrate . . .12g   Saturates 10g

🍬 🍬

🧈 10 MINS   🕐 40 MINS

SERVES 4

I N G R E D I E N T S

bsp butter

b 9 oz mushrooms, sliced

onion, finely chopped

shallot, finely chopped

bsp plain all-purpose flour

3 tbsp dry white wine or sherry

ups chicken or vegetable stock

cup light cream

bsp chopped fresh parsley

sh lemon juice (optional)

t and pepper

bsp sour cream or crème fraîche,
o garnish

Melt half the butter in a skillet over a medium heat. Add the mushrooms d season with salt and pepper. Cook for out 8 minutes until they are golden own, stirring occasionally at first, then re often after they start to color. move the mushrooms from the heat.

2 Melt the remaining butter in a saucepan over a medium heat, add the onion and shallot, and cook for 2–3 minutes until just softened. Stir the flour into the pan and continue cooking for 2 minutes. Add the wine and stock and stir well.

3 Set aside about one-quarter of the mushrooms. Add the remainder to the pan. Reduce the heat, cover and cook gently for 20 minutes, stirring occasionally.

4 Allow the soup to cool slightly, then transfer to a blender or food processor and purée until smooth, working in batches, if necessary. (If using a food processor, strain off the cooking liquid and reserve. Purée the soup solids with enough cooking liquid to moisten them, then combine with the remaining liquid.)

5 Return the soup to the saucepan and stir in the reserved mushrooms, the cream and parsley. Cook for about 5 minutes to heat through. Taste and adjust the seasoning, adding a few drops of lemon juice if wished. Ladle into warm bowls and decorate with sour cream.

Celery & Stilton Soup

This soup combines two ingredients that have been paired since Victorian times.

NUTRITIONAL INFORMATION

Calories	380	Sugar	.........6g
Protein	........10g	Fats	..........35g
Carbohydrates	....7g	Saturates	.....21g

15 MINS   40 MINS

SERVES 4

INGREDIENTS

2 tbsp butter

1 onion, finely chopped

4 large celery stalks, peeled and finely chopped

1 large carrot, finely chopped

4 cups chicken or vegetable stock

3–4 thyme sprigs

1 bay leaf

½ cup heavy cream

5½ oz Stilton cheese, crumbled

freshly grated nutmeg

salt and pepper

1 Melt the butter in a large saucepan over a medium-low heat. Add the onion and cook for 3–4 minutes, stirring frequently, until just softened. Add the celery and carrot and continue cooking for 3 minutes. Season lightly with salt and pepper.

2 Add the stock, thyme, and bay leaf and bring to a boil. Reduce the heat, cover, and simmer gently for about 25 minutes, stirring occasionally, until the vegetables are very tender.

3 Allow the soup to cool slightly and remove the bouquet garni. Transfer the soup to a blender or food processor and purée until smooth, working in batches, if necessary. (If using a food processor, strain off the cooking liquid and reserve. Purée the soup solids with enough cooking liquid to moisten them, then combine with the remaining liquid.)

4 Return the puréed soup to the saucepan and stir in the cream. Simmer over a low heat for 5 minutes.

5 Add the Stilton slowly, stirring constantly, until smooth. (Do not allow the soup to boil.) Taste and adjust the seasoning, adding salt, if needed, plenty of pepper and nutmeg to taste.

6 Ladle into warm bowls, garnish with celery leaves and serve.

VARIATION

Substitute ripened Cheddar or Gruyére for the Stilton.

Trout & Celeriac Soup

The cooking liquid in which the fish is poached becomes a delicious fish stock. If you just want stock, poach fish heads and trimmings.

NUTRITIONAL INFORMATION

Calories . . . . . . .369 Sugars 4g
Protein . . . . .24g Fat 21g
Carbohydrate . . .17g Saturates 10g

25 MINS | 1¼ HOURS

SERVES 4

INGREDIENTS

b 9 oz whole trout

oz celeriac, peeled and diced

cup heavy cream

bsp cornstarch, dissolved in 3 tbsp water

opped fresh chervil or parsley, to garnish

FISH STOCK BASE

bsp butter

nion, thinly sliced

arrot, thinly sliced

ek, thinly sliced

up dry white wine

cups water

ay leaf

3 Put the fish into the liquid (if necessary, cut the fish in pieces to fit in). Bring back to a boil and skim off any foam that rises to the top. Reduce the heat to low and simmer gently for 20 minutes.

4 Remove the fish and set aside. Strain the stock through a cheesecloth-lined strainer into a clean saucepan. Remove any fat from the stock. (There should be about 6 cups stock.)

5 Bring the stock to a boil. Add the celeriac and boil gently, uncovered, for 15–20 minutes until it is tender and the liquid has reduced by about one-third.

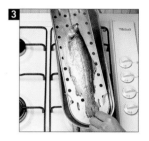

6 When the fish is cool enough to handle, peel off the skin and remove the flesh from the bones. Discard the skin, bones, head, and tail.

7 Add the cream to the soup and when it comes back to a boil, stir in the dissolved cornstarch. Boil gently for 2–3 minutes until slightly thickened, stirring frequently. Return the fish to the soup. Cook for 3–4 minutes to reheat. Taste and adjust the seasoning, if necessary. Ladle into warm bowls and garnish with chervil or parsley.

To make the fish stock base, melt the butter in a fish kettle, a large ucepan or cast-iron casserole over a dium-high heat. Add the onion, carrot, d leek and cook for about 3 minutes, or til the onion starts to soften.

Add the wine, water, and bay leaf. Bring to a boil, reduce the heat, cover, d boil gently for 15 minutes.

Haddock & Potato Soup

This chunky aromatic soup is perfect for a cold weather lunch or supper served with crusty bread and a salad.

NUTRITIONAL INFORMATION

Calories	404	Sugar	. . . . .17g
Protein	. . . . .24g	Fats	. . . . .11g
Carbohydrates	. . .55g	Saturates	. . . . . .4g

15 MINS   40 MINS

SERVES 4

I N G R E D I E N T S

1 tbsp oil

2 oz smoked sliced bacon, cut into thin matchsticks

1 large onion, finely chopped

2 tbsp all-purpose flour

4 cups milk

1 lb 9 oz potatoes, cut into ½ inch cubes

6 oz skinless smoked haddock

salt and pepper

finely chopped fresh parsley, to garnish

1 Heat the oil in a large saucepan over a medium heat. Add the bacon and cook for 2 minutes. Stir in the onion and continue cooking for 5–7 minutes, stirring frequently, until the onion is soft and the bacon golden. Tip the pan and spoon off as much fat as possible.

2 Stir in the flour and continue cooking for 2 minutes. Add half of the milk and stir well, scraping the bottom of the pan to mix in the flour.

3 Add the potatoes and remaining milk and season with pepper. Bring just to a boil, stirring frequently, then reduce the heat and simmer, partially covered, for 10 minutes.

4 Add the fish and continue cooking, stirring occasionally, for about 15 minutes, or until the potatoes are tender and the fish breaks up easily.

5 Taste the soup and adjust the seasoning (salt may not be needed). Ladle into a warm tureen or bowls and sprinkle generously with chopped parsley.

COOK'S TIP

Cutting the potatoes into small cubes not only looks attractive, but it allows them to cook more quickly and evenly.

Salmon & Leek Soup

Salmon is a favorite with almost everyone. This delicately flavored and pretty soup is perfect for entertaining.

NUTRITIONAL INFORMATION

Calories 322	Sugar 6g	
Protein 18g	Fats 21g	
Carbohydrates ...15g	Saturates 8g	

15 MINS   40 MINS

SERVES 4

INGREDIENTS

tbsp olive oil

arge onion, finely chopped

arge leeks, including green parts, thinly sliced

potato, finely diced

cups fish stock

cups water

ay leaf

½ oz skinless salmon fillet, cut into ½ inch cubes

cup heavy cream

lt and pepper

sh lemon juice (optional)

pped fresh chervil or parsley, to garnish

Heat the oil in a heavy-bottomed saucepan over a medium heat. Add e onion and leeks and cook for about 3 nutes until they begin to soften.

Add the potato, stock, water, and bay leaf with a large pinch of salt. ng to a boil, reduce the heat, cover, and ok gently for about 25 minutes until the getables are tender. Remove the bay f.

Allow the soup to cool slightly, then transfer about half of it to a blender or food processor and purée until smooth. (If using a food processor, strain off the cooking liquid and reserve. Purée half the soup solids with enough cooking liquid to moisten them, then combine with the remaining liquid.)

4 Return the puréed soup to the saucepan and stir to blend. Reheat gently over a medium-low heat.

5 Season the salmon with salt and pepper and add to the soup. Continue cooking for about 5 minutes, stirring occasionally, until the fish is tender and starts to break up. Stir in the cream, taste and adjust the seasoning, adding a little lemon juice if wished. Ladle into warm bowls, sprinkle with chervil or parsley and serve.

Shrimp Bisque

This soup utilizes every part of the shrimp. You could leave the shrimp flesh out of the soup as most of the flavor comes from the shells.

NUTRITIONAL INFORMATION

Calories 227   Sugars 7g
Protein ....25g   Fat 4g
Carbohydrate ...22g   Saturates 1g

🍮 15 MINS   🕐 1 HOUR 20 MINS

SERVES 4

I N G R E D I E N T S

1 lb cooked shrimp in the shell

2 tsp oil

2 large onions, halved and sliced

1 carrot, grated

1 celery stalk, sliced

1–2 garlic cloves, finely chopped or minced

6¼ cups water

1 bay leaf

2 tsp butter

6 tbsp white rice

1 tbsp tomato paste

fresh lemon juice

salt and pepper

snipped fresh dill or chopped parsley, to garnish

1 Peel the shrimp and keep the shells for the soup. Reserve the shrimp flesh, covered, in the refrigerator.

2 Heat the oil in a large saucepan. Add the shrimp shells and cook over a high heat, stirring frequently, until they start to brown. Reduce the heat and add one-quarter of the onions, the carrot, celery and garlic. Cover and cook for 4–5 minutes, stirring frequently, until the

onions soften. Add the water and bay leaf with a small pinch of salt. Bring to a boil, reduce the heat, cover and simmer gently for 25 minutes. Strain the shrimp stock

3 Heat the butter in a large saucepan over a medium heat and add the remaining onions. Cover and cook for 5–6 minutes, stirring frequently, until they soften and just begin to color. Add the shrimp stock, rice, and tomato paste. Bring to a boil. Reduce the heat, cover, and simmer for 30 minutes, or until rice is very soft.

4 Allow the soup to cool slightly, then transfer to a blender or food processor and purée until smooth, working in batches if necessary. (If using a food processor, strain off the cooking liquid and reserve. Purée the soup solids with enough cooking liquid to moisten them, then combine with the remaining liquid.)

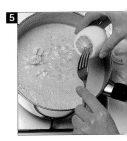

5 Return the soup to the saucepan and place over a medium-low heat. Add the reserved shrimp and a few drops of lemon juice, or to taste. Simmer for about 8 minutes, stirring occasionally, until the soup is reheated. Taste and adjust the seasoning if necessary. Ladle into warm bowls, sprinkle with dill or parsley and serve.

Vegetable Beef Soup

A wonderful way to use fresh garden produce, but frozen vegetables are equally colorful and nutritious. No need to defrost them first.

NUTRITIONAL INFORMATION

Calories	186	Sugar	........9g
Protein	........22g	Fats	...........5g
Carbohydrates	...15g	Saturates	......1g

10 MINS   2 HOURS

SERVES 6

INGREDIENTS

lb stewing steak

x 14 oz cans chopped tomatoes in juice

onions, finely chopped

-3 garlic cloves, finely chopped

carrots, diced

celery stalks, sliced

/2 oz green cabbage, thinly sliced

bay leaf

-6 allspice berries

tsp dried thyme

tsp dried marjoram

cups water

cups beef stock

oz dwarf beans, cut into short pieces

/2 oz English peas

/2 oz corn

alt and pepper

1 Trim all visible fat from the steak and cut into ½ inch cubes. Put in a large saucepan with the tomatoes, onions, garlic, carrots, celery, cabbage, bay leaf, allspice, thyme, marjoram, and water.

2 Bring to a boil over a medium-high heat, skimming off any foam that rises to the surface. Stir in the stock, reduce the heat and regulate it so that the soup boils very gently. Season with salt and pepper. Cook, partially covered, for 1 hour, stirring occasionally.

3 Add the dwarf beans, peas, and corn. Continue cooking for 1 hour longer, or until the meat and vegetables are very tender.

4 Taste and adjust the seasoning, adding salt and pepper as necessary. Ladle into warm bowls and serve.

COOK'S TIP

For quick beef stock, dilute 1 bouillon cube in 4 cups water, or use a can of beef consommé made up to that quantity with water. Alternatively, you can use all water and add 1 tsp salt.

Beef, Herb, & Vegetable Brot

This light, lean soup is studded with small diced vegetables and fragrant herbs. The stock may be used as a basis for other soups.

NUTRITIONAL INFORMATION

Calories	25	Sugars	. . . . .4g
Protein	. . . . .1g	Fat	. . . . .0g
Carbohydrate	. . . .5g	Saturates	. . . . . .0g

 15 MINS   5 HOURS

SERVES 4

I N G R E D I E N T S

7 oz celeriac, peeled and finely diced

2 large carrots, finely diced

2 tsp chopped fresh marjoram leaves

2 tsp chopped fresh parsley

2 plum tomatoes, skinned, seeded and diced

salt and pepper

B E E F   S T O C K

1 lb boneless beef shin or stewing steak, cut into large cubes

1 lb 10 oz veal, beef or pork bones

2 onions, quartered

2½ quarts water

4 garlic cloves, sliced

2 carrots, sliced

1 large leek, sliced

1 celery stalk, cut into 2 inch pieces

1 bay leaf

4–5 sprigs fresh thyme, or ¼ tsp dried thyme

salt

1 To make the stock, trim as much fat as possible from the beef and put in a large roasting pan with the bones and onions. Roast in a preheated oven at 375°F for 30–40 minutes until browned, turning once or twice. Transfer the ingredients to a large soup kettle or flameproof casserole and discard the fat.

2 Add the water (it should cover by at least 2 inches) and bring to a boil. Skim off any foam that rises to the surface. Reduce the heat and add the sliced garlic, carrots, leek, celery, bay leaf, thyme, and a pinch of salt. Simmer very gently, uncovered, for 4 hours, skimming occasionally. Do not stir. If the ingredients emerge from the liquid, top up with water.

3 Gently ladle the stock through a cheesecloth-lined strainer into a large container and remove as much fat as possible. Save the meat for another purpose, if wished, and discard the bones and vegetables. (There should be about 8 cups of stock.)

4 Boil the stock very gently until it reduced to 6¼ cups, or if the sto already has concentrated flavor, measu out that amount and save the rest f another purpose. Taste the stock a adjust the seasoning if necessary.

5 Bring a saucepan of salted wat to a boil and drop in the celeriac a carrots. Reduce the heat, cover and be gently for about 15 minutes until tend Drain.

6 Add the herbs to the boiling be stock. Divide the cooked vegetabl and tomatoes among warm bowls, lac over the boiling stock and serve.

Scotch Broth

This traditional winter soup is full of goodness, with lots of tasty golden vegetables along with tender barley and lamb.

NUTRITIONAL INFORMATION

Calories 166	Sugar 7g	
Protein 13g	Fats 5g	
Carbohydrates ...18g	Saturates 2g	

 15 MINS   1¹⁄₂ MINS

SERVES 4

INGREDIENTS

⅓ cup pearl barley

10½ oz lean boneless lamb, such as shoulder or neck fillet, trimmed of fat and cut into ½ inch cubes

cups water

onion, finely chopped

garlic cloves, finely chopped or minced

cups chicken or meat stock

bay leaf

large leek, quartered lengthways and sliced

large carrots, finely diced

parsnip, finely diced

½ oz peeled rutabaga, diced

tbsp chopped fresh parsley

salt and pepper

COOK'S TIP

This soup is lean when the lamb is trimmed. By making it beforehand, you can remove any hardened fat before reheating.

1 Rinse the barley under cold running water. Put in a saucepan and cover generously with water. Bring to a boil and boil for 3 minutes, skimming off the foam from the surface. Set aside, covered, in the saucepan.

2 Put the lamb in a large saucepan with the water and bring to a boil. Skim off the foam that rises to the surface.

3 Stir in the garlic, stock, onion, and bay leaf. Reduce the heat and boil very gently, partially covered, for 15 minutes.

4 Drain the barley and add to the soup. Add the leek, carrots, parsnip, and rutabaga. Continue simmering for about 1 hour, or until the lamb and vegetables are tender, stirring occasionally.

5 Taste and adjust the seasoning. Stir in the parsley and ladle into warm bowls to serve.

Chicken & Noodle Broth

A flavorful stock is essential, but meat stock would be equally good.

20 MINS   15 MINS

SERVES 4

INGREDIENTS

1 egg yolk

⅓ cup freshly grated Parmesan cheese

2 tbsp all-purpose flour

freshly grated nutmeg

1 tsp water, or as needed

5 cups chicken stock

1 tbsp shredded basil leaves or chopped
   tarragon leaves

2 tsp finely chopped fresh parsley

salt and pepper

freshly grated Parmesan cheese,
   to serve

1 Combine the egg yolk, Parmesan cheese, and flour in a mixing bowl. Add a good grating of nutmeg, a pinch of salt, and plenty of freshly ground pepper.

2 Add the water and stir with a fork until the dough comes together and pulls away from the sides of the bowl. (It should be very stiff.) If the dough is too crumbly, add more water by half teaspoons. If the dough is too sticky, add more flour by teaspoons until it holds together and does not stick to your hands.

3 Cut the dough in quarters. Working with one quarter at a time, roll the dough into a sausage shape until it exceeds the width of your two hands. Break in half and roll into thin strings, ⅛ inch in diameter or less (as thin as possible); break into shorter lengths as needed. Lay the strings on a cutting board, well spaced. Repeat with the remaining dough. Leave to dry for 15–45 minutes and cut into 1 inch lengths.

4 Put the stock in a large saucepan and bring to a boil. Reduce the heat and regulate it so the liquid bubbles gently. Taste and season with salt and pepper. Drop in the noodles and cook for 5– minutes until they are tender. Stir in the shredded basil and chopped parsley. Ladle into warm bowls and serve with fresh grated Parmesan cheese.

Pumpkin Soup

This is an American classic that has now become popular worldwide. When pumpkin is out of season use butternut squash in its place.

NUTRITIONAL INFORMATION

Calories	112	Sugars	7g
Protein	4g	Fat	7g
Carbohydrate	8g	Saturates	2g

10 MINS   30 MINS

SERVES 6

INGREDIENTS

about 2 lb pumpkin

tbsp butter or margarine

onion, sliced thinly

garlic clove, crushed

cups vegetable stock

tsp ground ginger

tbsp lemon juice

-4 thinly pared strips of orange rind (optional)

-2 bay leaves or 1 bouquet garni

cups milk

alt and pepper

TO GARNISH

-6 tablespoons light or heavy cream, unsweetened yogurt, or fromage frais

nipped chives

3 Add the pumpkin and toss with the onion for 2–3 minutes.

4 Add the stock and bring to a boil over a medium heat. Season to taste with salt and pepper and add the ginger, lemon juice, strips of orange peel, if using, and bay leaves or bouquet garni. Cover and simmer over a low heat for about 20 minutes, until the pumpkin is tender.

5 Discard the orange peel, if using, and the bay leaves or bouquet garni. Cool the soup slightly, then press through a sieve or process in a food processor until smooth. Pour into a clean saucepan.

6 Add the milk and reheat gently. Adjust the seasoning. Garnish with a swirl of cream, unsweetened yogurt, or fromage frais and snipped chives, and serve.

1 Peel the pumpkin, remove the seeds, and then cut the flesh into 1 inch cubes.

2 Melt the butter or margarine in a large, heavy-based saucepan. Add the onion and garlic and fry over a low heat until soft but not colored.

Chicken & Asparagus Soup

This delectable soup is best made with fairly large asparagus with long stems.

NUTRITIONAL INFORMATION

Calories 308   Sugar 5g
Protein ....17g   Fats 24g
Carbohydrates ....7g   Saturates 14g

20 MINS   45 MINS

SERVES 4

I N G R E D I E N T S

12 oz asparagus

2 tsp butter

1 onion, halved and sliced

1 leek, sliced

4 tbsp white rice

4 cups chicken stock

1 bay leaf

⅔ cup heavy cream

6 oz cooked chicken, cut into thin slices

salt and pepper

1 Remove and discard woody bases of the asparagus. Using a vegetable peeler, peel the asparagus stems. Cut off the tips and set aside. Chop the stems into small pieces.

2 Bring a small saucepan of salted water to a boil and drop in the asparagus tips. Cook for 1–2 minutes until

bright green and barely tender. If they are large, slice in half lengthways. Reserve the asparagus tips.

3 Heat the butter in a large saucepan over a medium heat and add the onion and leek. Cover and cook for 3–4 minutes, stirring frequently, until the onion is soft.

4 Add the asparagus stems, rice, stock, and bay leaf with a pinch of salt. Bring just to a boil, reduce the heat, cover, and simmer for 30–35 minutes or until the rice and vegetables are very soft. Remove the bay leaf.

5 Allow the soup to cool slightly, then transfer to a blender or food processor and purée until smooth, working in batches if necessary. (If using a food processor, strain off the cooking liquid and reserve. Purée the soup solids with enough cooking liquid to moisten them, then combine with the remaining liquid.)

6 Return the soup to the saucepan and place over a medium-low heat. Stir in the chicken and reserved asparagus tips, then the cream. Taste and adjust the seasoning, adding salt, if needed, and pepper. Simmer for 5–10 minutes until heated through, stirring occasionally. Ladle the soup into warm bowls and serve.

Chicken, Leek, & Celery Soup

This gently flavored pale green soup is well balanced and very satisfying. It is suitable either for a starter or light lunch.

NUTRITIONAL INFORMATION

Calories	258	Sugars	.........3g
Protein	........19g	Fat	..........12g
Carbohydrate	...20g	Saturates	......6g

15 MINS   1¼ HOURS

SERVES 4

INGREDIENTS

cups chicken stock

bay leaf

oz skinless boned chicken breast

tbsp all-purpose flour

tsp butter

small onion, finely chopped

large leeks, including green parts, thinly sliced

celery stalks, peeled and thinly sliced

tbsp heavy cream

eshly grated nutmeg

alt and pepper

esh cilantro leaves or parsley, to garnish

1 Heat the stock in a small saucepan with the bay leaf until it is steaming. Add the chicken breast and simmer gently for 20 minutes, or until firm to the touch. Discard the bay leaf. Remove the chicken and, when cool enough to handle, cut into small cubes.

2 Put the flour in a bowl. Very slowly whisk in enough of the stock to make a smooth liquid, adding about half the chicken stock.

3 Heat the butter in a heavy-bottomed saucepan over a medium-low heat. Add the onion, leeks, and half of the celery. Cook for about 5 minutes, stirring frequently, until the leeks begin to soften.

4 Slowly pour in the flour and stock mixture and bring to a boil, stirring constantly. Stir in the remaining stock, with a large pinch of salt if it is unsalted. Reduce the heat, cover, and cook gently for about 25 minutes until the vegetables are tender.

5 Allow the soup to cool slightly, then transfer to a blender or food processor and purée until smooth, working in batches, if necessary. (If using a food processor, strain off the cooking liquid and reserve for later. Purée the soup solids with enough cooking liquid to moisten them, then combine with the remaining liquid.)

6 Return the soup to the saucepan and stir in the cream and nutmeg. Season with salt, if needed, and pepper. Place over a medium-low heat. Add the chicken breast and remaining celery to the soup. Simmer for about 15 minutes, until the celery is just tender, stirring occasionally. Taste and adjust the seasoning, ladle into warm bowls and sprinkle with cilantro or parsley.

Lentil & Parsnip Pottage

Smooth and delicious, this soup has the most glorious golden color and a fabulous flavor.

NUTRITIONAL INFORMATION

Calories	82	Sugars	........4g
Protein	.........6g	Fat	...........1g
Carbohydrate	...13g	Saturates	.....0.3g

5 MINS   55 MINS

SERVES 4

INGREDIENTS

3 slices lean sliced bacon, chopped

1 onion, chopped

2 carrots, chopped

2 parsnips, chopped

⅓ cup red lentils

4 cups vegetable stock or water

salt and pepper

chopped fresh chives to garnish

1 Heat a large saucepan, add the bacon and dry-fry for 5 minutes until crisp and golden.

2 Add the onion, carrots, and parsnips and cook for about 5 minutes without browning.

3 Add the lentils to the saucepan and stir to mix with the vegetables.

4 Add the stock or water to the pan and bring to a boil. Cover and simmer for 30–40 minutes until tender.

5 Transfer the soup to a blender or food processor and blend for about 15 seconds until smooth. Alternatively, press the soup through a strainer.

6 Return to the saucepan and reheat gently until almost boiling.

7 Season the soup with salt and pepper to taste.

8 Garnish the lentil and parsnip pottage with chopped fresh chives and serve at once.

COOK'S TI

For a meatier soup, use knuckle of ham in place of t streaky bacon. Cook it for 1½-hours before adding the vegetabl and lentils and use the ham's cooki liquid as the sto

Beef & Vegetable Soup

This comforting broth is perfect for a cold day and is just as delicious made with lean lamb or pork surloin.

NUTRITIONAL INFORMATION

Calories 138   Sugars 2g
Protein ....13g   Fat 3g
Carbohydrate ...15g   Saturates 1g

🍲 12 HOURS   🕐 1 ¼ HOURS

SERVES 4

I N G R E D I E N T S

cup pearl barley, soaked overnight

cups beef stock

tsp dried mixed herbs

oz lean rump or sirloin beef

large carrot, diced

leek, shredded

medium onion, chopped

celery sticks, sliced

lt and pepper

tbsp fresh parsley, chopped, to garnish

usty bread, to serve

1 Place the pearl barley in a large saucepan. Pour over the stock and dd the mixed herbs. Bring to a boil, cover nd simmer gently over a low heat for 10 inutes.

VARIATION

vegetarian version can be ade by omitting the beef and eef stock and using vegetable ock instead. Just before serving, ir in 6 oz fresh bean curd, rained and diced.

2 Meanwhile, trim any fat from the beef and cut the meat into thin strips.

3 Skim away any scum that has risen to the top of the stock with a flat ladle.

4 Add the beef, carrot, leek, onion, and celery to the pan. Bring back to a boil, cover and simmer for about 1 hour or until the barley, meat, and vegetables are just tender.

5 Skim away any remaining scum that has risen to the top of the soup with a flat ladle. Blot the surface with absorbent paper towels to remove any fat. Adjust the seasoning according to taste.

6 Ladle the soup into warm bowls and sprinkle with freshly chopped parsley. Serve very hot, accompanied with crusty bread.

Chunky Potato & Beef Soup

This is a real winter warmer—pieces of tender beef and chunky mixed vegetables are cooked in a liquor flavored with sherry.

NUTRITIONAL INFORMATION

Calories 187	Sugars 3g	
Protein 14g	Fat 9g	
Carbohydrate ...12g	Saturates 2g	

5 MINS   35 MINS

SERVES 4

INGREDIENTS

2 tbsp vegetable oil

8 oz lean braising or frying steak, cut into strips

8 oz new potatoes, halved

1 carrot, diced

2 celery stalks, sliced

2 leeks, sliced

3¾ cups beef stock

8 baby-corn-on-the-cobs, sliced

1 bouquet garni

2 tbsp dry sherry

salt and pepper

chopped fresh parsley, to garnish

1 Heat the vegetable oil in a large saucepan.

2 Add the strips of meat to the saucepan and cook for 3 minutes, turning constantly.

3 Add the halved potatoes, diced carrot, sliced celery, and leeks. Cook for a further 5 minutes, stirring.

4 Pour the beef stock into the saucepan and bring to a boil. Reduce the heat until the liquid is simmering, then add the sliced baby-corn-on-the-cobs and the bouquet garni.

5 Cook the soup for a further 20 minutes or until cooked through.

6 Remove the bouquet garni from the saucepan and discard. Stir the dry sherry into the soup and then season to taste with salt and pepper.

7 Pour the soup into warmed bowls and garnish with the chopped fresh parsley. Serve at once with crusty bread.

COOK'S TI

Make double the quantity soup and freeze the remainder in rigid container for later use. Whe ready to use, leave in the refrigerat to defrost thoroughly, the heat until very ho

entil & Ham Soup

This is a good hearty soup, based on a stock made from a ham knuckle, with plenty of vegetables and red lentils to thicken it and add flavor.

NUTRITIONAL INFORMATION

Calories 219   Sugars 4g
Protein . . . . .17g   Fat 3g
Carbohydrate . . .33g   Saturates 1g

2¹/₄ HOURS   1³/₄ HOURS

SERVES 4–6

INGREDIENTS

cup red lentils

cups stock or water

onions, chopped

garlic clove, minced

large carrots, chopped

lean ham knuckle or 6 oz lean bacon, chopped

large tomatoes, skinned and chopped

fresh or dried bay leaves

oz potatoes, chopped

tbsp white wine vinegar

tsp ground allspice

alt and pepper

hopped scallions or chopped fresh parsley, to garnish

occasionally to prevent the lentils from sticking to the bottom of the pan.

4 Add the potatoes and continue to simmer for about 20 minutes until the potatoes and ham knuckle are tender.

5 Discard the bay leaves. Remove the knuckle and chop ¾ cup of the meat and reserve. If liked, press half the soup through a strainer or blend in a food processor or blender until smooth. Return to the pan with the rest of the soup.

6 Adjust the seasoning, add the vinegar and allspice and the reserved chopped ham. Simmer gently for a further 5–10 minutes. Serve sprinkled liberally with spring scallions or chopped parsley.

1 Put the lentils and stock or water in a saucepan and leave to soak or 1–2 hours.

2 Add the onions, garlic, carrots, ham knuckle or bacon, tomatoes, bay aves, and seasoning.

3 Bring the mixture in the saucepan to a boil, cover, and simmer for about 1 our until the lentils are tender, stirring

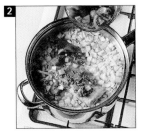

Lamb & Barley Broth

Warming and nutritious, this broth is perfect for a cold winter's day. The slow cooking allows you to use one of the cheaper cuts of meat.

NUTRITIONAL INFORMATION

Calories	304	Sugars	........4g
Protein	........29g	Fat	..........14g
Carbohydrate	...16g	Saturates	......6g

 15 MINS   2¼ HOURS

SERVES 4

I N G R E D I E N T S

1 tbsp vegetable oil

1 lb lean neck of lamb

1 large onion, sliced

2 carrots, sliced

2 leeks, sliced

4 cups vegetable stock

1 bay leaf

few sprigs of fresh parsley

⅓ cup pearl barley

1 Heat the vegetable oil in a large, heavy-bottomed saucepan and add the pieces of lamb, turning them to seal and brown on both sides.

2 Lift the lamb out of the pan and set aside until required.

3 Add the onion, carrots, and leeks to the saucepan and cook gently for about 3 minutes.

4 Return the lamb to the saucepan and add the vegetable stock, bay leaf, parsley, and pearl barley to the saucepan.

5 Bring the mixture in the pan to a boil, then reduce the heat. Cover and simmer for 1½–2 hours.

6 Discard the parsley sprigs. Lift the pieces of lamb from the broth and allow them to cool slightly.

7 Remove the bones and any fat and chop the meat. Return the lamb to the broth and reheat gently.

8 Ladle the lamb and parsley broth into warmed bowls and serve immediately.

COOK'S TIP

This broth will taste even better if made the day before, as this allows the flavors to fully develop. It also means that any fat will solidify on the surface so you can then lift it off. Keep the broth in the refrigerator until required.

Chicken & Leek Soup

This satisfying soup can be served as a main course. You can add rice and bell peppers to make it even more hearty, as well as colorful.

NUTRITIONAL INFORMATION

Calories	...183	Sugar	...4g
Protein	...21g	Fats	...9g
Carbohydrates	...4g	Saturates	...5g

   5 MINS   1¹/₄ HOURS

SERVES 4–6

INGREDIENTS

tbsp butter

oz boneless chicken

oz leeks, cut into 1-inch pieces

cups fresh chicken stock
(see page 14)

bouquet garni enevelope

pitted prunes, halved

salt and white pepper

cooked rice and diced bell peppers
(optional)

1 Melt the butter in a large saucepan.

2 Add the chicken and leeks to the saucepan and fry for 8 minutes.

3 Add the chicken stock and bouquet garni envelope and stir well.

4 Season well with salt and pepper to taste.

5 Bring the soup to a boil and simmer for 45 minutes.

6 Add the prunes to the saucepan with some cooked rice and diced bell peppers (if using) and simmer for about 20 minutes.

7 Remove the bouquet garni from the soup and discard. Serve the chicken and leek soup immediately.

VARIATION

Instead of the bouquet garni envelope, you can use a bunch of fresh mixed herbs, tied together with string. Choose herbs such as parsley, thyme, and rosemary.

Partan Bree

This traditional Scottish soup is thickened with a purée of rice and crab meat cooked in milk. Add sour cream, if liked, at the end of cooking.

NUTRITIONAL INFORMATION

Calories 112   Sugars 5g
Protein . . . . .7g   Fat 2g
Carbohydrate . . .18g   Saturates 0.3g

 1 HOUR   🕐 35 MINS

SERVES 6

I N G R E D I E N T S

1 medium-sized boiled crab

scant ½ cup long-grain rice

2½ cups skimmed milk

2½ cups Fish Stock
   (see page 15)

1 tbsp anchovy paste

2 tsp lime or lemon juice

1 tbsp chopped fresh parsley or I tsp
   chopped fresh thyme

3–4 tbsp sour cream (optional)

salt and pepper

snipped chives, to garnish

1 Remove and reserve all the brown and white meat from the crab, then crack the claws and remove and chop that meat; reserve the claw meat.

COOK'S TIP

If you are unable to buy a whole crab, use about 6 oz frozen crab meat and thaw thoroughly before use; or a 6 oz can of crab meat which just needs thorough draining.

2 Put the rice and milk into a saucepan and bring slowly to a boil. Cover and simmer gently for about 20 minutes.

3 Add the reserved white and brown crabmeat and seasoning and simmer for a further 5 minutes.

4 Cool a little, then press through a strainer, or blend in a food processor or blender until smooth.

5 Pour the soup into a clean saucep and add the fish stock and t reserved claw meat. Bring slowly to a bo then add the anchovy paste and lime lemon juice and adjust the seasoning.

6 Simmer for a further 2–3 minute Stir in the parsley or thyme and th swirl sour cream (if using) through ea serving. Garnish with snipped chives.

Smoked Haddock Soup

Smoked haddock gives this soup a wonderfully rich flavor, while the mashed potatoes and cream thicken and enrich the stock.

NUTRITIONAL INFORMATION

Calories	169	Sugars	........8g
Protein	........16g	Fat	..........5g
Carbohydrate	...16g	Saturates	......3g

25 MINS · 40 MINS

SERVES 4–6

INGREDIENTS

8 oz smoked haddock fillet

1 onion, chopped finely

1 garlic clove, minced

2½ cups water

2½ cups skimmed milk

1–1½ cups hot mashed potatoes

2 tbsp butter

about 1 tbsp lemon juice

5 tbsp low-fat unsweetened fromage blanc

4 tbsp fresh parsley, chopped

salt and pepper

1 Put the fish, onion, garlic, and water into a saucepan. Bring to a boil, cover and simmer for 15–20 minutes.

2 Remove the fish from the pan, strip off the skin, and remove all the bones. Flake the flesh finely.

3 Return the skin and bones to the cooking liquor and simmer for 10 minutes. Strain, discarding the skin and bone. Pour the liquor into a clean pan.

4 Add the milk, flaked fish, and seasoning to the pan, bring to a boil and simmer for about 3 minutes.

5 Gradually whisk in sufficient mashed potato to give a fairly thick soup, then stir in the butter and sharpen to taste with lemon juice.

6 Add the fromage blanc and 3 tablespoons of the chopped parsley. Reheat gently and adjust the seasoning. Sprinkle with the remaining parsley and serve immediately.

COOK'S TIP

Undyed smoked haddock may be used in place of the bright yellow fish; it will give a paler color but just as much flavor. Alternatively, use smoked cod or smoked whiting.

LOW-FAT SOUPS

Soups are a traditional first course, but served with fresh crusty bread they can also be a satisfying meal in their own right—and, depending on the choice of ingredients—one that is low in calories. For the best results, use homemade stock from the liquid left over from cooking vegetables and the juices from casseroles. Potatoes can also be added to the soup to thicken it as opposed to the traditional thickeners of flour or fat and water.

Cucumber & Tomato Soup

Although this chilled soup is not an authentic Indian dish, it is wonderfu
served as a 'cooler' between hot, spicy courses.

NUTRITIONAL INFORMATION

Calories ....73 Sugar 16g
Protein ....2g Fats 1g
Carbohydrates ...16g Saturates 0.2g

12 HOURS   0 MINS

SERVES 6

INGREDIENTS

4 tomatoes, peeled and seeded

5 oz watermelon, seedless if available

4 inch piece cucumber, peeled and seeded

2 scallions, green part only, chopped

1 tbsp chopped fresh mint

salt and pepper

fresh mint sprigs, to garnish

1 Using a sharp knife, cut 1 tomato into
½ inch dice.

2 Remove the rind from the melon, and
remove the seeds if it is not seedless.

3 Put the 3 remaining tomatoes into
a blender or food processor and,
with the motor running, add the
seeded cucumber, chopped scallions and
watermelon. Blend until smooth.

4 If not using a food processor, push
the seeded watermelon through a
strainer. Stir the diced tomatoes and mint
into the melon mixture. Adjust the
seasoning to taste. Chop the cucumbe
scallions and the 3 remaining tomatoe
finely and add to the melon.

5 Chill the cucumber and tomato sou
overnight in the refrigerator. Chec
the seasoning and transfer to a servin
dish. Garnish with mint sprigs.

COOK'S TIP

Although this soup does improve
if chilled overnight, it is also
delicious as a quick appetizer if
whipped up just before a meal, and
served immediately.

Chilled Cucumber Soup

Serve this soup over ice on a warm summer day as a refreshing starter. It has the fresh tang of yogurt and a dash of spice from the Tabasco sauce.

NUTRITIONAL INFORMATION

Calories 83   Sugars 7g
Protein ....12g   Fat 1g
Carbohydrate ....7g   Saturates 0.3g

1¼ HOURS   0 MINS

SERVES 4

I N G R E D I E N T S

cucumber, peeled and diced

⅔ cups Fresh Fish Stock, chilled (see page 15)

cup tomato juice

cup low-fat unsweetened yogurt

cup low-fat fromage blanc (or double the quantity of yogurt)

½ oz peeled shrimp, thawed if frozen, roughly chopped

ew drops Tabasco sauce

tbsp fresh mint, chopped

alt and white pepper

ce cubes, to serve

T O   G A R N I S H

origs of mint

ucumber slices

hole peeled shrimp

1 Place the diced cucumber in a blender or food processor and work for a few seconds until smooth. Alternatively, chop the cucumber finely and push through a strainer.

2 Transfer the cucumber to a bowl. Stir in the stock, tomato juice, yogurt, fromage blanc (if using), and shrimp, and mix well.

3 Add the Tabasco sauce and season to taste.

4 Stir in the chopped mint, cover, and chill for at least 2 hours.

5 Ladle the soup into glass bowls and add a few ice cubes. Serve garnished with mint, cucumber slices, and whole shrimp.

VARIATION

nstead of shrimp, dd white crabmeat or ground nicken. For a vegetarian version of is soup, omit the shrimp and add n extra 4½ oz finely diced ucumber. Use fresh vegetable stock stead of fish stock.

Beet & Potato Soup

A deep red soup makes a stunning first course. Adding a swirl of sour cream and a few sprigs of dill gives a very pretty effect.

NUTRITIONAL INFORMATION

Calories 120	Sugars 11g
Protein 4g	Fat 2g
Carbohydrate . . .22g	Saturates 1g

20 MINS   30 MINS

SERVES 6

I N G R E D I E N T S

1 onion, chopped

12 oz potatoes, diced

1 small cooking apple, peeled, cored, and grated

3 tbsp water

1 tsp cumin seeds

1 lb cooked beet, peeled and diced

1 dried bay leaf

pinch of dried thyme

1 tsp lemon juice

2½ cups hot vegetable stock

4 tbsp sour cream

salt and pepper

few sprigs of fresh dill, to garnish

1 Place the onion, potatoes, apple, and water in a large bowl. Cover and cook on HIGH power for 10 minutes.

2 Stir in the cumin seeds and cook on HIGH power for 1 minute.

3 Stir in the beet, bay leaf, thyme, lemon juice, and stock. Cover and cook on HIGH power for 12 minutes, stirring halfway through. Leave to stand, uncovered, for 5 minutes.

4 Remove and discard the bay leaf. Strain the vegetables and reserve the liquid in a pitcher.

5 Purée the vegetables with a little of the reserved liquid in a food processor or blender, until they are smooth and creamy. Alternatively, either mash the soup or press it through a strainer.

6 Pour the vegetable purée into a clea bowl with the reserved liquid and m well. Season with salt and pepper to tast Cover and cook on HIGH power for 4- minutes until very hot.

7 Serve the soup in warmed bowl Swirl 1 tablespoon of sour cream in each serving and garnish with a few spri of fresh dill.

Yogurt & Spinach Soup

Whole young spinach leaves add vibrant color to this unusual soup.
Serve with hot, crusty bread for a nutritious light meal.

NUTRITIONAL INFORMATION

Calories	227	Sugars	........13g
Protein	........14g	Fat	...........7g
Carbohydrate	...29g	Saturates	......2g

15 MINS   30 MINS

SERVES 4

INGREDIENTS

½ cups chicken stock

tbsp long-grain rice, rinsed and drained

tbsp water

tbsp cornstarch

½ cups low-fat unsweetened yogurt

ice of 1 lemon

egg yolks, lightly beaten

2 oz young spinach leaves, washed and drained

alt and pepper

1 Pour the stock into a large pan, season and bring to a boil. Add the ce and simmer for 10 minutes, until arely cooked. Remove from the heat.

2 Combine the water and cornstarch to make a smooth paste.

3 Pour the yogurt into a second pan and stir in the cornstarch mixture. Set he pan over a low heat and bring the ogurt slowly to a boil, stirring with a ooden spoon in one direction only. This ill stabilize the yogurt and prevent it om separating or curdling on contact ith the hot stock. When the yogurt has ached boiling point, stand the pan on a heat diffuser and leave to simmer slowly for 10 minutes. Remove the pan from the heat and allow the mixture to cool slightly before stirring in the beaten egg yolks.

4 Pour the yogurt mixture into the stock, stir in the lemon juice and stir to blend thoroughly. Keep the soup warm, but do not allow it to boil.

5 Blanch the washed and drained spinach leaves in a large pan of boiling, salted water for 2–3 minutes until they begin to soften but have not wilted. Tip the spinach into a colander, drain well, and stir it into the soup. Let the spinach warm through. Taste the soup and adjust the seasoning if necessary. Serve in wide shallow soup plates, with hot, fresh crusty bread.

Red Lentil Soup with Yogurt

Tasty red lentil soup flavored with chopped cilantro. The yogurt adds a light piquancy to the soup .

NUTRITIONAL INFORMATION

Calories 280   Sugars 6g
Protein ....17g   Fat 7g
Carbohydrate ...40g   Saturates 4g

 5 MINS   30 MINS

SERVES 4

INGREDIENTS

2 tbsp butter

1 onion, chopped finely

1 celery stalk, chopped finely

1 large carrot, grated

1 dried bay leaf

1 cup red lentils

5 cups hot vegetable or chicken stock

2 tbsp chopped fresh cilantro

4 tbsp low-fat unsweetened yogurt

salt and pepper

fresh cilantro sprigs, to garnish

1 Place the butter, onion, and celery in a large bowl. Cover and cook on HIGH power for 3 minutes.

2 Add the carrot, bay leaf, and lentils. Pour over the stock. Cover and cook on HIGH power for 15 minutes, stirring halfway through.

3 Remove from the microwave oven and stand, covered, for 5 minutes.

4 Remove the bay leaf, then blend in batches in a food processor, until smooth. Alternatively, press the soup through a strainer.

5 Pour into a clean bowl. Season with salt and pepper to taste and stir in the cilantro. Cover and cook on HIGH power for 4–5 minutes until very hot.

6 Serve in warmed bowls. Stir 1 tablespoon of yogurt into each serving and garnish with sprigs of fresh cilantro.

COOK'S T

For an extra creamy soup t adding low-fat crème fraîche or so cream instead of yogu

Spicy Lentil Soup

For a warming, satisfying meal on a cold day, this lentil dish is packed full of taste and goodness.

NUTRITIONAL INFORMATION

Calories 155   Sugars 4g
Protein . . . . .11g   Fat 3g
Carbohydrate . . .22g   Saturates 0.4g

1 HOUR   1¼ HOURS

SERVES 4

INGREDIENTS

cup red lentils

tsp vegetable oil

large onion, chopped finely

garlic cloves, minced

tsp ground cumin

tsp ground coriander

tsp garam masala

tbsp tomato paste

½ cups Fresh Vegetable Stock
(see page 14)

bout 12 oz can corn, drained

alt and pepper

TO SERVE

w-fat unsweetened yogurt

hopped fresh parsley

armed pocket bread

1 Rinse the red lentils in cold water. Drain the lentils well and put to ne side.

2 Heat the oil in a large non-stick saucepan and fry the onion and garlic ently until soft but not browned.

3 Stir in the cumin, coriander, garam masala, tomato paste and 4 ablespoons of the stock. Mix well and mmer gently for 2 minutes.

4 Add the lentils and pour in the remaining stock. Bring to a boil, reduce the heat and simmer, covered, for 1 hour until the lentils are tender and the soup thickened. Stir in the corn and heat through for 5 minutes. Season well.

5 Ladle into warmed soup bowls and top each with a spoonful of yogurt and a sprinkling of parsley. Serve with warmed pocket bread.

COOK'S TIP

Many of the ready-prepared ethnic breads available today either contain fat or are brushed with oil before baking. Always check the ingredients list for fat content.

Mushroom & Ginger Soup

Thai soups are very quickly and easily put together, and are cooked so that each ingredient can still be tasted in the finished dish.

NUTRITIONAL INFORMATION

Calories ....74 Sugars 1g
Protein ....3g Fat 3g
Carbohydrate ....9g Saturates 0.4g

  1½ HOURS   15 MINS

SERVES 4

INGREDIENTS

¼ cup dried shiitake mushrooms or
  1⅓ cups field or crimini mushrooms

4 cups hot fresh vegetable stock
  (see page 14)

4½ oz thread egg noodles

2 tsp sunflower oil

3 garlic cloves, minced

1 inch piece ginger, shredded finely

½ tsp mushroom catsup

1 tsp light soy sauce

2 cups mung bean sprouts

cilantro leaves, to garnish

1 Soak the dried shiitake mushrooms (if using) for at least 30 minutes in 1¼ cups of the hot vegetable stock. Remove the stalks and discard, then slice the mushrooms. Reserve the stock.

2 Cook the noodles for 2–3 minutes in boiling water. Drain and rinse. Set them aside.

3 Heat the oil over a high heat in a wok or large, heavy skillet. Add the garlic and ginger, stir and add the mushrooms. Stir over a high heat for 2 minutes.

4 Add the remaining vegetable stock with the reserved stock and bring to a boil. Add the mushroom catsup and soy sauce.

5 Stir in the bean sprouts and cook until tender. Put some noodles in each bowl and ladle the soup on top. Garnish with cilantro leaves and serve immediately.

COOK'S TIP

Rice noodles contain no fat and are ideal for anyone on a low-fat diet.

Carrot & Cumin Soup

Carrot soups are very popular and here cumin, tomato, potato, and celery give the soup both richness and depth.

NUTRITIONAL INFORMATION

Calories 114   Sugars 8g
Protein . . . . .3g   Fat 6g
Carbohydrate . . .12g   Saturates 4g

2½ HOURS   45 MINS

SERVES 4–6

I N G R E D I E N T S

tbsp butter or margarine

large onion, chopped

-2 garlic cloves, minced

oz carrots, sliced

cups Chicken or Vegetable Stock
(see page 15)

tsp ground cumin

celery stalks, sliced thinly

oz potato, diced

tsp tomato paste

tsp lemon juice

fresh or dried bay leaves

out 1¼ cups skimmed milk

lt and pepper

lery leaves to garnish

1 Melt the butter or margarine in a large saucepan. Add the onion and garlic and fry very gently until the onion begins to soften.

2 Add the carrots and continue to fry gently for a further 5 minutes, stirring frequently and taking care they do not brown.

3 Add the stock, cumin, seasoning, celery, potato, tomato paste, lemon juice, and bay leaves and bring to a boil. Cover and simmer gently for about 30 minutes until all the vegetables are very tender.

4 Discard the bay leaves, cool the soup a little, and then press it through a strainer or blend in a food processor or blender until smooth.

5 Pour the soup into a clean pan, add the milk and bring slowly to a boil. Taste and adjust the seasoning.

6 Garnish each serving with a small celery leaf and serve.

OOK'S TIP

is soup can be frozen
r up to 3 months. Add the
lk when reheating.

Consommé

A traditional clear soup made from beef bones and lean ground beef. Thin strips of vegetables provide a colorful garnish.

NUTRITIONAL INFORMATION

Calories 109	Sugars 6g
Protein 13g	Fat 3g
Carbohydrate 7g	Saturates 1g

6¼ HOURS   1¼ HOURS

SERVES 4–6

INGREDIENTS

5 cups strong beef stock

1 cup extra lean ground beef

2 tomatoes, skinned, seeded, and chopped

2 large carrots, chopped

1 large onion, chopped

2 celery storks, chopped

1 turnip, chopped (optional)

1 Bouquet Garni

2–3 egg whites

shells of 2–4 eggs, crushed

1–2 tbsp sherry (optional)

salt and pepper

Melba Toast, to serve

TO GARNISH

julienne strips of raw carrot, turnip, celery, or celeriac or a one-egg omelet, cut into julienne strips

1 Put the stock and ground beef in a saucepan. Leave for 1 hour. Add the tomatoes, carrots, onion, celery, turnip (if using), bouquet garni, 2 of the egg whites, the crushed shells of 2 of the eggs, and plenty of seasoning. Bring to almost boiling point, whisking hard all the time with a flat whisk.

2 Cover and simmer for 1 hour, taking care not to allow the layer of froth on top of the soup to break.

3 Pour the soup through a jelly bag, keeping the froth back until the last, then pour the ingredients through the cloth again into a clean pan. The resulting liquid should be clear.

4 If the soup is not quite clear, return to the pan with another egg whi and the crushed shells of 2 more egg Repeat the whisking process as before a then boil for 10 minutes; strain again.

5 Add the sherry (if using) to the so and reheat gently. Place the garni in the warmed soup bowls and carefu pour in the soup. Serve with melba toast

Bacon, Bean, & Garlic Soup

A mouth-wateringly healthy vegetable, bean, and bacon soup with a garlic flavor. Serve with granary or whole-wheat bread.

NUTRITIONAL INFORMATION

Calories 261	Sugars 5g	
Protein 23g	Fat 8g	
Carbohydrate . . .25g	Saturates 2g	

 5 MINS   20 MINS

SERVES 4

I N G R E D I E N T S

oz lean smoked Canadian bacon slices

carrot, sliced thinly

celery stalk, sliced thinly

onion, chopped

tbsp oil

garlic cloves, sliced

cups hot vegetable stock

oz can chopped tomatoes

tbsp chopped fresh thyme

bout 14 oz can cannellini beans, drained

tbsp tomato paste

alt and pepper

rated Cheddar cheese, to garnish

COOK'S TIP

r a more substantial soup add
oz cup small pasta shapes or short
ngths of spaghetti when you add
e stock and tomatoes. You will
so need to add an extra $^2/_3$ cup
getable stock.

1 Chop 2 slices of the bacon and place in a bowl. Cook on HIGH power for 3–4 minutes until the fat runs out and the bacon is well cooked. Stir the bacon halfway through cooking to separate the pieces. Transfer to a plate lined with paper towels and leave to cool. When cool, the bacon pieces should be crisp and dry. Place the carrot, celery, onion, and oil in a large bowl. Cover and cook on HIGH power for 4 minutes.

2 Chop the remaining bacon and add to the bowl with the garlic. Cover and cook on HIGH power for 2 minutes.

3 Add the stock, the contents of the can of tomatoes, the thyme, beans, and tomato paste. Cover and cook on HIGH power for 8 minutes, stirring halfway through. Season to taste. Ladle the soup into warmed bowls and sprinkle with the crisp bacon and grated cheese.

Special Occasion Soups

The selection of soups in this chapter offers something a little different. Special occasion soups are appropriate for entertaining, either because of their festive ingredients or their suitability for an informal gathering, or perhaps because they requires a little more preparation time than a family supper normally demands. The cold soups included in the chapter are also great for special occasions and home entertaining, and are equally welcome on a hot summer's day as a refreshing treat.

Minted Pea & Yogurt Soup

A deliciously refreshing, summery soup that is full of goodness. It is also extremely tasty served chilled.

NUTRITIONAL INFORMATION

Calories	208	Sugars	.........9g
Protein	........10g	Fat	...........7g
Carbohydrate	...26g	Saturates	.......2g

 15 MINS   25 MINS

SERVES 6

I N G R E D I E N T S

2 tbsp vegetable ghee or sunflower oil

2 onions, coarsely chopped

8 oz potato, coarsely chopped

2 garlic cloves, minced

1 inch gingerroot, chopped

1 tsp ground coriander

1 tsp ground cumin

1 tbsp all-purpose flour

3½ cups vegetable stock

1 lb frozen English peas

2-3 tbsp chopped mint

salt and pepper

⅔ cup strained Greek yogurt,
   plus extra to serve

½ tsp cornstarch

1¼ cups milk

mint sprigs, to garnish

1 Heat the vegetable ghee or sunflower oil in a saucepan, add the onions and potato and cook over a low heat, stirring occasionally, for about 3 minutes, until the onion is soft and translucent.

2 Stir in the garlic, ginger, coriander, cumin, and flour and cook, stirring constantly, for 1 minute.

3 Add the vegetable stock, peas, and the chopped mint and bring to a boil, stirring. Reduce the heat, cover, and simmer gently for 15 minutes, or until the vegetables are tender.

4 Process the soup, in batches, in a blender or food processor. Return the mixture to the pan and season with salt and pepper to taste. Blend the yogurt wi the cornstarch to a smooth paste and s into the soup.

5 Add the milk and bring almost to boil, stirring constantly. Cook ve gently for 2 minutes. Serve the soup h garnished with the mint sprigs and a sw of extra yogurt.

Stilton & Walnut Soup

Full of flavor, this rich and creamy soup is very simple to make and utterly delicious to eat.

NUTRITIONAL INFORMATION

Calories 392	Sugars 8g	
Protein 15g	Fat 30g	
Carbohydrate ...15g	Saturates 16g	

10 MINS   30 MINS

SERVES 4

I N G R E D I E N T S

tbsp butter

shallots, chopped

celery stalks, chopped

garlic clove, minced

tbsp all-purpose flour

cups vegetable stock

cups milk

cups blue Stilton cheese, crumbled, plus extra to garnish

tbsp walnut halves, roughly chopped

cup unsweetened yogurt

t and pepper

opped celery leaves, to garnish

1 Melt the butter in a large, heavy-bottomed saucepan and sauté the shallots, celery, and garlic, stirring occasionally, for 2–3 minutes, until soft.

2 Lower the heat, add the flour and cook, stirring constantly, for 30 seconds.

3 Gradually stir in the vegetable stock and milk and bring to a boil.

4 Reduce the heat to a gentle simmer and add the crumbled blue Stilton cheese and walnut halves. Cover and simmer for 20 minutes.

5 Stir in the yogurt and heat through for a further 2 minutes without boiling.

6 Season the soup to taste with salt and pepper, then transfer to a warm soup tureen or individual serving bowls, garnish with chopped celery leaves and extra crumbled blue Stilton cheese and serve at once.

COOK'S TIP

well as adding protein, amins, and useful fats to the t, nuts add important flavor d texture to vegetarian meals.

Carrot & Almond Soup

Carrots and almonds have a natural affinity that is obvious in this soup.

NUTRITIONAL INFORMATION

Calories	313	Sugars	........11g
Protein	........10g	Fat	.........23g
Carbohydrate	...17g	Saturates	......2g

 15 MINS   55 MINS

SERVES 4

I N G R E D I E N T S

2 tsp olive oil

1 onion, finely chopped

1 leek, thinly sliced

1 lb carrots, thinly sliced

6 cups water

1¾ oz soft white bread crumbs

1½ cups ground almonds

1 tbsp fresh lemon juice, or to taste

salt and pepper

snipped fresh chives, to garnish

3 Soak the bread crumbs in cold water to cover for 2–3 minutes, then strain them and press out the remaining water.

4 Put the almonds and bread crumbs in a blender or food processor with a ladleful of the carrot cooking water and purée until smooth and paste-like.

5 Transfer the soup vegetables and remaining cooking liquid to the blender or food processor and purée until smooth, working in batches if necessary. (If using a food processor, strain off the cooking liquid and reserve. Purée the soup solids with enough cooking liquid to moisten them, then combine with the remaining liquid.)

6 Return the soup to the saucepan and simmer over a low heat, stirring occasionally, until heated through. Add lemon juice, salt, and pepper to taste. Ladle the soup into warm bowls, garnish with chives and serve.

1 Heat the oil in a large saucepan over a medium heat and add the onion and leek. Cover and cook for about 3 minutes, stirring occasionally, until just soft; do not allow them to brown.

2 Add the carrots and water and season with a little salt and pepper. Bring to a boil, reduce the heat, and simmer gently, partially covered, for about 45 minutes until the vegetables are tender.

Avocado & Mint Soup

A rich and creamy pale green soup made with avocados and enhanced by a touch of chopped mint. Serve chilled in summer or hot in winter.

NUTRITIONAL INFORMATION

Calories 199	Sugars 3g
Protein 3g	Fat 18g
Carbohydrate 7g	Saturates 6g

 15 MINS   35 MINS

SERVES 6

I N G R E D I E N T S

tbsp butter or margarine

scallions, sliced

garlic clove, minced

cup all-purpose flour

½ cups vegetable stock

ripe avocados

–3 tsp lemon juice

nch of grated lemon rind

cup milk

cup light cream

–1½ tbsp chopped mint

lt and pepper

int sprigs, to garnish

MINTED GARLIC BREAD

cup butter

–2 tbsp chopped mint

–2 garlic cloves, minced

whole wheat or

white French bread stick

1 Melt the butter or margarine in a large, heavy-bottomed saucepan. Add e scallions and garlic clove and fry over low heat, stirring occasionally, for about minutes, until soft and translucent.

2 Stir in the flour and cook, stirring, for 1–2 minutes. Gradually stir in the stock, then bring to a boil. Simmer gently while preparing the avocados.

3 Peel the avocados, discard the pits and chop coarsely. Add to the soup with the lemon juice and rind and seasoning. Cover and simmer for about 10 minutes, until tender.

4 Cool the soup slightly, then press through a strainer with the back of a spoon or process in a food processor or blender until a smooth purée forms. Pour into a bowl.

5 Stir in the milk and cream, adjust the seasoning, then stir in the mint. Cover and chill thoroughly.

6 To make the minted garlic bread, soften the butter and beat in the mint and garlic. Cut the loaf into slanting slices but leave a hinge on the bottom crust. Spread each slice with the butter and reassemble the loaf. Wrap in foil and place in a preheated oven, 350°F, for about 15 minutes.

7 Serve the soup garnished with a sprig of mint and accompanied by the minted garlic bread.

Lobster Bisque

This rich and elegant starter soup is perfect for a special dinner. The lobster shell, made into a stock, contributes greatly to the flavor.

NUTRITIONAL INFORMATION

Calories ....398 Sugars 6g
Protein ....14g Fat 22g
Carbohydrate ...30g Saturates 14g

20 MINS   50 MINS

SERVES 4

I N G R E D I E N T S

1 lb cooked lobster

3 tbsp butter

1 small carrot, grated

1 celery stalk, finely chopped

1 leek, finely chopped

1 small onion, finely chopped

2 shallots, finely chopped

3 tbsp brandy

¼ cup dry white wine

5 cups water

1 tbsp tomato paste

½ cup whipping cream, or to taste

6 tbsp all-purpose flour

salt and pepper

snipped fresh chives, to garnish

1 Pull off the lobster tail. With the legs up, cut the body in half lengthways. Scoop out the tomalley (the soft pale greenish-grey part) and, if it is a female, the roe (the solid red-orange part). Reserve these together, covered and refrigerated. Remove the meat and cut into bite-sized pieces; cover and refrigerate. Chop the shell into large pieces.

2 Melt half the butter in a large saucepan over a medium heat and add the lobster shell pieces. Fry until brown bits begin to stick on the bottom of the pan. Add the carrot, celery, leek, onion, and shallots. Cook, stirring, for 1½–2 minutes (do not let it burn). Add the alcohol and bubble for 1 minute. Pour over the water, add the tomato paste, a large pinch of salt, and bring to a boil. Reduce the heat, simmer for 30 minutes and strain the stock, discarding the solids.

3 Melt the remaining butter in a small saucepan and add the tomalley and roe, if any. Add the cream, whisk to mix well, remove from the heat and set aside.

4 Put the flour in a small mixing bowl and very slowly whisk in 2 tablespoons of cold water. Stir in a little of the hot stock mixture to make a smooth liquid.

5 Bring the remaining lobster stock to a boil and whisk in the flour mixture. Boil gently for 4–5 minutes until the soup thickens, stirring frequently. Press the tomalley, roe, and cream mixture through a strainer into the soup. Reduce the heat and add the reserved lobster meat. Simmer gently until heated through.

6 Taste the soup and adjust the seasoning, adding more cream if wished. Ladle into warm bowls, sprinkle with chives, and serve.

Creamy Oyster Soup

This soup makes a rich and elegant starter. Serve it in shallow bowls so the oysters are visible, warm the bowls to keep the soup hot.

NUTRITIONAL INFORMATION

Calories ....299 Sugars 3g
Protein ....3g Fat 24g
Carbohydrate ...16g Saturates 15g

20 MINS   30 MINS

SERVES 4

I N G R E D I E N T S

2 oysters

tbsp butter

shallots, finely chopped

tbsp white wine

¼ cups fish stock

cup whipping or heavy cream

tbsp cornstarch, dissolved in
  2 tbsp cold water

alt and pepper

aviar or lumpfish roe, to garnish (optional)

2 Melt half the butter in a saucepan over a low heat. Add the shallots and cook gently for about 5 minutes until just soft, stirring frequently; do not allow them to brown.

3 Add the wine, bring to a boil and boil for 1 minute. Stir in the fish stock, bring back to a boil and boil for 3–4 minutes. Reduce the heat to a gentle simmer.

4 Add the oysters and their liquid and poach for about 1 minute until they become more firm but are still tender. Remove the oysters with a draining spoon and reserve, covered. Strain the stock.

5 Bring the strained stock to the boil in a clean saucepan. Add the cream and bring back to a boil.

6 Stir the dissolved cornstarch into the soup and boil gently for 2–3 minutes, stirring frequently, until slightly thickened. Add the oysters and cook for I–2 minutes to reheat them. Taste and adjust the seasoning, if necessary, and ladle the soup into warm bowls. Top each serving with a teaspoon of caviar or roe, if using.

1 To open the oysters, hold flat-side up, over a strainer set over a bowl to atch the juices, and push an oyster knife to the hinge. Work it around until you an pry off the top shell. When all the ysters have been opened, strain the liquid hrough a strainer lined with damp heesecloth. Remove any bits of shell tuck to the oysters and reserve them in heir liquid.

Bouillabaisse

This soup makes a festive seafood extravaganza worthy of a special celebration.

NUTRITIONAL INFORMATION

Calories	432	Sugar	.........9g
Protein	........43g	Fats	..........20g
Carbohydrates	...21g	Saturates	......3g

20 MINS   1 HOUR

SERVES 4

INGREDIENTS

450 g/1 lb king prawns (large shrimp)

750 g/1 lb 10 oz lb firm white fish fillets, such as sea bass, snapper and monkfish

4 tbsp olive oil

grated rind of 1 orange

1 large garlic clove, finely chopped

½ tsp chilli purée (paste) or harissa

1 large leek, sliced

1 onion, halved and sliced

1 red (bell) pepper, cored, deseeded and sliced

3–4 tomatoes, cored and cut into eighths

4 garlic cloves, sliced

1 bay leaf

pinch of saffron threads

½ tsp fennel seeds

600 ml/1 pint/2½ cups water

1.2 litres/2 pints/5 cups fish stock

1 fennel bulb, finely chopped

1 large onion, finely chopped

225 g/8 oz potatoes, peeled, halved and thinly sliced

250 g/9 oz scallops

salt and pepper

toasted French bread slices, to serve

ready-prepared aioli (garlic mayonnaise), to serve

1 Peel the prawns (shrimp) and reserve the shells. Cut the fish fillets into serving pieces about 5 cm/2 inches square. Trim off any ragged edges and reserve. Put the fish in a bowl with 2 tablespoons of the olive oil, the orange rind, crushed garlic and chilli purée (paste) or harissa. Turn to coat well, cover and chill the prawns (shrimp) and fish separately.

2 Heat 1 tablespoon of the olive oil in a large saucepan over a medium heat. Add the leek, sliced onion and red (bell) pepper. Cover and cook for about 5 minutes, stirring frequently, until the onion softens. Stir in the tomatoes, sliced garlic, bay leaf, saffron, fennel seeds, prawn (shrimp) shells, water and fish stock. Bring to the boil, reduce the heat and simmer, covered, for 30 minutes. Strain the stock, pressing with the back of a spoon to extract all the liquid.

3 To finish the soup, heat the remaining olive oil in a large saucepan. Add the fennel and finely chopped onion and cook for 4–5 minutes until the onion softens, stirring frequently. Add the stock and potatoes and bring to the boil. Reduce the heat slightly, cover and cook for 12–15 minutes, or until the potatoes are just tender.

4 Adjust the heat so the soup simmers gently and add the fish, starting with any thicker pieces and putting in the thinner ones after 2 or 3 minutes. Add the prawns (shrimp) and scallops and continue simmering gently until all the seafood is cooked and opaque throughout.

5 Taste the soup and adjust the seasoning. Ladle into warm bowls. Spread the garlic sauce on the toasted bread slices and arrange on top of the soup.

Cioppino

This tomato-based Californian soup is brimming with seafood, which can be varied according to availability. Serve it with olive bread or ciabatta.

NUTRITIONAL INFORMATION

Calories 211	Sugar 7g
Protein 26g	Fats 4g
Carbohydrates . . .10g	Saturates 1g

20 MINS   1¼ HOURS

SERVES 4

INGREDIENTS

00 g/1 lb 2 oz mussels

00 g/1 lb 2 oz clams, rinsed

00 ml/10 fl oz/1¼ cups dry
  white wine

tbsp olive oil

large onion, finely chopped

stalk celery, finely chopped

yellow or green (bell) pepper, cored,
  deseeded and finely chopped

00 g/14 oz can chopped tomatoes
  in juice

garlic cloves, very finely chopped

tbsp tomato purée (paste)

bay leaf

50 ml/12 fl oz/1½ cups fish
  stock or water

75 g/6 oz small squid, cleaned and cut
  into small pieces

25 g/8 oz skinless white fish fillets, such
  as cod, sole or haddock

50 g/5½ oz small scallops, or cooked
  shelled prawns (shrimp)

hopped fresh parsley, to garnish

1 Discard any broken mussels and those
  with open shells that do not close
hen tapped. Rinse, pull off any 'beards',
nd if there are barnacles, scrape them
ith a knife under cold running water. Put

the mussels in a large heavy-based saucepan. Cover tightly and cook over a high heat for about 4 minutes, or until the mussels open, shaking the pan occasionally.

2 When cool enough to handle, remove the mussels from the shells, adding any additional juices to the cooking liquid. Strain the cooking liquid through a muslin-lined sieve and reserve.

3 Put the clams into a heavy saucepan with 50 ml/2 fl oz/¼ cup of the wine. Cover tightly, place over a medium-high heat and cook for 2–4 minutes, or until they open. Remove the clams from the shells and strain the cooking liquid through a muslin-lined sieve and reserve.

4 Heat the olive oil in a large saucepan over a medium-low heat. Add the

onion, celery and (bell) pepper and cook for 3–4 minutes, until the onion softens, stirring occasionally. Add the remaining wine, tomatoes, garlic, tomato purée (paste) and bay leaf. Continue cooking for 10 minutes.

5 Stir in the fish stock or water, squid and reserved mussel and clam cooking liquids. Bring to the boil, reduce the heat and simmer for 35–40 minutes until the vegetables and squid are tender.

6 Add the fish, mussels and clams and simmer, stirring occasionally, for about 4 minutes until the fish becomes opaque. Stir in the scallops or prawns (shrimp) and continue simmering for 3–4 minutes until heated through. Remove the bay leaf, ladle into warm bowls and sprinkle with chopped parsley.

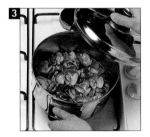  

Bean & Sausage Tureen

The Mexican-style garnishes make this a festive dish for informal entertaining. Include some smoky or spicy sausages for added flavor.

NUTRITIONAL INFORMATION

Calories	.624	Sugar	11g
Protein	34g	Fats	27g
Carbohydrates	65g	Saturates	10g

🥘 20 MINS   🕐 2 HOURS

SERVES 4

INGREDIENTS

3⅔ cups dried black beans

1 tbsp olive oil

2 onions, finely chopped

4 garlic cloves, finely chopped

2 quarts cups water

2 x 14 oz cans plum tomatoes in juice

1 tbsp tomato paste

1 bay leaf

½ tsp ground cumin

¼ tsp dried oregano

½ tsp chili paste

1 lb 9 oz lean sausages

salt and pepper

TO GARNISH

2–3 ripe avocados

3–4 tbsp lime juice

3 tomatoes, skinned, seeded, and chopped

about 1¼ cups sour cream

1 bunch scallions, finely chopped

1 large bunch fresh cilantro leaves, chopped

1 Pick over the beans, cover generously with cold water and leave to soak for 6 hours or overnight. Drain the beans, put in a saucepan and add enough cold water to cover by 2 inches. Bring to a boil and boil for 10 minutes. Drain and rinse well.

2 Heat the oil in a very large pot or flameproof casserole over a medium heat. Add the onions and cook for about 5 minutes, stirring frequently, until they start to color. Add the garlic and continue cooking for 1 minute.

3 Add the water, tomatoes, tomato paste, and drained beans. When the mixture begins to bubble, reduce the heat to low. Add the bay leaf, cumin, oregano, and chili paste and stir to mix well. Cover and simmer gently for 1½–2 hours, stirring occasionally, until the beans are

very tender. Season with salt and, needed, pepper.

4 Meanwhile, bake the sausages in preheated oven at 350°F for 40–4 minutes, turning 2 or 3 times for eve browning. Drain, slice, and add to th beans after they have been cooking fo about 1 hour.

5 Peel and dice the avocado. Mix wit the lime juice in a bowl and turn t coat. Put all the other garnishes i separate bowls.

6 When the beans are tender, tast the soup and adjust the seasonin Ladle the soup into warm bowls. Serv with garnishes.

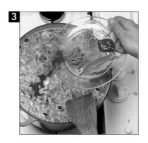  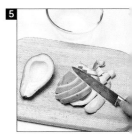

Poached Beef Soup

This lean, pretty soup makes an elegant light main course for 4, or it will serve 6 as a starter. A bit of last minute assembly is needed.

NUTRITIONAL INFORMATION

Calories ....178 Sugars 6g
Protein ....16g Fat 4g
Carbohydrate ...19g Saturates 2g

15 MINS   40 MINS

SERVES 4

I N G R E D I E N T S

2 small new potatoes, quartered

slim carrots, quartered lengthways and cut into 1½ inch lengths

½ oz tiny green beans, cut into 1½ inch lengths

cups rich beef or meat stock

tbsp soy sauce

tbsp dry sherry

2 oz beef tenderloin, about 2 inches thick

½ oz shiitake mushrooms, sliced

tbsp chopped fresh parsley

tbsp chopped fresh chives

alt and pepper

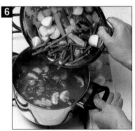

1 Bring a saucepan of salted water to a boil and drop in the potatoes and carrots. Reduce the heat, cover, and boil gently for about 15 minutes until tender. Bring another saucepan of salted water to the boil, drop in the beans and boil for about 5 minutes until just tender. Drain the vegetables and reserve.

2 Bring the stock to a boil in a saucepan and add the soy sauce and sherry. Season with salt and pepper to taste. Reduce the heat and adjust so that the stock bubbles very gently around the edges. Add the beef and simmer for 10 minutes. (The beef should be very rare, as it will continue cooking in the bowls.)

3 Add the mushrooms and continue simmering for 3 minutes. Warm the bowls in a low oven.

4 Remove the meat from the stock and leave to rest on a carving board. Taste the stock and adjust the seasoning, if necessary. Bring the stock back to a boil.

5 Cut the meat in half lengthways and slice each half into pieces about ⅛ inch thick. Season the meat lightly with salt and pepper and divide among the warm bowls.

6 Drop the reserved vegetables into the stock and heat through for about 1 minute. Ladle the stock over the meat, dividing the vegetables as evenly as possible. Sprinkle over the herbs and serve.

Chicken Soup with Pastry

This soup needs a rich, flavorful stock, and mushrooms that contribute plenty of flavor. The pastry top is baked separately to simplify serving.

NUTRITIONAL INFORMATION

Calories . . . . . . .560 Sugars 2g
Protein . . . . .28g Fat 33g
Carbohydrate . . .40g Saturates 10g

15 MINS   1 HOUR

SERVES 4

I N G R E D I E N T S

2¾ pints stock

4 skinless boned chicken breasts

2 garlic cloves, minced

small bunch of fresh tarragon or
  ¼ tsp dried tarragon

1 tbsp butter

14 oz cremini mushrooms, sliced

3 tbsp dry white wine

6 tbsp all-purpose flour

¾ cup whipping or heavy cream

13½ oz puff pastry

2 tbsp finely chopped fresh parsley

salt and pepper

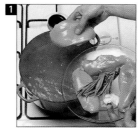

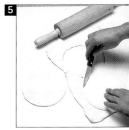

1 Put the stock in a saucepan and bring just to a boil. Add the chicken, garlic and tarragon, reduce the heat, cover, and simmer for 20 minutes, or until the chicken is cooked through. Remove the chicken and strain the stock. When the chicken is cool, cut into bite-sized pieces.

2 Melt the butter in a large skillet over a medium heat. Add the mushrooms and season with salt and pepper. Cook for 5–8 minutes until they are golden brown, stirring occasionally at first, then stirring more often after they start to color. Add the wine and bubble briefly. Remove the mushrooms from the heat.

3 Put the flour in a small mixing bowl and very slowly whisk in the cream to make a thick paste. Stir in a little of the stock to make a smooth liquid.

4 Bring the stock to a boil in a large saucepan. Whisk in the flour mixture and bring back to a boil. Boil gently for 3–4 minutes until the soup thickens, stirring frequently. Add the mushrooms and liquid, if any. Reduce the heat to low and simmer very gently, just to keep warm.

5 Cut out 6 rounds of pastry smaller i diameter than the soup bowls, usin a plate as a guide. Put on a baking shee prick with a fork and bake in a preheate oven at 400°F for about 15 minutes or until deep golden.

6 Meanwhile, add the chicken meat t the soup. Taste and adjust th seasoning. Simmer for about 10 minute until the soup is heated through. Stir i the parsley. Ladle the soup into warr bowls and place the pastry rounds on top Serve immediately.

Garbanzo Bean & Fruit Soup

This main-course soup is Mexican in origin. Its appeal comes from an unusual combination of fruits and vegetables.

25 MINS   1½ HOURS

SERVES 4

INGREDIENTS

lb 12 oz chicken legs or thighs, skinned

celery stalk, sliced

large carrot, halved and sliced

large onion, finely chopped

garlic cloves, finely chopped

½ quarts chicken stock

–5 parsley stems

bay leaf

½ oz lean smoked ham, diced

4 oz can garbanzo beans, drained and rinsed

large turnip, diced

zucchini, halved and sliced

large potato, diced

sweet potato, diced

oz corn kernels

large pears, peeled, cored, and cut into bite-sized pieces

tbsp fresh lime juice, or to taste

tbsp olive oil

very green, unripe bananas, cut into ¼ inch slices

alt and pepper

hopped fresh parsley, to garnish

1 Put the chicken into a large 4 quart pot with the celery, carrot, onion, garlic, stock, parsley stems, and bay leaf. Bring just to a boil over a medium-high heat and skim off any foam that rises to the surface. Reduce the heat and simmer, partially covered, for about 45 minutes, or until the chicken is tender.

2 Remove the chicken from the stock. When it is cool, remove the meat from the bones, cut into bite-sized pieces and reserve. Skim the fat as from the stock. Discard the parsley stems and bay leaf.

3 Bring the stock just to a boil. Add the ham, garbanzo beans, turnip, zucchini, potato, sweet potato, and corn.

Return the meat to the stock. Adjust the heat so the soup simmers gently and cook, partially covered, for about 30 minutes, or until all the vegetables are tender.

4 Add the pears and lime juice to the soup and continue cooking for about 5 minutes, just until they are barely poached. Season to taste, add more lime juice if wished.

5 Heat the oil in a skillet over a medium-high heat. Fry the bananas until golden. Drain on paper towels and keep warm. Ladle the soup into bowls and top with fried banana slices.

Pheasant & Cider Soup

This an excellent soup to serve in the fall,
when pheasant are widely available.

NUTRITIONAL INFORMATION

Calories	.471	Sugar	.8g
Protein	.12g	Fats	.32g
Carbohydrates	.32g	Saturates	.19g

🥔 30 MINS   🕐 1³/₄ HOURS

SERVES 4

INGREDIENTS

2 tbsp butter

3 shallots, finely chopped

2 garlic cloves, thinly sliced

1¼ cups hard cider

5 cups pheasant or chicken stock

1 carrot, finely chopped

1 celery stalk, finely chopped

1 bay leaf

1 pheasant

10½ oz potatoes, diced

9 oz small button mushrooms, halved or
   quartered

1 large eating apple, peeled and diced

1¼ cups heavy cream

4 tbsp cornstarch, diluted with 3 tbsp cold
   water

salt and pepper

TO GARNISH

2 tbsp olive oil, or as needed

30 sage leaves

1 Melt half of the butter in a large
   saucepan over a medium heat. Add
the shallots and garlic and cook for 3–4
minutes, stirring frequently, until soft.
Pour over the cider and bring to a boil.

Add the stock, carrot, celery, bay leaf, and
pheasant, which should be submerged.
Bring back to a boil, reduce the heat,
cover, and simmer for about 1 hour, or
until the pheasant is very tender. (Older
pheasant may take longer.)

2 When the pheasant is cool enough to
   handle, remove the meat from the
bones and cut into bite-sized pieces,
discarding any fat. Strain the stock,
pressing with the back of a spoon to
extract all the liquid. Discard the
vegetables and bay leaf. Remove as much
fat as possible from the stock.

3 Put the pheasant stock in a large
   saucepan and bring to a boil. Adjust
the heat so the liquid boils very gently.
Add the potatoes and cook for about 15
minutes until they are just barely tender.

4 Meanwhile, melt the remaining butter
   in a large skillet over a medium heat.

Add the mushrooms and season with sa
and pepper. Cook for 5–8 minutes unt
they are golden brown, stirring o
occasion, then more often once they sta
to change color.

5 Add the mushrooms to the soup
   together with the apple and cream
and cook for about 10 minutes until th
apple and potatoes are tender. Whisk th
diluted cornstarch into the soup. Bo
gently for 2–3 minutes, whisking, unt
slightly thickened. Then, add the pheasar
meat and simmer gently until the soup
hot.

6 Heat the oil in a small skillet until
   starts to smoke. Add the sage leave
and fry for about 20 seconds until crisp
Drain on paper towels. Ladle the soup int
warm bowls and garnish with crumble
fried sage.

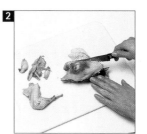

Duck, Cabbage, & Bean Soup

If you can't find the preserved duck or goose that is traditionally used for this dish, you could braise duck legs in stock.

NUTRITIONAL INFORMATION

Calories 479	Sugars 8g
Protein 29g	Fat 16g
Carbohydrate . . .57g	Saturates 7g

🕒 20 MINS   🕐 1¹/₄ HOURS

SERVES 4

I N G R E D I E N T S

preserved duck legs

tbsp duck fat or olive oil

onion, finely chopped

garlic cloves, finely chopped

carrots, sliced

large leek, halved lengthways and sliced

turnips, diced

oz dark leafy cabbage, such as Savoy

cups chicken or duck stock

potatoes, diced

oz dried white beans, soaked and cooked, or 2 x 14 oz cans white beans

bay leaf

tbsp roughly chopped fresh parsley

2 slices baguette

½ oz grated Gruyére cheese

salt and pepper

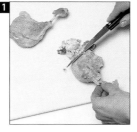

1 Scrape as much fat as possible from the preserved duck. Remove the duck meat from the bones, keeping it in large pieces; discard the skin and bones.

2 Heat the duck fat or oil in a large soup kettle or flameproof casserole over a medium heat. Add the onion and three-quarters of the garlic. Cover and cook for 3–4 minutes until just soft. Add the carrots, leek, and turnips, cover and continue cooking for 20 minutes, stirring occasionally. If the vegetables start to brown, add a tablespoon of water.

3 Meanwhile, bring a large saucepan of salted water to a boil. Drop in the cabbage and boil gently for 5 minutes. Drain well.

4 Add the stock to the stewed vegetables. Stir in the potatoes, beans, parboiled cabbage, and bay leaf, adjust seasoning. Bring to a boil, reduce the heat and simmer for 15 minutes.

5 Chop together the parsley and remaining garlic. Stir into the soup with the preserved duck, cover again and simmer for about 20 minutes, stirring occasionally. Season to taste.

6 Toast the bread under a preheated hot broiler on one side. Turn and top with the cheese. Broil until the cheese melts. Ladle the soup into warm bowls and top with the cheese toasts.

Parmesan Pancakes in Broth

This delicious soup has a rich homemade Italian-style meat stock as a base. A perfect dinner party starter, it is very light.

NUTRITIONAL INFORMATION

Calories	37	Sugars	.........0g
Protein	.........3g	Fat	..........2g
Carbohydrate	....3g	Saturates	......1g

🥘 25 MINS   🕐 2¹/₂ HOURS

SERVES 4

I N G R E D I E N T S

1 tbsp all-purpose flour

2 tbsp milk

2 eggs

2 tbsp chopped fresh basil

3 tbsp freshly grated Parmesan cheese, plus extra to serve

M E A T   S T O C K

1 lb chicken wings and/or legs

9 oz lean boneless stewing beef, such as shin

6 cups water

1 celery stalk, thinly sliced

1 carrot, thinly sliced

1 onion, halved and sliced

2 garlic cloves, minced

3–4 parsley stems

1 bay leaf

½ tsp salt

pepper

1 To make the stock, put the chicken and beef in a large pot with the water, celery, carrot, onion, garlic, parsley stems, bay leaf, and salt. Bring just to a boil and skim off the foam that rises to the surface. Reduce the heat and simmer very gently, uncovered, for 2 hours.

2 Strain the stock and remove as much fat as possible. Discard the vegetables and herbs. (Save the meat for another purpose.)

3 Bring the stock to a boil in a clean saucepan. If necessary, boil to reduce the stock to 4 cups. Taste and adjust the seasoning (be restrained with salt). Reduce the heat and simmer gently while making the pancakes.

4 To make the pancakes, put the flour in a bowl and add half the milk. Whisk until smooth, add the remaining milk and whisk again. Break in the eggs and whisk to combine well. Season with salt and pepper and stir in the basil and Parmesan.

5 Film the bottom of a small non-stic 6–7 inch skillet with oil and heat unt it begins to smoke. Pour in one-third o the batter (about 4 tablespoons) and ti the pan so the batter covers the botton Cook for about 1 minute until mostly s around the edges. Turn the pancake an cook the other side for about 15 second Turn out on to a plate. Continue makin the remaining pancakes, adding more o to the pan if needed.

6 Roll the pancakes up while warn then cut into ⅛ inch slices across th roll to make spirals. Divide the pancak spirals among bowls. Ladle over the ho broth and serve with Parmesan.

French Onion Soup

A rich, flavorful homemade stock is the key to this satisfying soup. While beef stock is traditional, chicken stock would be delicious as well.

NUTRITIONAL INFORMATION

Calories 417	Sugar 10g		
Protein 16g	Fats 19g		
Carbohydrates . . .41g	Saturates 9g		

15 MINS   1½ HOURS

SERVES 4

INGREDIENTS

tbsp butter

tbsp olive oil

lb large yellow onions, halved and sliced into half-circles

large garlic cloves, finely chopped

tbsp all-purpose flour

cup dry white wine

quarts beef stock

tbsp brandy

slices French bread

oz Gruyére cheese, grated

Salt and pepper

1 Melt the butter with the oil in a large heavy-bottomed saucepan over a medium heat. Add the onions and cook, covered, for 10–12 minutes until they soften, stirring occasionally. Add the garlic and sprinkle with salt and pepper.

COOK'S TIP

Don't try to hurry this soup. The rich flavor comes from cooking the onions slowly so their natural sugar caramelizes, then brewing them with the stock.

2 Reduce the heat a little and continue cooking, uncovered, for 30–35 minutes, or until the onions turn a deep, golden brown, stirring from time to time until they start to color, then stirring more frequently and scraping the bottom of the pan as they begin to stick (see Cook's Tip).

3 Sprinkle over the flour and stir to blend. Stir in the white wine and bubble for 1 minute. Pour in the stock and bring to a boil, scraping the bottom of the pan and stirring to combine well. Reduce the heat to low, add the brandy and simmer gently, stirring occasionally, for 45 minutes.

4 Toast the bread under a preheated hot broiler on one side. Turn over and top with the cheese, dividing it evenly. broil until the cheese melts.

5 Place a piece of cheese toast in each of the 6 warmed bowls, then ladle the hot soup over. Serve at once.

Jerusalem Artichoke Soup

Select artichokes with the fewest knobs, as there is less waste and they will be easier to peel.

NUTRITIONAL INFORMATION

Calories . . . . . . .337 Sugar 7g
Protein . . . . .6g Fats 28g
Carbohydrates . . .19g Saturates 12g

20 MINS   30 MINS

SERVES 4

INGREDIENTS

1 lb Jerusalem artichokes

2 tsp butter

1 onion, finely chopped

4 oz peeled rutabaga, cubed

1 strip pared lemon rind

3 cups chicken or vegetable stock

3 tbsp heavy cream

1 tbsp fresh lemon juice, or to taste

4 tbsp lightly toasted pine nuts

1 Peel the Jerusalem artichokes and cut large ones into pieces. Drop into a bowl of cold water to prevent discoloration.

2 Melt the butter in a large saucepan over a medium heat. Add the onion and cook for about 3 minutes, stirring frequently, until just soft.

3 Drain the Jerusalem artichokes and add them to the saucepan with the rutabaga and lemon rind. Pour in the stock, season with a little salt and pepper and stir to combine. Bring just to a boil, reduce the heat and simmer gently for about 20 minutes until the vegetables are tender.

4 Allow the soup to cool slightly, then transfer to a blender or food processor and purée until smooth. (If using a food processor, strain off the cooking liquid and reserve. Purée the soup solids with enough cooking liquid to moisten them, then combine with the remaining liquid.)

5 Return the soup to the saucepan, st in the cream and simmer for about minutes until reheated. Add the lemo juice. Taste and adjust the seasonin adding more lemon juice if wished. Lad the soup into warm bowls and very gent place the pine nuts on top, dividing the evenly. Serve at once.

Roasted Garlic Soup

The combination of potato, garlic, and onion works brilliantly in soup. In this recipe the garlic is roasted to give it added dimension and depth.

NUTRITIONAL INFORMATION

Calories ....247 Sugar 7g
Protein ....8g Fats 10g
Carbohydrates ...34g Saturates 5g

15 MINS   1 HOUR

SERVES 4

INGREDIENTS

large bulb garlic with large cloves, peeled (about 3½ oz)

tsp olive oil

large leeks, thinly sliced

large onion, finely chopped

potatoes, diced (about 1 lb)

cups chicken or vegetable stock

bay leaf

cup light cream

freshly grated nutmeg

fresh lemon juice (optional)

salt and pepper

snipped fresh chives, to garnish

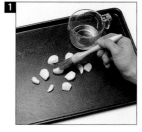  

1 Put the garlic cloves in a baking dish, lightly brush with oil and bake in a preheated oven at 350°F for about 20 minutes until golden.

2 Heat the oil in a large saucepan over a medium heat. Add the leeks and onion, cover and cook for about 3 minutes, stirring frequently, until they begin to soften.

3 Add the potatoes, roasted garlic, stock, and bay leaf. Season with salt (unless the stock is salty) and pepper. Bring to a boil, reduce the heat, cover, and cook gently for about 30 minutes until the vegetables are tender. Remove the bay leaf.

4 Allow the soup to cool slightly, then transfer to a blender or food processor and purée until smooth, working in batches if necessary. (If using a food processor, strain off the cooking liquid and reserve. Purée the soup solids with enough cooking liquid to moisten them, then combine with the remaining liquid.)

5 Return the soup to the saucepan and stir in the cream and a generous grating of nutmeg. Taste and adjust the seasoning, if necessary, adding a few drops of lemon juice, if wished. Reheat over a low heat. Ladle into warm soup bowls, garnish with chives or parsley and serve.

Saffron Mussel Soup

Mussels are easy to prepare, economical, and very tasty. This soup has pure, delicate flavors and the fresh aromas of the sea.

NUTRITIONAL INFORMATION

Calories 381   Sugars 3g
Protein . . . . .16g   Fat 29g
Carbohydrate . . . .11g   Saturates 17g

 15 MINS   40 MINS

SERVES 4

I N G R E D I E N T S

4 lb 8 oz mussels

⅔ cup dry white wine

1 tbsp butter

2 large shallots, finely chopped

1 leek, halved lengthways and thinly sliced

pinch of saffron threads

1 ¼ cups heavy cream

1 tbsp cornstarch, dissolved in 2 tbsp water

salt and pepper

2 tbsp chopped fresh parsley

3 When they are cool enough to handle, remove the mussels from the shells, adding any additional juices to the cooking liquid. Strain the cooking liquid through a cheesecloth-lined strainer. Top up the cooking liquid with water to make 4 cups.

4 Melt the butter in heavy-bottomed saucepan. Add the shallots and leek, cover and cook until they begin to soften, stirring occasionally.

5 Stir in the mussel cooking liquid and the saffron. Bring to a boil, reduce the heat and simmer for 15–20 minutes until the vegetables are very tender.

6 Add the cream, stir and bring just to a boil. Stir the dissolved cornstarch into the soup and boil gently for 2–3 minutes until slightly thickened, stirring frequently. Add the mussels and cook for I–2 minutes to reheat them. Taste and adjust the seasoning, if necessary. Stir in the parsley, ladle into warm bowls and serve.

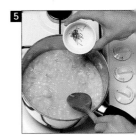

1 Discard any broken mussels and those with open shells that do not close when tapped. Rinse, pull off any 'beards', and if there are barnacles, scrape them off with a knife under cold running water.

2 Put the mussels in a large heavy-bottomed saucepan over a high heat with the wine and a little pepper. Cover tightly and cook for 4–5 minutes, or until the mussels open, shaking the pan occasionally.

Watercress Vichyssoise

Traditional vichyssoise is simply cold leek and potato soup flavored with chives. The addition of watercress gives it a refreshing flavor.

NUTRITIONAL INFORMATION

Calories	149	Sugars	.........3g
Protein	.........4g	Fat	...........9g
Carbohydrate	...13g	Saturates	......4g

15 MINS   40 MINS

SERVES 4

INGREDIENTS

1 tbsp olive oil

3 large leeks, thinly sliced (about 12 oz)

1 large potato, finely diced (about 12 oz)

2½ cups chicken or vegetable stock

2 cups water

1 bay leaf

6 oz prepared watercress

¼ cup light cream

salt and pepper

watercress leaves, to garnish

cook gently for about 25 minutes until the vegetables are tender. It may be difficult to find the bay leaf, however it is best removed.

3 Add the watercress and continue to cook for a further 2–3 minutes, stirring frequently, just until the watercress is completely wilted.

4 Allow the soup to cool slightly, then transfer to a blender or food processor and purée until smooth, working in batches if necessary. (If using a food processor, strain off the cooking liquid and reserve. Purée the soup solids with enough cooking liquid to moisten them, then combine with the remaining liquid.)

5 Put the soup in a large bowl and stir in half the cream. Season with salt, if needed, and plenty of pepper.

6 Refrigerate until cold. Taste and adjust the seasoning, if necessary. Ladle into chilled bowls, drizzle the remaining cream on top and garnish with watercress leaves. Serve at once.

1 Heat the oil in a heavy-bottomed saucepan over a medium heat. Add the leeks and cook for about 3 minutes, stirring frequently, until they begin to soften.

2 Add the potato, stock, water, and bay leaf. Add salt if the stock is unsalted. Bring to a boil, reduce the heat, cover and

Piquant Oatmeal Soup

This unusual soup, of Mexican origin, is simple and comforting. It has a hint of chili heat, but its character is more sweet than spicy.

NUTRITIONAL INFORMATION

Calories	137	Sugars	.........4g
Protein	.........3g	Fat	..........8g
Carbohydrate	...14g	Saturates	......4g

 10 MINS   35 MINS

SERVES 4

INGREDIENTS

80 g/3 oz/1 cup oatmeal

3 tbsp butter

1 large sweet onion

2–3 garlic cloves

12 oz tomatoes, skinned, seeded and chopped

6 cups chicken stock

⅛ tsp ground cumin

1 tsp harissa, or ½ tsp chili paste

1–2 tbsp lime juice

salt and pepper

chopped scallions, to garnish

1 Place a heavy-bottomed skillet over a medium heat. Add the oats and toast for about 25 minutes, stirring frequently, until lightly and evenly browned. Remove the oats from the pan and allow to cool.

2 Heat the butter in a large saucepan over a medium heat. Add the onion and garlic and cook until the onion is soft.

3 Add the tomatoes, stock, cumin, harissa or chili paste, and a good pinch of salt to the softened onion and garlic.

4 Stir in the oats and bring to a boil. Regulate the heat so that the soup boils gently and cook for 6 minutes.

5 Stir in 1 tablespoon of the lime juice. Taste and adjust the seasoning. Add more lime juice if desired. Ladle the soup into warm bowls and sprinkle with scallions, to garnish.

COOK'S TIP

This soup is very quick to prepare once the oats are toasted. The oats could be prepared in advance at a convenient time.

VARIATION

Substitute lemon juice for the lime juice, using a little less.

Cucumber & Salmon Soup

When cucumber is cooked it becomes a much more subtle vegetable, perfect to set off the taste of smoked salmon.

NUTRITIONAL INFORMATION

Calories	308	Sugar	.........7g
Protein	........13g	Fats	..........22g
Carbohydrates	...15g	Saturates	.....12g

15 MINS   25 MINS

SERVES 4

INGREDIENTS

tsp oil

large onion, finely chopped

large cucumber, peeled, seeded and sliced

small potato, diced

celery stalk, finely chopped

cups chicken or vegetable stock

⅔ cup heavy cream

5½ oz smoked salmon, finely diced

tbsp chopped fresh chives

salt and pepper

fresh dill sprigs, to garnish

1 Heat the oil in a large saucepan over a medium heat. Add the onion and cook for about 3 minutes until it begins to soften.

2 Add the cucumber, potato, celery, and stock, along with a large pinch of salt, if using unsalted stock. Bring to a boil, reduce the heat, cover, and cook gently for about 20 minutes until the vegetables are tender.

3 Allow the soup to cool slightly, then transfer to a blender or food processor, working in batches if necessary.

4 Purée the soup until smooth. If using a food processor, strain off the cooking liquid and reserve it. Purée the soup solids with enough cooking liquid to moisten them, then combine with the remaining liquid.

5 Transfer the puréed soup into a large container. Cover, and refrigerate until cold.

6 Stir the cream, salmon, and chives into the soup. If time permits, chill for at least 1 hour to allow the flavors to blend. Taste and adjust the seasoning, adding salt, if needed, and pepper. Ladle into chilled bowls and garnish with dill.

Spicy Icy Red Bell Pepper

This brilliantly colored soup makes a great summer starter, especially when bell peppers are abundant in markets–or in your garden.

NUTRITIONAL INFORMATION

Calories	97	Sugars 13g
Protein	.........3g	Fat 3g
Carbohydrate	...15g	Saturates 0g

🔪 15 MINS   🕐 50 MINS

SERVES 4

I N G R E D I E N T S

1 tbsp olive oil

1 lb leeks, thinly sliced

1 large onion, halved and thinly sliced

2 garlic cloves, finely chopped or minced

6 red bell peppers, cored, seeded and sliced

4 cups water

½ tsp ground cumin

½ tsp ground coriander

1 tsp chili paste, or to taste

1–2 tsp fresh lemon juice

salt and pepper

finely chopped scallion greens or chives, to garnish

2 Stir in the bell peppers and cook for a further 2–3 minutes. Add the water, cumin, coriander and chili paste together with a large pinch of salt. Bring to a boil, reduce the heat, cover, and simmer for about 35 minutes until all the vegetables are tender.

3 Allow the soup to cool slightly, then transfer to a blender or food processor and purée until smooth, working in batches if necessary. (If using a food processor, strain off the cooking liquid and reserve. Purée the soup solids with enough cooking liquid to moisten them, then combine with the remaining liquid.)

4 Put the soup in a large bowl, then season with salt and pepper and add lemon juice, to taste. Allow to cool completely, cover, and chill in the refrigerator until cold.

5 Before serving, taste and adjust the seasoning, if necessary. Add a little more chili paste if a spicy taste is preferred. Ladle into chilled bowls and garnish with scallion greens or chives.

1 Heat the oil in a large saucepan over a medium heat. Add the leeks, onion, and garlic and cook, covered, for about 5 minutes until the onion is softened, stirring frequently.

Melon & Ginger Soup

Almost any variety of melon is appropriate, including Honeydew, Galia, Ogen, Charentais or Cantaloupe, but it is essential that the melon is ripe.

NUTRITIONAL INFORMATION

Calories 179	Sugars 16g	
Protein 2g	Fat 12g	
Carbohydrate ...16g	Saturates 7g	

15 MINS   0 MINS

SERVES 4

INGREDIENTS

large ripe melon (about 2 lb)

 tsp grated peeled fresh gingerroot or more

tbsp fresh lemon juice, or to taste

tsp superfine sugar

cup whipping cream

salt

snipped fresh chives, to garnish

1 Halve the melon, discard the seeds, and scoop the flesh into a blender or food processor. Purée until smooth, stopping to scrape down the sides as necessary. (You may need to work in batches.)

COOK'S TIP

To determine the ripeness of melon, gently press the end opposite the stem—it should give a little, and there is usually a characteristic aroma on pressing that helps to confirm the verdict.

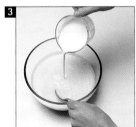

2 Add the grated ginger, lemon juice, and sugar with a pinch of salt and process to combine. Taste and add a little more ginger, if wished. Scrape into a bowl, cover and chill completely, usually for about 30 minutes, or until cold.

3 Add the cream and stir to combine well. Taste and adjust the seasoning, adding a little more salt and lemon juice if necessary.

4 To serve, divide the melon purée among four chilled bowls and garnish with chives.

Cucumber & Walnut Soup

Parsley tames the pungent garlic flavor of this traditional Balkan soup. The cucumber and yogurt make it a refreshing summer starter.

NUTRITIONAL INFORMATION

Calories 254	Sugars 4g	
Protein 8g	Fat 23g	
Carbohydrate 4g	Saturates 6g	

 20 MINS 0 MINS

SERVES 4

INGREDIENTS

1 large cucumber

½ cup walnut pieces, toasted (see Cook's Tip)

½ oz parsley, leaves only

1 small garlic clove, very finely chopped

2 tbsp olive oil

4 tbsp water

1 tbsp fresh lemon juice, or to taste

1¼ cups strained Greek yogurt

salt and pepper

fresh mint leaves, to garnish

COOK'S TIP

Toasting the walnuts gives them extra flavor. Just heat them in a dry skillet over a medium-low heat until they begin to color and smell aromatic.

1 Peel the cucumber, slice lengthways, and scoop out the seeds with a small sharp spoon. Cut the flesh into 1 inch pieces.

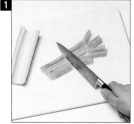

2 Put the walnuts, parsley leaves, garlic, oil, and water in a blender or food processor with half of the cucumber and purée until smooth, stopping to scrape down the sides as necessary.

3 Add the remaining cucumber to the blender or processor with a pinch of salt and the lemon juice. Purée until smooth.

4 Scrape the purée into a large bow and stir in the yogurt. Season to tast with salt and pepper and add a little mor lemon juice, if wished.

5 Cover and chill for about 30 minute or until cold. Taste and adjust th seasoning, if necessary. Ladle into chille bowls and garnish with mint leaves.

Cold Fresh Cilantro Soup

This soup brings together Thai flavors for a cool refreshing starter. It highlights fresh cilantro, now much more widely available.

NUTRITIONAL INFORMATION

Calories	107	Sugars	.........5g
Protein	.........4g	Fat	..........2g
Carbohydrate	...19g	Saturates	......0g

15 MINS   35 MINS

SERVES 4

INGREDIENTS

tsp olive oil

large onion, finely chopped

leek, thinly sliced

garlic clove, thinly sliced

cups water

zucchini, about 7 oz, peeled and chopped

tbsp white rice

inch piece lemongrass

lime leaves

oz fresh cilantro leaves and soft stems

hili paste, (optional)

alt and pepper

nely chopped red bell pepper and/or red chilies, to garnish

2 Add the water, zucchini, and rice with a large pinch of salt and some pepper. Stir in the lemongrass and lime leaves. Bring just to a boil and reduce the heat to low. Cover and simmer for about 15–20 minutes until the rice is soft and tender.

3 Add the fresh cilantro leaves, pushing them down into the liquid. Continue cooking for 2–3 minutes until they are wilted. Remove the lemongrass and lime leaves.

4 Allow the soup to cool slightly, then transfer to a blender or food processor and purée until smooth, working in batches if necessary. (If using a food processor, strain off the cooking liquid and reserve for later. Purée the soup solids with enough cooking liquid to moisten them, then combine with the remaining liquid.)

5 Scrape the soup into a large container. Season to taste with salt and pepper. Cover and refrigerate until cold.

6 Taste and adjust the seasoning. For a more spicy soup, stir in a little chili paste to taste. For a thinner soup, add a small amount of iced water. Ladle into chilled bowls and garnish with finely chopped red bell pepper and/or chilies.

1 Heat the oil in a large saucepan over a medium heat. Add the onion, leek, and arlic, cover and cook for 4–5 minutes ntil the onion is soft, stirring frequently.

Shrimp Dumpling Soup

These small dumplings filled with shrimp and pork may be made slightly larger and served as dim sum on their own, if you prefer.

NUTRITIONAL INFORMATION

Calories	311	Sugars	.........2g
Protein	........18g	Fat	...........8g
Carbohydrate	...41g	Saturates	.......2g

 20 MINS 10 MINS

SERVES 4

INGREDIENTS

DUMPLINGS

1⅝ cups all-purpose flour

¼ cup boiling water

⅛ cup cold water

1½ tsp vegetable oil

FILLING

4½ oz ground pork

4½ oz cooked peeled shrimp, chopped

1¾ oz canned water chestnuts, drained, rinsed, and chopped

1 celery stalk, chopped

1 tsp cornstarch

1 tbsp sesame oil

1 tbsp light soy sauce

SOUP

3¾ cups fish stock

1¾ oz cellophane noodles

1 tbsp dry sherry

chopped chives, to garnish

1 To make the dumplings, mix together the flour, boiling water, cold water, and oil in a bowl until a pliable dough is formed.

2 Knead the dough on a lightly floured surface for 5 minutes. Cut the dough into 16 equal sized pieces.

3 Roll the dough pieces into rounds about 3 inches in diameter.

4 Mix the filling ingredients together in a large bowl.

5 Spoon a little of the filling mixture into the center of each round. Bring the edges of the dough together, scrunching them up to form a 'moneybag' shape. Twist the gathered edges to seal.

6 Pour the fish stock into a large saucepan and bring to a boil.

7 Add the cellophane noodles, dumplings, and dry sherry to the pan and cook for 4–5 minutes, until the noodles and dumplings are tender. Garnish with chopped chives and serve immediately.

Shrimp Gumbo

This soup is thick with onions, red bell peppers, rice, shrimp, and okra, which both adds flavor and acts as a thickening agent.

NUTRITIONAL INFORMATION

Calories ....177 Sugar 5g
Protein ....12g Fats 8g
Carbohydrates ...15g Saturates 1g

1 HOUR   45 MINS

SERVES 4–6

INGREDIENTS

1 large onion, chopped finely

2 slices lean bacon, chopped finely (optional)

1–2 garlic cloves, minced

2 tbsp olive oil

1 large or 2 small red bell peppers, chopped finely or minced coarsely

3½ cups fish orvegetable stock (see pages 14–15)

1 fresh or dried bay leaf

1 blade mace

good pinch of ground allspice

3 tbsp long-grain rice

1 tbsp white wine vinegar

4½–6 oz okra, trimmed and sliced very thinly

½–⅔ cup peeled shrimp

1 tbsp anchovy paste

2 tsp tomato paste

1–2 tbsp chopped fresh parsley

salt and pepper

TO GARNISH

whole shrimp

sprigs of fresh parsley

1 Gently fry the onion, bacon (if using), and garlic in the oil in a large saucepan for 4–5 minutes until soft. Add the bell peppers to the pan and continue to fry gently for a couple of minutes.

2 Add the stock, bay leaf, mace, allspice, rice, vinegar, and seasoning and bring to a boil. Cover and simmer gently for about 20 minutes, giving an occasional stir, until the rice is just tender.

3 Add the okra, shrimp, anchovy paste, and tomato paste, cover and simmer gently for about 15 minutes until the okra is tender and the mixture slightly thickened.

4 Discard the bay leaf and mace from the soup and adjust the seasoning. Stir in the parsley and serve each portion garnished with a whole shrimp and parsley sprigs.

Index